PRAISE FOR *FRUITFUL*, BY BRIAN NICHOLSON AND SARAH HUCK:

"'All hands and dirt and heart and soul'—a description of Red Jacket founder, Joe Nicholson, in Brian Nicholson's introduction, but it could just as easily be the motto of Red Jacket Orchards itself. Never has the job of growing both community as well as product appeared more meaningful than in the pages of this wonderful book, whose recipes take you through the seasons with grace and aplomb, leaving you wiser—and more joyful—for the journey."

—Dan Barber, chef and co-owner,
Blue Hill and Blue Hill at Stone Barns

"*Fruitful* is the book we need now! This heartfelt work about growing, tending and finally putting this glorious fruit on the table inspires me to my roots. You just know that this is fruit as it's supposed to be: rich with flavor, promise, and goodness, the result of generations fine-tuning their most important art."

—Deborah Madison,
author of *Seasonal Fruit Desserts* and *Vegetable Literacy*

FRUITFUL

Fruitful

FOUR SEASONS OF FRESH FRUIT RECIPES

BRIAN NICHOLSON **RED ★ JACKET** SARAH HUCK
— EST. 1958 • NEW YORK —

RUNNING PRESS
PHILADELPHIA • LONDON

Nov - 72

THIS BOOK IS DEDICATED TO OUR FIRST AND
FOURTH GENERATIONS OF OUR RED JACKET FARMING FAMILY.
IN LOVING MEMORY OF EMILY NICHOLSON AND JOE NICHOLSON SR.
FOR LEADING US DOWN AN AGRARIAN PATH, WITH COMMITMENT
AND INTEGRITY—AND TO OUR CHILDREN
WHO FILL US WITH ENDLESS STRENGTH AND
HOPE FOR THE FUTURE.

ISBN 978-0-7624- 4565-3
Library of Congress Control Number: 2013943524

E-book ISBN 978-0-7624- 5175-3

9 8 7 6 5 4 3 2 1
Digit on the right indicates the number of this printing

Designed by Frances J. Soo Ping Chow
Edited by Kristen Green Wiewora
Food Stylist: Emma Feigenbaum
Prop Stylist: Mariellen Melker
Typography: Abraham Lincoln, Centaur MT, Janda Stylish Script,
Raleway Thin, Samantha, and Univers

Running Press Book Publishers
2300 Chestnut Street
Philadelphia, PA 19103-4371

Visit us on the web!
www.offthemenublog.com

TABLE of CONTENTS

Acknowledgments

I WANT TO THANK THE MANY PEOPLE WHO CONTRIBUTED TO THIS BEAUTIFUL CULMINATION OF LIVING HISTORY AND CULINARY ART. THE BOOK WOULD NOT HAVE HAPPENED WITHOUT AN IDEA HATCHED LONG AGO BY MY CO-AUTHOR SARAH HUCK AND OUR FRIENDS RICH ROSSMASSLER AND JUSTONE BOSSERT, SO I THANK THE THREE OF YOU IMMENSELY. SARAH, YOU BELIEVED IN, COAXED, STIRRED, AND CAJOLED MY FAMILY TO EXPRESS THE DEEP LOVE OF OUR CRAFT. YOUR TALENT AND PASSION FULFILL THIS BOOK.

Sarah and I both extend a warm and heartfelt thanks to the following: our superb agent, Jenni Ferrari-Adler for having faith in this project and patiently seeing it through the years; our editor, Kristen Green Wiewora and everyone at Running Press for your outstanding professionalism and care in helping us craft something so near to our hearts; talented book designer Frances Soo Ping Chow; photographer Steve Legato and food stylist Emma Feigenbaum for bringing our fruit to life; recipe tester extraordinaire Arielle Cooper; Allon, Daniella, Noa, and Amelia Azulai for their infinite and steadfast wonderfulness.

We would also like to thank all of the remarkable chefs, fellow farmers, and food professionals who generously shared some of their favorite recipes, including Dan Barber, Jeff and Adina Bialas, Daniel Boulud and DBGB's pastry chef Mymi Eberhardt, Melissa Clark, Mary Cleaver, Karen DeMasco, Melissa and Emily Elsen, Sara Kate Gillingham-Ryan, Rune and Giulietta Hilt, Molly Killeen, Agatha Kulaga and Erin Patinkin, Kari and Tyler Morris, Jessica Quon and Sabrina Valle, Chris Ronis, June Russell, Sarah Sanneh, Adam Shepard, Francine Stephens and Andrew Feinberg, Andrew Tarlow and the Marlow & Sons pastry chef Ashley

Whitmore, Julie Tarras Wallach, Bill Telepan, Molly Wessel, and Jody Williams. We particularly express our deep gratitude to Chef Daniel Humm, for your eloquent and kind foreword.

Red Jacket would not be a success without the dedicated individuals who work here every day—growing, packing, juicing, trucking, retailing and administering—to help us make the best-tasting product in the world. Your tireless commitment is an everlasting inspiration: thank you!

It's essential to recognize my family. First, of course, Mom: you are the glue that keeps this whole thing together (you and your jam). You persevered in raising a farm family, with humor and your patented "Irish Ways"; because of that, we now have a fourth generation waiting in the wings. To my eldest brother JJ, with passion in your heart and no fear, you led us to the streets of New York City and its Greenmarkets. Red Jacket Orchards would be very different without your love of that space. To my sister, Amy May, of equal passion and creativity, you labored in the New York City streets and brought our relationship with the city's culinary scene to a new level. To my "better half since the egg split" twin brother, Mark, with your love of politics, plow, family, and now sales, taking every step with you keeps me sane and makes the whole thing that much more fun.

To my father, Joe, whose deep passion and endless pursuit of superior flavors informs our every decision. You took the raw potential of a small orchard and willed it into a generational business that is our Red Jacket today. Your vision, contrarian nature, and absolute intolerance of obstacles has lead us to a better place—and created a wonderful ride for all involved.

Finally, to my wife and kids, Kirstin, Emily, Colin, and Anna: You inspire me daily as I watch the beauty of life unfolding around me. Your patience and love empower this journey and fill me with pride.

And most importantly, to our many dedicated customers, it's not enough to say thank you. Without your priorities taking shape for better food and a better planet, none of this is possible. As I like to say, "You keep eating, we'll keep growing!"

Foreword

GREW UP IN A SMALL TOWN IN SWITZERLAND, A TOWN WHERE THE ONLY PLACE TO SHOP FOR PRODUCE, MEAT, AND DAIRY WAS THE LOCAL FARMERS' MARKET. I HAVE VIVID CHILDHOOD MEMORIES OF STROLLING THROUGH THE MARKET WITH MY MOTHER ON ALMOST A DAILY BASIS. WE'D SELECT WHAT LOOKED BEST, ALWAYS CHATTING WITH THE PURVEYORS, WHETHER IT WAS ABOUT THE TOWN GOSSIP OR NEW FRUIT THEY WERE GROWING, AND THEN HAUL HOME OUR FINDS TO BE WASHED, PEELED, AND SHUCKED. THESE EARLY EXPERIENCES AT THE MARKET TAUGHT ME A LOT. THEY TAUGHT ME ABOUT THE DELICIOUS INGREDIENTS AT MY FINGERTIPS AND THE COMMITMENT THAT FARMERS HAVE TO THEIR PRODUCTS. THEY GREATLY INFLUENCED MY PHILOSOPHY AS A CHEF AND MY APPROACH TO FOOD IN GENERAL. AND THOSE EARLY EXPERIENCES ARE WHAT LED ME INTO THIS PROFESSION IN THE FIRST PLACE. WHEN I EVENTUALLY MOVED TO AMERICA I WAS WORRIED I WOULD LOSE SOME OF THIS CONNECTION TO THE FOOD, TO THE FARMERS. I WAS CONCERNED THAT THIS CULTURE WOULDN'T EXIST.

But when I first moved here my concerns were put to rest. And once I came to New York City I found Red Jacket Orchards at the Union Square Greenmarket and fell in love. I could tell that it had a personal connection, both to the earth and to the customers coming to buy goods. It was great to see this and it reminded me so much of home and my early memories of the markets in Switzerland. The Nicholsons were so proud of their product, their land, and their farmers. They just wanted to tell you all the great stories from the orchards. And there was such a clear respect for their craft, which led to really amazing products. At their stand you could always overhear the sharing of recipes for seasonal pies and jams and tips on how to tell when a fruit was ripe.

Joe Nicholson, the second-generation owner, has perfected so many fruits. The farms' apricots, peaches, and plums are delicious and inspirational. He's passed along decades of knowledge to his family and to his staff, and all while, the level of quality remains unmatched. Their vast experience and quality product have made Red Jacket Orchards a household name in New York City, while paving the way for many other local farms and farmers with its unique sense of hospitality at the market. And the Nicholsons have been building meaningful connections with their clients, from the home cook to the restaurant chef, since they first started their company. Everyone walking away from their stand does so with only the best products, always at the peak of their seasonality and ripeness. They look forward to coming back the following week to get their hands on a new batch of delicious ingredients.

Over the years I've truly loved watching Red Jacket blossom. What started as a small farm stand has grown into a remarkable business, and somehow Red Jacket has managed to keep that vibe. It maintains that human element, with face-to-face connections and real passion for produce. This cookbook is a true extension of the business. It brings the same personal touch and dedication to quality into the home. And having a piece of Red Jacket Orchards permanently in my home gives me, as a client, a sense of ownership. It enhances the sense of community that the Nicholson family has always embodied since the day they bought those first acres of farmland, decades ago.

by Daniel Humm
Chef/Owner,
Eleven Madison Park and The NoMad

The Red Jacket Story
from Joe Nicholson

THE FIRST TIME I SAW RED JACKET ORCHARDS IT WAS BURIED UNDER A FOOT OF SNOW. IT WAS FEBRUARY 1957. I WAS A 15-YEAR-OLD KID FROM BETHPAGE, LONG ISLAND, WHERE MY PARENTS, JOE AND EMILY NICHOLSON, OWNED NICHOLSON'S POULTRY FARM. BETHPAGE WAS BEGINNING TO EXPERIENCE SUBURBAN SPRAWL AND THE STATE OF NEW YORK DECIDED IT WAS TIME TO ACCOMMODATE THAT GROWTH AND BUILD THE WANTAGH-SEAFORD EXPRESSWAY. OUR LAND WAS GOING TO BECOME AN OFF-RAMP. MY FAMILY WOULD BE DISPLACED.

My father had no intention of quitting the farming life, and dreamed of moving us to the Finger Lakes. He described it as a stunning region of scenic lakes, beautiful vistas, and quaint towns, far different from increasingly crowded Long Island. He spotted an advertisement in *The Wall Street Journal* for a 110-acre farm and with me in tow, headed upstate to take a look. Boy, was my father right. We were instantly enchanted by the romance of the snow-covered landscape, fruit trees, barns, and beautiful old Greek revival farmhouse. The following spring, my family packed up and moved to our new home in Geneva, New York.

From the beginning, it was a challenge. My dad didn't know anything about fruit growing and wasn't prepared for the steep learning curve. In the early years we struggled. Much of our revenue came from selling cherries, plums, and apples at depressed prices to the local cannery. In Bethpage, we'd sold directly to consumers, so that's what we did in Geneva; my mother became the manager of the roadside stand while my dad concentrated on fruit production. From June to October our stand sold strawberries in spring, stone fruit in summer (especially peaches), and apples in autumn. In 1968, my father bought an old rack-and-cloth cider press and began pressing juice in the barn, which we also sold.

During the summer, I worked alongside my dad from dawn until dusk, six days a week (Saturday was a treat, as we would quit at 4pm). He loaded me with responsibilities—running picking crews, trucking fruit to the cannery, and planting orchards the old-fashioned way, with a shovel. I loved it, but like many farm kids I never expected to return. Farming was a hard life and I was itching to see the possibilities of the world. So I went to college and graduate school, joined the Navy and served on a minesweeper, got married and spent several years on Wall Street in a research department. When I was 28, I took a personality test while interviewing for a brokerage house. The test told me that I was entrepreneurial, had a high need for adventure and change, and would be happiest building the farm business, so in 1972, I surprised myself and returned to Geneva with my wife, our two year-old son and two-week old twin boys. I have never looked back.

All four of my children—JJ, Mark, Brian, and Amy—grew up in the farming life and much like me, they've all felt the tug to return at various times. Over the years, we've accomplished a lot together. We've expanded our orchards and developed new fruit varieties like our prized apricots and plums; established ourselves at the NYC Greenmarket; built a thriving wholesale operation; and revived my father's juicing tradition with a full line of fresh fruit juices, winning some national awards. Every day we push to be innovative and sustainable leaders in the fruit business. It's an adventure that's just as exciting and engaging as it was 41 years ago, and as magical as that first snowy day. You can do many things in life and still find happiness, but I'm so grateful that I found my way back home. It's been very satisfying journey.

A WORD FROM
BRIAN NICHOLSON

IF MY FATHER, JOE NICHOLSON, HAD HIS WAY, HE WOULD TEACH EVERYONE HE MET HOW TO PLANT AN APRICOT TREE. THAT'S WHO MY DAD IS, ALL HANDS AND DIRT AND HEART AND SOUL, AND FOR ALL OF US AT RED JACKET ORCHARDS, THAT SPIRIT OF TENDING AND CULTIVATING FLAVOR—THE SWEET, JUICY, DRIP-DOWN-YOUR-CHIN FLAVOR OF FRESH FRUIT—IS THE MOST DIRECT PATH TO ALL THAT IS GOOD IN LIFE. FOR US, IT'S AN ACT THAT SYMBOLIZES FAMILY, SUSTENANCE, COMMUNITY, PERSEVERANCE, AND A LEGACY THREE GENERATIONS DEEP.

This cookbook is that apricot tree. Not everyone has the time, yard space, fertile soil, or inclination to plant a tree, but everyone can learn to appreciate and cook with fresh fruit. When you crunch into a crisp apple on a blustery fall day, or eye a basket of burnished nectarines, part of what you consume is the grower's story. For us, that story is five decades of sharing the best possible produce at market. It might not be news that sharing food is the fastest way to bring people together, but when you're a farmer you witness this first-hand every day. Just spend a morning eavesdropping at any local farmers' market. You're sure to discover one thing: the favorite topic is recipes. Whether shoppers are swapping peach cobbler secrets or doling out gooseberry advice, our market stand often feels like a walking, talking cookbook.

I always joke that at our house that there's no such thing as the farm-to-table movement. The farm and table are inseparable. While we were growing up, our old oak table sat in the middle of our kitchen, in the middle of the farmhouse, just adjacent to the orchard. It was the center of our existence and the center of who we were. Without fail, my parents, siblings, and I ate all our family meals at that table (except for one short stint in the '70s when Mom tried TV trays). When there was an emergency or an important decision to be made, we had family meetings at that table. When my dad stopped for lunch during a day of farming, he and my grandparents convened at that table. I've sat with my wife and children at that table. It's seen an incredible richness of joy, struggle, and of course, food. You can't be this close to the farming life and not have the passion we do for fruit.

This cookbook continues our family heritage of committed growing and we hope you will find it to be a comprehensive resource, no matter where your local farmers' market may be. We believe that if you do something, do it properly and with integrity. We strive to emulate these values in all that we do on the farm and among the community that surrounds us. We are passionate about introducing others to amazing farm-fresh flavor and quality that's fit for every family table, including our own.

Spring
and Early
Summer

RHUBARB AND SPRING BERRIES

I'T'S EASY TO TAKE FOR GRANTED THE CYCLES OF OUR SEASONS AND, AT LEAST IN THE NORTHEAST REGION WHERE OUR ORCHARD IS, THE INCREDIBLE CHANGES THAT OCCUR AS WE PASS FROM ONE TO THE NEXT. LIKE ANY FAMILY TIED TO THE LAND, WE ARE ALWAYS BRACING FOR THE CHALLENGES OF A PARTICULAR SEASON AND I TRULY ENJOY ALL OF THEM. BUT I DO HAVE FAVORITES.

Spring, the "Great Awakening," happens to be one of them. There's so much to look forward to once winter's chill begins to break: the return of migrant birds like our colorful orioles, the swell of warm sunshine, and of course, the scent of dirt! The raw, crisp, Canadian air that blows into the Finger Lakes from the Northwest during the cold months scatters, and the earth's subtle outdoor aromas return. It's invigorating, and it gets me excited for the work ahead.

As the thaw melts, we're hit by the rich, loamy scent of mud. It calls to farmers early, before spring has even officially begun: "Time to feed me!" So although activity halts in the orchards for most of winter, by late February we are usually right back at it. Our fruit trees won't bear peaches, cherries, apricots, or apples for several months, but they are the first to get our attention.

As any orchardist will tell you, trees are living things. Just like us, they breathe, drink, and reproduce—but with limited resources—so it's our job to ensure they have healthy soil, structure, and maintenance. An unkempt orchard quickly becomes gangly and nonproductive, so it is important that we care for them properly from the outset of spring. Trees need pruning to cut back excessive wood growth and maintain ideal limb structure. To allow for proper light and airflow, we trim the limbs by hand, encouraging the tree to focus energy on fruit-producing branches.

As the weeks progress, we prepare for the trees' blooming and leafing out, and we wait, holding our breath, for the trees to safely pass the last frost, usually in late May. Frost can easily kill delicate blossoms, a devastation that will either thin a crop, or in a really bad year, completely wipe it out. (This last happened in 2012, when the Northeast yielded the smallest crops since 1948 and many growers produced less than half of their potential harvest.) When the threat of frost is behind us, we turn to bees for the heavy lifting, bringing in 165 hives to pollinate over 500 acres. Having our little friends "set the crop" is an amazing symbiotic relationship. The trees need pollination, and the bees love being so close to a massive food source. But it's fast work: flowers sometimes bloom for just a few short days, and in cool weather the bees stay busy inside keeping the hive healthy, so steady temperatures are crucial for optimal pollination.

The now-fertilized blossoms go into "petal fall," leaving behind tiny fruitlets. The tree dedicates extraordinary energy into nurturing them, pulling on all of its water and nutrient reserves. As harvest approaches, we vigilantly watch for disease and insect and animal destruction, relying on a combination of biodynamic, organic, conventional, and sustainable approaches to keep them healthy.

Meanwhile, other spring tasks need doing. We're removing the straw that had covered strawberry plants from winter chill; it will now be bedding that keeps weeds down and dirt from splashing up on berries during heavy rains. Pruning the canes of our berry bushes, mowing, road repair, bin repair, and other preparations keep us all busy. We're also selling the last of our "cellared" fruit, the apples we store all year in temperature-controlled rooms to prevent spoilage (this is why you can find such tasty apples in the dead of winter). Our apple packhouse hums along through spring, transferring the fruit from enormous twenty-bushel harvest bins into smaller bushel boxes to be sold at various markets.

Although we sell juice and apples all year, it is a happy day at market when our first crop of the year, rhubarb, is finally harvested. Customers ask for weeks about its impending arrival and are thrilled to see the red-green stalks coming off our trucks. By mid-June, the strawberries are also ready, followed soon after by other berries, too. At this point, spring takes on a fevered pitch, with our dedicated pickers working from sunrise to delicately pluck ripe fruit from the trees. The full swing of summer is just around the bend, and we can't wait.

Rhubarb

ONE OF THE FIRST SPRINGTIME SHOOTS TO PUSH ITS WAY skyward is rhubarb, its broad canopy of leaves gradually unfurling to protect the rosy, mouth-puckering stalks beneath. Botanically speaking, rhubarb is a vegetable, but it has such a history of being sweetened and prepared in fruit-filled desserts (its nickname is the "pie plant") that over time it has become a tried-and-true honorary member of the fruit family.

toss it into any old salad or dessert as you might, say, an apple, or chomp on a raw stalk as you walk home from the market (although a snack of raw stalks dipped in bowls of sugar is pretty tasty, like Nature's Fun Dip). Cooking with rhubarb demands some thoughtfulness. But I always encourage shoppers to look at that tartness as an advantage, since this is what enables rhubarb to slip comfortably between sweet and savory dishes. For

JOE'S GROWING TIPS:

• Thriving best in Northern climates, rhubarb loves bright light and rich soil, so find a sunny, fertile patch of your garden in which to grow it.

• Rhubarb begins its growth as the weather warms. You can help it along by placing an overturned bucket or pot on top of the shoot to increase the ambient temperature and trick it into growing more quickly, a practice called "forcing." The stalks don't wither until the weather turns chilly, so while you may think of it as a spring crop, you can actually enjoy it throughout the summer and into early fall, though later crops may yield a more fibrous stalk. At the end of the season, leave about 50 percent of the stalks and their leaves in the ground to ensure a crop the following year.

• It can take a few years before you see a good crop of this perennial plant, so be patient. Avoid the temptation to harvest the first year, since you really want to give the root system time to grow strong and healthy. From the second year onward, aim to harvest only a third or so of the plant's growth to avoid stressing the plant. After five years, dig up the plant in early spring, separate the "pedials" (bulbs) into 3- to 5-inch / 7.5 to 12.5 cm pieces, and share with neighbors or replant them with 10 to 14 inches / 25.5 to 35.5 cm between each one; this will help them remain vigorous.

• When harvesting rhubarb, make sure never to cut the stalk with scissors or a knife, as this can inhibit future growth. Instead, pull gently on the stalk while twisting it until it snaps cleanly at the base.

In spite of that, customers sometimes fret that rhubarb's sourness makes it a tricky kitchen companion. To an extent, that's valid—you can't just slice it up and

example, it is a home run in pies, jams, sauces, cobblers, and compotes, working well with all those flavors we associate with dessert: rich creams, yogurts, and butters;

full-bodied sweeteners like maple syrup and honey; zesty citrus; and warm spices like cinnamon, cardamom, and ginger. But it's also an excellent foil to fatty meat and fish—few things perk up a leg of lamb, slice of baked ham, or fillet of mackerel like a rhubarb chutney or salsa. It really takes to rich, salty cheeses like veiny blues and creamy bries and is great with toasted almonds or walnuts. You can pickle it, juice it, boil it into a delicious mash (my favorite) or use it as a base for a tasty cocktail (as we did in our Rhubarb Tom Collins, page 26). In fact, its root is used in bitters as well as in the Italian *amaro* Fernet-Blanca. Of course, one of my favorite ways to enjoy rhubarb is paired with other fruits, particularly apples and berries of any kind. You just can't beat fruit on top of fruit.

To prepare rhubarb, first trim and discard the leaves, which contain toxic oxalic acid. We do this for our customers before the stalks even reach the market, but if you ever see them, they need to go. Wash the stalk under cold running water. If you dislike the stringiness or if you plan to use it raw, lightly peel away the outer layer with a vegetable peeler or paring knife. Rhubarb is notorious for falling apart quickly once cooked, and this is fine and expected, although a very high-heat cooking method like roasting will help it maintain its shape.

SELECTION: Seek out stalks that are firm and glossy with no shriveling. Stalks are usually 1 to 3 inches / 2.5 to 7.5 cm thick. The thicker stalks (often hothouse grown) are sometimes considered to have a milder, less sour flavor; whether that makes it more or less desirable is up to you. At any rate, the smaller stalks are also usually less fibrous, and may not even require any peeling. Most rhubarb appears deep maroon or blushing red-green in color, but a fully green stalk does not mean that it is not ripe or unfit for cooking; it is likely just a different variety.

STORAGE: Fresh rhubarb does not last long once harvested, usually up to a week (wrapped in plastic) in the refrigerator. Do not wash stalks until just before use, as the moisture can hasten deterioration. Rhubarb also freezes well (see Freezing Fruit, page 247).

SPICY ROAST CHICKEN *with* RHUBARB CHUTNEY

Just the smell of chutney cooking on the stove brings back a favorite memory of my grandparents, making it together in their later years. So while it has a special place in my heart to begin with, I can't resist its sweet-tart play of flavors. Rhubarb chutney is especially delicious, extra tangy from the fruit with a touch of warmth from the ginger and clove. You can spoon it over everything from roast chicken and lamb to slabs of fresh goat cheese. It simply teems with flavor and is a great way to use up any excess fruit hanging out in your kitchen.

Makes 4 servings

RHUBARB CHUTNEY	SPICY ROAST CHICKEN
1½ pounds / 680 g rhubarb, diced	2 dried red chiles, such as chile de arbol
¾ cup / 150 g packed light brown sugar	1 teaspoon yellow mustard seeds
½ cup / 80 g golden raisins	1 teaspoon coriander seeds
⅓ cup / 80 ml cider vinegar	1 teaspoon black peppercorns
⅓ cup / 50 g finely chopped red onion	1 (3½-pound / 1.6 kg) whole chicken, patted dry
1 tablespoon peeled and finely chopped fresh ginger	1 tablespoon olive oil
¼ teaspoon ground cloves	2½ teaspoons kosher salt
Pinch kosher salt	Greek yogurt, for serving
1 teaspoon freshly grated lemon zest	Chopped cilantro, for serving

To make the chutney, combine the rhubarb, brown sugar, raisins, vinegar, red onion, ginger, cloves, and salt in a heavy-bottomed saucepan over medium heat. Bring to a boil over high heat, then reduce the heat to medium-low and simmer gently, stirring often, until the rhubarb is tender and the mixture has thickened, 10 to 15 minutes. Stir in the lemon zest and remove the pan from the heat to cool completely. You should have about 2½ cups / 590 ml of chutney.

To make the chicken, in a medium-sized, dry skillet over medium heat, toast the chiles, mustard seeds, coriander, and peppercorns until fragrant, 1 to 2 minutes. Transfer the mixture to a spice grinder or mortar and pestle, and grind or crush it together until it forms a coarse powder. Transfer the spice rub to a small bowl and whisk in the oil.

Season the chicken inside and out with salt. Rub the spice mixture all over the bird. Place chicken on a platter and cover loosely with plastic wrap. Refrigerate at least 1 hour or overnight. Let stand at room temperature for 20 minutes before roasting. Preheat the oven to 400°F / 205°C.

Lightly oil a small roasting pan or baking dish that is just big enough to fit the chicken (a 9- or 10-inch / 23 or 25.5 cm pie plate is great for this). Roast the chicken, breast-side up, for 20 minutes. Flip the chicken and roast it 20 minutes more. Then flip it breast-side up, and continue cooking until it is golden brown and juices run clear when pierced in the deepest part of the thigh, 15 to 20 minutes longer. Let the chicken rest on a cutting board for 15 minutes before carving. Serve the chicken topped with chutney, a small dollop of yogurt, and cilantro.

ROASTED RHUBARB,
WATERCRESS, *and* GOAT CHEESE SALAD

If rhubarb's usual tartness scares you off, this is the rhubarb recipe for you. Roasting is a great way to mellow its bite, leaving just a touch of tang, and it's one of the few cooking methods that allow rhubarb chunks to stay intact. It's an outstanding alternative to more conventional pears or apples in a crisp salad, and you could also drizzle in a little extra syrup and spoon the luscious results over ice cream, Greek yogurt, or waffles.

Makes 6 servings

8 ounces / 230 g rhubarb, cut into ½-inch / 1.3 cm pieces

3 tablespoons maple syrup, or to taste

3 tablespoons plus 1 teaspoon extra-virgin olive oil, divided

1½ tablespoons sherry vinegar

¼ teaspoon kosher salt

2 tablespoons thinly sliced shallot

2 teaspoons minced tarragon

1 pound / 450 g watercress, tough stems removed

¼ cup / 30 g toasted chopped walnuts

3 ounces / 85 g soft goat cheese, crumbled (about ¾ cup)

Preheat the oven to 450°F / 230°C. Line a rimmed baking sheet with aluminum foil. Toss together the rhubarb, syrup, and 1 teaspoon of the oil. Spread the mixture on the prepared baking sheet and roast until the rhubarb is tender, 7 to 10 minutes. Remove the baking sheet from the oven and set it aside to cool.

In a small bowl, whisk together the vinegar, salt, shallot, and tarragon. Whisk in the remaining 3 tablespoons of oil.

In a large bowl, combine the watercress, walnuts, and rhubarb. Gently toss in the goat cheese and dressing.

RHUBARB-OAT BREAD *with* STRAWBERRY BUTTER

On drizzly spring mornings when summer is dragging its feet, a warm slice of this moist, dense quickbread raises the spirits. Make sure to use the smaller, jewel-like strawberries from your local farmers' market versus the supersized grocery variety—their more concentrated juices meld with the butter and sweetly offset rhubarb's zing. Keep extra butter wrapped tightly in plastic for up to one week in the refrigerator or for up to six months in the freezer.

Makes 1 loaf

STRAWBERRY BUTTER	RHUBARB-OAT BREAD
½ cup / 115 g unsalted butter, at room temperature	1 pound / 455 g rhubarb, cut into ¼-inch / 6 mm pieces (2 cups)
2 tablespoons confectioners' sugar	¾ cup plus 2 tablespoons / 190 g granulated sugar, divided
⅛ teaspoon kosher salt	1¼ cups / 175 g all-purpose flour
⅓ cup /70 g hulled and coarsely chopped strawberries	⅓ cup / 40 g toasted chopped walnuts
	½ cup / 60 g old-fashioned rolled oats
	½ teaspoon baking soda
	¼ teaspoon fine sea salt
	¼ teaspoon ground cinnamon
	Grated zest of 1 orange
	2 large eggs
	½ cup / 120 ml walnut or vegetable oil

To make the butter, whip the butter, sugar, and salt in a food processor until fluffy. Add the berries and continue to whip until fully incorporated. Scrape the mixture onto a large sheet of plastic wrap. Shape it into a log and wrap tightly with the plastic. Chill until ready to use.

To make the bread, combine the rhubarb and 2 tablespoons of the sugar in a small saucepan over medium heat. Cook, stirring occasionally, until the fruit is just tender, 5 to 7 minutes; remove the pan from the heat and set it aside to cool.

Preheat the oven to 350°F / 180°C. Lightly grease a 9 x 5-inch / 23 x 12.5 cm loaf pan.

In a large bowl, whisk together the flour, the remaining ¾ cup / 190 g of sugar, the walnuts, oats, baking soda, salt, and cinnamon. In a separate bowl, whisk together the rhubarb, orange zest, eggs, and oil. Gently fold the dry ingredients into the wet ingredients until just combined.

Scrape the batter into the prepared pan. Bake until golden brown and a toothpick inserted in the center of the cake emerges clean, 50 minutes to 1 hour. Transfer to a wire rack to cool in the pan for 15 minutes, then turn out the loaf onto the rack and cool completely.

Meanwhile, allow the butter to come to room temperature. Slice the bread and slather it with the butter.

RHUBARB TOM COLLINS

An all-American cocktail, the Tom Collins is said to have been created on the East Coast in the late nineteenth century. The original was an easygoing libation of simple syrup, carbonated water, lemon juice, and a douse of gin. Since then, all kinds of variations have popped up, substituting rum or whiskey for the gin, and limes for the lemons. Here's an orchard-inspired version to add to the mix—rhubarb's light herbaceous notes work beautifully with the gin.

Makes 1 serving

RHUBARB SYRUP
1½ cups / 300 g granulated sugar
1½ cups / 170 g thinly sliced rhubarb

1½ ounces / 40 ml gin
1 ounce / 30 ml freshly squeezed lemon juice
Seltzer, as needed

For the rhubarb syrup: In a small pot, bring 1 cup / 240 ml of water to a boil, add the sugar, and cook until the sugar is completely dissolved. Stir in the rhubarb. Remove the pot from the heat and set it aside to cool completely. Store the rhubarb in its syrup in an airtight container in the refrigerator.

Fill a collins glass with ice cubes. Stir in the gin and the lemon juice. Top with seltzer, and drizzle in rhubarb syrup to taste. Garnish with some rhubarb slices from the syrup.

RHUBARB SORBETTO

To call Franny's in Brooklyn a pizza place doesn't do it justice. The menu is heavy on traditional Italian pizza and pasta, but it's all done with the seasons in mind: spring pie toppings include dandelion greens and ramps alongside the standard mozzarella, tomato, and basil. Husband and wife team Andrew Feinberg and Francine Stephens are pros at bringing out the best in just a few ingredients, like this blush-colored sorbet, which relies on raw rhubarb for its extra-refreshing appeal. At the restaurant, they use a professional gelato stabilizer to achieve a wonderfully smooth texture that is maintained even after freezing, but you can use a small pinch of xanthan gum at home. Look for it at your local health food store.

Makes about 1 quart / 1 liter

1½ to 1¾ pounds / 680 to 790 g rhubarb, as needed, chopped	⅛ teaspoon kosher salt
1¼ cups / 250 g granulated sugar	Pinch of xanthan gum

In the bowl of a food processor, process 1½ pounds / 680 g of the rhubarb until almost smooth and very juicy. Transfer the pulp to a fine-mesh sieve set over a large bowl; strain well. You should have about 2 cups/ 470 ml of strained juice; if not, purée and strain the remaining rhubarb. Discard the pulp.

In a large, heavy-bottomed pot, whisk together the sugar, salt, and xanthan gum. Slowly whisk in 1¼ cups / 300 ml of water and cook the mixture over medium heat, whisking occasionally, until the sugar is completely dissolved and the mixture thickens slightly, 5 to 10 minutes. Remove the pot from the heat and pour in the rhubarb juice.

Chill until completely cold, either in a bowl set over an ice bath or in the refrigerator overnight.

Churn in an ice-cream machine according to the manufacturer's instructions. Serve immediately or transfer to a quart-sized, freezer-proof container for longer storage.

RHUBARB-CARDAMOM CRÈME BRÛLÉE

This recipe was inspired by my sister Amy, who is a fan of rhubarb and the classic French dessert. It's a fantastic double whammy—first you get to tap away at the crisp, caramelized crust, and then you dig into the creamy, fruit-filled custard below.

Makes 8 servings

1½ pounds / 680 g rhubarb, trimmed and diced into ¼-inch / 6 mm pieces	2 tablespoons cardamom pods, lightly crushed
⅔ cup plus ¼ cup / 180 g granulated sugar, divided	8 large egg yolks
2⅔ cups / 630 ml heavy whipping cream	1 teaspoon pure vanilla extract
	2 tablespoons demarara sugar

In a small pot, combine the rhubarb and ¼ cup / 50 g of the sugar. Cook over medium heat, stirring occasionally, until the rhubarb is just tender, 5 to 7 minutes. Remove the rhubarb to a bowl with a slotted spoon. Continue cooking the liquid until it has reduced to a thick, syrupy consistency, about 5 minutes. Pour the syrup over the rhubarb in the bowl; set it aside to cool.

In a medium, heavy-bottomed pot over medium heat, combine the cream and cardamom. Simmer for 5 minutes; remove from the heat, cover, and let the mixture steep for 1 hour. Return the pot to the stove and bring the mixture back to a simmer, uncovered; strain the flavored cream through a fine-mesh sieve into a medium bowl, pressing down on the cardamom pods with a spatula. Discard the cardamom.

In a large bowl, whisk together the egg yolks and the remaining ⅔ cup / 140 g of sugar. Whisking constantly, pour in the hot cream mixture in a steady stream until combined. Whisk in the vanilla.

Preheat the oven to 325°F / 165°C. Divide the rhubarb and syrup equally among 8 (4-ounce / 120 ml) ramekins. Pour the custard base over the rhubarb in the ramekins. Transfer the ramekins to a roasting pan. Place the pan on the oven rack and pour enough boiling water into the pan to come halfway up the sides of the ramekins. Cover the roasting pan with foil and bake the custards until they are set around the edges but the centers jiggle slightly when shaken, 25 to 30 minutes. Remove the ramekins from the pan and cool to room temperature; transfer to the refrigerator to chill thoroughly, at least 4 hours.

Preheat the broiler. Sprinkle the tops of the custards lightly with demarara sugar. Transfer the ramekins to a baking sheet, and place them under the broiler, watching carefully, until they are caramelized and bubbly, 1 to 2 minutes.

Strawberries

HARVEST SEASON: LATE SPRING to EARLY SUMMER

IT IS A FREQUENTLY BEMOANED TRUTH THAT STRAWBER-ries, at least the most commercially available ones, are not what they once were. The sumptuous, slow-ripened kind we've all picked at a local farm or along some quiet, wooded path are part of a taste memory that forever lingers, and one that bland and bloated supermarket berries, which have sacrificed delicacy for resiliency and day. It's the most perishable crop we grow and it's a great way to get back into the season—on fire. Crimson and flower-fragranced, they are most likely found at the farmers' market, where it is feasible for farmers to pick, pack, and bring them to consumers within a day. The sweetest are tiny, wild varieties like Tri-Stars and Sea-scape, saturated with syrupy concentrated juices. At

JOE'S GROWING TIPS:

• Strawberries are herbaceous, low-growing perennials that proliferate in temperate zones, particularly in colder climates. Plant them as soon as the dirt is workable in spring. They need moist, light soil that drains easily (if your soil has poor drainage, consider planting them in a raised bed or container), and they prefer full sun away from shade-casting trees to better develop and deepen their sugars. Water them liberally.

• As the berry's name might imply, a layer of straw or other mulch at the base of each plant keeps the fruit clean and away from rot-inducing moisture. It also protects against weeds and provides some insulation against any early spring cold snaps.

• To help the plants create strong roots before bearing fruit, pinch off all (yes, all) of the snowy blossoms during the first summer of planting. This allows them to channel their energy into establishing healthy growth patterns, and though it means no fruit the first year, it will yield a more abundant crop for the next several years.

• Harvest strawberries in the early morning, while the fruit is still cool. Twist the berry from the vine, holding onto the stem. If possible, leave the stem intact, as it will help preserve the berry's freshness. Before plucking, check the berry's underbelly for unripe coloring, since the side facing the sun is often the first to turn ripe and red.

shelf life, cannot and will not ever match. And yet for some reason we keep trying, sometimes buying them all year long, hoping for a taste of the deeply flavored, sun-soaked berries of our minds.

Come spring, they're out there in local farm fields, soaking up the warm summer sun. I love strawberries because their delicate nature dictates what we pick each Red Jacket, we bring intensely-flavored Honeoye, Jewel, and Allstar strawberries to market. Perfectly ripe straw-berries need little adornment—dust them with sugar and plop them on top of tangy sour cream or crème fraîche, slice and sprinkle them with balsamic vinegar and minced tarragon or mint, or soak them in a cupful of red wine, such as a fruity Beaujolais. When I want a quick and healthy snack, I just "cap and smash" the berries straight into a bowl, sweeten them with a drop of fruit juice, and start spooning them in.

They're also delicious churned into ice cream and sorbet, paired with vanilla-scented sponge cakes, or folded into pastry cream and spooned into tart shells. Strawberries love everything citrus—orange zest, lime juice, lemon, even a splash of Grand Marnier or limoncello—and mate well with other berries and rhubarb, too. Dipping them in melted chocolate is an undisputed classic, though bittersweet chocolate is a better choice than milk or white chocolates, since the dark acidic notes nicely offset the fruit's sugars. Few jams are as deserving of buttered breakfast toast than strawberry.

Never wash your berries until just before you are going to use them. Moisture makes them extremely susceptible to mold. Rinse them before hulling, to make sure that no water seeps into the cavity. To hull a strawberry, shallowly angle a paring knife into the base of the strawberry stem, run it around the core and pop out the green leaves and stem.

SELECTION: Ripe strawberries are intensely aromatic (their Latin name, *fragaria*, means "fragrance"). If you aren't immediately hit with a heady, honeyed scent, move on. Fresh berries are glossy and garnet-hued with no matte appearance, which indicates they are beginning to spoil. At the market, tilt the carton gently and take a peek at the underside—the berries should move freely in the container and the bottom should be dry and juice-free. If they stick together or appear damp, you likely have a few moldy berries hiding in there. Strawberries will not continue to ripen once picked, so purchase them at their peak, with little or no white coloring at the tips or shoulders.

STORAGE: Ripe strawberries really ought to be enjoyed the same day you bring them home. Highly perishable, they will last only a few days in the refrigerator, and the cold air tends to mute their flavor and fragrance. On the other hand, they will rapidly begin to rot on the countertop. If you're bent on keeping them for a few days, pack them loosely in a paper towel–lined resealable plastic bag and refrigerate, taking care to stack nothing on top of them as they bruise easily. You can also freeze them (see Freezing Fruit, page 247).

BRIOCHE FRENCH TOAST *with* FRESH RICOTTA
AND LEMON THYME STRAWBERRIES

As a rule, lemon-scented herbs like lemon thyme, lemon verbena, and lemon balm really take to succulent fruits like berries, peaches, and plums. They deliver soft herbal notes that don't overwhelm and add interest to sweet and savory fruit dishes. In the summer, a handful of leaves dropped into pitchers of ice-cold water make for a refreshing alternative to lemon slices. Here, lemon thyme gives a lift to a grown-up version of French toast.

Makes 6 servings

LEMON THYME STRAWBERRIES	BRIOCHE FRENCH TOAST
1 pint / 340 g fresh ripe strawberries	4 large eggs
1½ teaspoons granulated sugar, more as needed	¼ cup / 50 g granulated sugar
1½ teaspoons minced lemon thyme (see note)	2½ cups / 590 ml whole milk
	1 teaspoon lemon zest
	Pinch of fine sea salt
	1 pound / 455 g day-old brioche or challah, sliced 1 inch / 2.5 cm thick
	¼ cup / 55 g unsalted butter, divided
	Fresh ricotta, for serving

To hull the strawberries, run a paring knife around the base of the strawberry stem and pop out the hull. Thinly slice the strawberries into a bowl (you should have about 2 cups sliced), and toss them with the sugar and lemon thyme. Let stand for 15 minutes. Taste and sweeten with more sugar if desired.

To make the French toast, in a wide, shallow bowl or casserole dish, whisk together the eggs, sugar, and milk. Whisk in the lemon zest and salt.

Dip each slice of bread into the egg mixture, turning to coat evenly. Soak it just long enough for the bread to absorb the liquid, about 15 to 30 seconds, depending on the dryness of your bread. Do not oversoak or the bread will break apart.

Melt 2 tablespoons of the butter in a large skillet over medium-high heat. Add half of the French toast in a single layer; cook, without moving, until the undersides are crisp and golden, 2 to 3 minutes. Flip and cook the other sides until golden, 2 to 3 minutes more. Transfer to a plate. Repeat with the remaining butter and bread.

Serve immediately, topped with ricotta and the strawberries.

Note: If you have trouble getting your hands on some lemon thyme, substitute ¼ teaspoon of lemon zest, ¼ teaspoon of minced thyme, and ¼ teaspoon of minced mint.

STRAWBERRY HAND PIES

Friends and family will get a kick out of these fruit-filled, flaky mini pies. Similar in shape to an empanada or a Cornish pasty, they fit right into the palm of your hand, no fork necessary (though maybe a few napkins!). They're amazing straight from the fryer, or you could pack them up for an afternoon picnic; the addition of egg to the crust makes them sturdy enough to withstand transportation and they're good at room temperature, too. Make sure to maintain a steady oil temperature using a deep-fat or candy thermometer. It can make all the difference between a crisp crust and a burnt or soggy one.

Makes 1 dozen individual pies

CRUST	FILLING
2⅔ cups / 390 g all-purpose flour	1 pound / 455 g strawberries, hulled and cut into ½-inch / 1.3 cm dice (about 2½ cups diced)
2 teaspoons granulated sugar	⅓ cup / 70 g granulated sugar
1 teaspoon kosher salt	1½ tablespoons cornstarch
1 cup / 225 g unsalted butter, chilled and cubed	⅛ teaspoon kosher salt
1 large egg, whisked with enough water to equal ½ cup / 120 ml	Canola oil, for frying
	Cinnamon sugar, for sprinkling

To make the dough, in a food processor, pulse together the flour, sugar, and salt. Pulse in the butter until the mixture forms large, pea-sized crumbs. Pulse in the egg mixture, a little at a time, as needed, until it forms a moist, crumbly dough. It should not be wet, but just damp enough to hold together when you squeeze it in your fist. On a clean surface, bring the dough together into a single ball, working it as little as possible. Cut the ball into 12 equal wedges. Roll each wedge into a ball and flatten each ball into a disk with the palm of your hand. Lay the dough rounds on a baking sheet, cover the sheet tightly with plastic wrap, and refrigerate for 1 hour.

To make the filling, toss together the berries, sugar, cornstarch, and salt in a medium pot. Let the mixture stand for 15 minutes. Simmer gently over medium heat until the juices are no longer cloudy and a thick, cohesive sauce forms around the berries, 5 to 10 minutes. Remove the pot from the heat and set it aside to cool completely.

On a lightly floured surface, roll one disk of dough into a 5-inch / 12.5 cm circle (store the remaining dough in the fridge until ready to use). Spoon a heaping tablespoon of the strawberry mixture onto one half of the dough round; brush the edges of the dough with water and fold the dough over filling, creating a half moon. Press down on the edges to seal. Crimp the edges with the tines of a fork (this will also ensure a good seal, since you don't want any filling to spill out while frying).. Transfer the filled pie to a floured baking sheet. Repeat with the remaining dough and filling. Transfer the baking sheet to the refrigerator and chill pies for 30 minutes.

Fill a large, heavy-bottomed pot with 3 to 4 inches / 7.5 to 10 cm of oil over medium-high heat. Heat the oil to 375°F / 190°C on a deep-fat or candy thermometer. Carefully fry the pies in batches until golden brown and firm, about 3 to 4 minutes per batch. Transfer the pies to a paper towel–lined plate and sprinkle them all over with cinnamon sugar. Let the oil return to 375°F / 190°C before frying the remaining pies.

STRAWBERRY-BLACK PEPPER GRANITA

This dessert is all about vibrancy. It practically hums with flavor, from the candy-sweet berries to the syrupy balsamic to the peppercorn's subtle warmth. It's the perfect end to a late-spring meal, when evenings are growing warm and you're craving a finish that refreshes and satisfies. You can even enhance the decadence factor by topping it with a dollop of mascarpone or some dark chocolate shavings.

Makes about 6 cups

⅓ cup / 70 g granulated sugar	½ teaspoon freshly ground black pepper
1 pound / 450 g strawberries, hulled and divided	Pinch of fine sea salt
2 teaspoons to 1 tablespoon aged balsamic vinegar, to taste	Mint, basil, or tarragon, chopped, for serving

Combine the sugar and ⅔ cup / 160 ml of water in a small pot over medium heat. Simmer until the sugar completely dissolves and the liquid is syrupy, about 5 minutes. Cool completely.

Coarsely chop 4 cups / 785 g of the berries; transfer to a food processor and purée until smooth. Strain through a fine-mesh sieve into a bowl.

Stir the cooled syrup, vinegar, pepper, and salt into the strained berry juice. Pour the mixture into a wide, shallow pan (a square baking pan is perfect for this), and transfer the pan, uncovered, to the freezer. Freeze, breaking up the mixture with a fork every 30 minutes, until completely frozen and crumbly, about 1½ hours.

To serve, finely dice the remaining strawberries. Spoon the granita into dishes. Top with finely diced berries and herbs. Store any leftover granita in an airtight container for up to 2 weeks.

STRAWBERRY-PECAN SHORTCAKES

It's no secret that strawberries and buttery shortcakes are a heavenly match, but strawberries and buttery pecans are a close second. These biscuits are crisp on the outside with a fluffy center perfect for soaking up all those macerated berry juices. If you like your shortcakes with more heft, split and toast them just before filling.

Makes 6 servings

STRAWBERRIES	PECAN SHORTCAKES
1 pint / 340 g ripe strawberries, hulled and sliced	1½ cups / 210 g all-purpose flour
3 tablespoons packed light brown sugar, plus more as needed	⅓ cup / 70 g granulated sugar
Pinch of kosher salt	2¼ teaspoons baking powder
Zest of ½ orange	½ teaspoon baking soda
	¼ teaspoon kosher salt
	½ cup / 60 g pecans, coarsely chopped
	5 tablespoons / 70 g unsalted butter, very cold and cut into cubes
	¾ cup / 180 ml sour cream, more as needed
	1 teaspoon pure vanilla extract
	Whipped cream, for serving

In a small bowl, combine the strawberries, sugar, salt, and orange zest. Let the mixture stand at room temperature while you prepare the biscuits.

Preheat the oven to 450°F / 230°C. Line a large baking sheet with parchment paper.

In the bowl of a food processor, pulse together the flour, sugar, baking powder, baking soda, and salt. Pulse in the pecans until finely ground. Pulse in the butter until the mixture forms pea-sized crumbs. Pulse in the sour cream and vanilla until the mixture just forms a sticky dough (if it seems dry, add additional sour cream, 1 tablespoon at a time, as needed).

Spoon scant ½-cup / 95 g portions of dough onto the prepared baking sheet. Bake until the shortcakes are golden brown, 12 to 15 minutes. Remove the baking sheet from the oven and transfer the cakes to a wire rack to cool.

Taste the strawberries and add more sugar if necessary. Split the shortcakes and top each serving with strawberries and whipped cream. Serve immediately.

MACERATED FRUIT

If you've ever marinated a juicy steak or chicken breast in herbs and spices, you know the benefits of allowing different flavors to marry over a period of time. Macerated fruit abides by the same principle, only it requires no cooking: just a few well-considered ingredients and some time. This is how easy it is: Place any juicy sliced fruit in a bowl (leave small blueberries and raspberries whole) and toss in a splash of liquor, vinegar, fruit juice, or syrup. You can experiment with quantities and types, but think along the lines of what complements that particular fruit. For instance, strawberries are good with balsamic vinegar and peaches are excellent with a sweet white wine. Orange juice is great with practically any fruit, and I love to experiment with our orchard juices, like Apricot Stomp with sweet cherries or Fuji Apple Juice with blackberries. You can also drop in one or two pieces of whole spices (or a tiny pinch of ground spices), chopped herbs like mint or tarragon, and other sweeteners like honey or sugar. Cover the fruit and let it stand for 30 minutes at room temperature or up to overnight in the refrigerator. As the mixture sits, the fruit's moisture is released and its flavor is infused with the surrounding ingredients, creating a syrupy, stove-free sauce for pound cakes, ice creams, and other desserts.

STRAWBERRY OLIVE OIL CAKE

It's almost impossible to eat just one slice of this cake. Incredibly moist and just sweet enough, it's dessert-worthy, snack-worthy, and (almost) breakfast-worthy, too. Formerly the pastry chef at Tom Colicchio's Craft restaurant, Karen DeMasco now heads the pastry kitchen at Locanda Verde, a rustic Manhattan taverna where her Italian-inflected desserts are inspired by the market's peak offerings. Karen's forte—creating unexpected layers of flavor and texture—is at play in this jam-swirled cake enriched with fruity olive oil.

Makes one 8-inch cake

2 large eggs, at room temperature	2 teaspoons freshly squeezed lemon juice
1 large egg yolk, at room temperature	1¼ cups / 130 g cake flour
Finely grated zest of 1 lemon	¾ teaspoon baking powder
½ cup plus 3 tablespoons / 160 g granulated sugar	¾ teaspoon kosher salt
½ cup / 120 ml extra-virgin olive oil	6 tablespoons / 85 g unsalted butter, melted and cooled
3 tablespoons milk	½ cup / 120 ml Quick Strawberry Jam (page 251), gently warmed

Preheat the oven to 350°F / 180°C. Grease an 8-inch / 20.5 cm springform cake pan. Arrange an oven rack in the bottom of the oven.

In the bowl of an electric mixer fitted with the whisk attachment, beat the eggs, yolk, lemon zest, and sugar on medium-high speed until doubled in volume, about 5 minutes.

While the eggs are whipping, in a separate bowl, combine the olive oil, milk, and lemon juice. In a third bowl, sift together the flour, baking powder, and salt.

Slowly drizzle the olive oil mixture into the eggs while the eggs continue to whip. After all of the liquid is incorporated, turn the mixer to low and add the dry ingredients in three additions, allowing each addition to incorporate fully before adding the next. With the mixer running, slowly drizzle in the melted butter until just combined.

Scrape the cake batter into the prepared pan. Bake on the bottom rack until the edges just begin to set, 15 to 20 minutes. Working quickly, remove the cake from the oven and spoon the jam over its surface, letting it sink in and create a swirling effect. Return the cake to the oven and bake until it feels firm to the touch and a cake tester emerges with crumbs, 20 to 25 minutes longer. Remove the pan from the oven and let the cake cool on a wire rack in the pan for 15 minutes, then release the cake from the pan and return it to the rack to cool. Serve warm or at room temperature.

MUDDLED STRAWBERRY SHANDY

This drink may be pink and frothy from muddled strawberries, but a generous draft of lager and a shot of rum anchor it firmly in the stiff drink category. Serve it up in a hefty mug that's spent an hour or so in the freezer getting good and frosty. You can make it with the lemon syrup or substitute your favorite lemonade (a good one to try is our Joe's Summer Blend juice (page 302).

Makes 2 servings

⅓ cup / 70 g granulated sugar
2 strips lemon peel, white pith removed
2 tablespoons freshly squeezed lemon juice, plus more as needed
2.25 ounces / 60 g strawberries, finely chopped (⅓ cup chopped)
1 ounce / 30 ml gold or light rum
Pale lager beer or wheat beer, as needed

In a small saucepan over medium heat, combine the sugar with ⅓ cup / 80 ml of water. Simmer until the sugar completely dissolves. Stir in the lemon peel, remove the pan from the heat, and cool to room temperature. Stir in the lemon juice and discard the lemon peel. Use the syrup immediately, or transfer to an airtight container and refrigerate for up to 1 week.

Muddle the strawberries in the bottom of a cocktail shaker. Strain in the lemon syrup and pour in the rum. Shake vigorously. Divide the mixture between 2 medium-sized frosty mugs. Top off with beer. Squeeze in extra lemon juice, if desired.

Currants

IT'S MYSTIFYING THAT FRESH CURRANTS REMAIN ON THE sidelines of America's culinary habits. For starters, few fruits are more beautiful than these tiny, lustrous orbs of red, black, and white. The flavor is intensely sweet-tart but laced with exotic undertones of cedar, clove, and dark cherry. Black currants are considered the muskiest and most astringent, followed by the clean, bright-tasting red, and the milder white (best for eating out of hand and also the most rare).

bake with them, too—try pairing the inky black ones with pears in an oat-topped crumble, or the crimson ones with raspberries or sweet cherries in a summer tart. Black currants are especially prized for their use in crème de cassis, an ambrosial French liqueur consumed as an aperitif (to make your own, see page 283). At the orchard, we turn them into our own richly flavored—but alcohol-free—refreshment, combining cold-pressed black currant and apple juices. Even the plant's leaves,

JOE'S GROWING TIPS:

• Currants grow in temperate northern regions, preferably with a southern exposure. Although they can grow in a wide range of soils, cool, heavy clay soil with good drainage keeps their shallow roots in place and helps provide the moisture they need to thrive.

• Don't rush the picking of currants. They can hang on the bush until all of them are plump and fully colored—for weeks or even all summer—and will only mellow in flavor as they do so.

• Because they are so delicate, wait for a dry day to pick them. Any clinging rain or dew can cause mold. To give them the longest life off the bush, remove whole clusters, rather than individual berries.

• Currant bushes are not apt to run wild, and require infrequent pruning. Spend an afternoon in early spring removing some of the older dead branches and leaving half a dozen or so of the new shoots to allow for maximum yield.

Really, though, you can use them interchangeably, especially when cooking. Cooking mellows their punch. They've known this for centuries in Europe, where they enjoy popularity in jams, jellies, puddings, and juices. Depending on how you prepare and season them, currants can make a great foil for rich savory foods, like roasted game meats and pâté, or a vibrant compote for sweet custards, cheesecakes, and ice creams. You can

which have a fresh muskiness similar to the fruit, can be stirred into pitchers of lemonade or steeped with the berries in alcohol for an extra layer of complexity. The berries take especially well to Middle Eastern flavors like rosewater, almonds, mint, orange, and spice. Members of the genus *ribes* (which also includes gooseberries), fresh currants are a true berry, not at all related to dried black currants, which are a species of grape.

When preparing currants, simply rinse them gently under cool water before removing them from the stems. Some suggest removing the berries' seeds. Don't go to the trouble. They are not nearly as seedy as raspberries and the pips are so small that it seems like the kind of task that would turn you off of them forever. When cooking, a few minutes on the stovetop is usually enough to bring out their syrupy juices.

SELECTION: Look for plump, dry berries with no soft or dark spots. Fresh red and white currants shine with an incandescent glow; black currants have a duller complexion similar to that of blueberries. They are often sold still attached to their delicate, twig like branches, clustered like grapes. Be sure to check the underside of their container for stains, a telltale sign of deterioration.

STORAGE: When you cradle a bunch of currants in your hands, you'll sense immediately that they demand careful handling. As soon as you get home from the market, line a plate with paper towels and transfer the clusters, still on the stem, to the plate in a single layer, discarding any that appear soft or crushed. Do not wash or trim them until just before preparing them. They will usually keep this way in the refrigerator for several days, and if they are really fresh, as long as a week. You can also freeze them (see Freezing Fruit, page 247).

FREEKEH SALAD *with* RED CURRANTS, ARUGULA, GOLDEN BEETS, AND FETA

A green spelt berry with Middle Eastern origins, freekeh is roasted over hot coals while in the hull, giving it a characteristic smokiness. Fresh red currants are often too tart to eat raw, but in this salad their brightness really balances the sweet beets, salty feta, and bitter arugula. If you can't find freekeh, any sturdy, nutty grain like farro, wheatberry, or even brown rice will do.

Makes 4 servings

1 pound / 455 g golden beets, peeled and cut into ½-inch / 1.3 cm cubes

1½ tablespoons plus ¼ cup / 80 ml extra-virgin olive oil, divided

¾ teaspoon kosher salt, divided, plus more as needed

Freshly ground black pepper

1¼ cups (8 ounces / 230 g) freekeh

½ cup / 80 g fresh red currants, rinsed

2 teaspoons honey

1 tablespoon red wine vinegar, preferably aged

2 tablespoons minced garlic scapes, or 1 small clove garlic, minced

4 cups / 110 g fresh arugula, torn into pieces

3 ounces / 85 g feta cheese, crumbled (¾ cup)

Preheat the oven to 400°F / 205°C. Toss the beets with 1½ tablespoons / 20 ml of the oil, ¼ teaspoon of the salt, and black pepper to taste. Spread the beets on a baking sheet in a single layer and roast, tossing occasionally, until tender, 30 to 40 minutes.

Meanwhile, bring a large pot of salted water to a boil. Add the freekeh and cook until tender but chewy, 25 to 30 minutes. Drain well.

Toss the currants gently with the honey. In a small bowl, whisk together the vinegar, garlic scapes, and the remaining ½ teaspoon of salt. Whisk in the remaining ¼ cup / 60 ml of oil. Stir in the currant mixture.

In a large bowl, toss together the arugula, beets, freekeh, and feta. Gently toss in the dressing. Taste and add more salt and pepper, if necessary. Serve immediately.

ROASTED RACK OF LAMB *with* CURRANT CUMBERLAND SAUCE

Rack of lamb is my all-time favorite food. Cumberland sauce is too fancy-sounding a name for the rustic condiment that it really is. Picture the ease of cranberry sauce with a dialed-up intensity (thanks to a glug of wine and the richly flavored currants) and you've pretty much nailed it. And just like cranberry sauce loves turkey, Cumberland sauce has a thing for bold red meats like this mustard-slathered rack of lamb. You can use red, black, or a mix of currants, adjusting the seasonings until you hit on the perfect blend of sweet, tart, and spicy.

Makes 4 to 6 servings

LAMB	CUMBERLAND SAUCE
⅓ cup / 80 ml Dijon mustard	1 orange
1 tablespoon chopped thyme	6 ounces / 170 g mixed red and black currants, stems removed
2 teaspoons extra-virgin olive oil	
4 garlic cloves, finely chopped	½ cup / 110 g packed dark brown sugar, or to taste
2 (1½- to 2-pound / 680 to 910 g) racks of lamb, "Frenched" (your butcher can do this for you)	⅓ cup / 80 ml Marsala wine
	2 teaspoons freshly squeezed lemon juice
1 tablespoon kosher salt	½ teaspoon dry mustard
1½ teaspoons freshly ground black pepper	2 tablespoons chopped tarragon

To prepare the lamb, in a small bowl, whisk together the mustard, thyme, oil, and garlic. Season the meat all over with salt and pepper, and then coat it evenly with the mustard mixture. Place the lamb in a roasting pan with the ribs curving downward (fat-side up). Cover with plastic wrap and let it stand at room temperature for 1 hour.

While the meat marinates, prepare the sauce: Using a vegetable peeler, remove the orange peel in strips, leaving behind as much white pith as possible; use a paring knife to trim away any pithy spots from the peel. Slice the strips thinly lengthwise. Juice the zested orange and reserve the juice. Bring a small pot of water to a boil and drop in the rind; simmer for 5 minutes to soften the rind, and then drain and discard the water.

In a medium pot, combine the orange peel, orange juice, brown sugar, wine, lemon juice, and mustard. Simmer until the sugar dissolves and the sauce is slightly thickened, 5 to 10 minutes. Stir in the currants and cook gently until they just begin to pop, about 5 minutes. Taste and stir in more sugar, if needed.

Preheat the oven to 425°F / 220°C. Roast the lamb until a thermometer inserted into the meat (do not touch bone) registers 130°F / 55°C for medium-rare, 20 to 25 minutes. Remove the pan from the oven, cover it loosely with foil, and let the lamb stand at room temperature for 10 minutes before carving into individual ribs. Spoon the sauce over the lamb (reheat it if you want to serve it warm); garnish with the tarragon and serve immediately.

SUGARED CURRANTS

Sugaring is the kind of trick you pick up if you hang around foodies at the farmers' market. All it takes is a little egg white and some sugar, and you've instantly got yourself a beautiful, glittering centerpiece or garnish. You can do it with anything small, including grapes and lady apples, but tiny currants are best for garnishing. Use them to top baked meringues, lemon tarts, chocolate mousse, or even homemade ice cream. If you are concerned about consuming raw egg, swap it out for pasteurized meringue powder (available at kitchen supply stores).

Makes 1 cup

½ pint / 160 g red currants	¼ cup / 50 g superfine sugar, plus more as needed
1 egg white, lightly beaten (or substitute powdered egg meringue)	

Pull the berries apart into smaller, single-serving-sized bunches.

Line a baking sheet with parchment paper. Whisk the egg white (or reconstitute the powdered meringue according to the package instructions). Place the sugar in a wide, shallow bowl.

Using a pastry brush, coat the berries lightly with egg white. Scatter the sugar over the berries (you may have to do this a few times before you get a complete coating) and shake off any excess.

Lay the currants on the prepared baking sheet and let them stand at room temperature until they are dry to the touch, 30 minutes to 1 hour. The sugared currants will keep for 24 hours at room temperature.

BLACK CURRANT–ANISE SORBET

Like people, each fruit seems to have its own personality. Black currant is the undisputed drama queen, with a haunting muskiness and natural affinity for aromatic spices like clove, mace, and here, star anise. Equally striking is this sorbet's velvety purple hue, especially when garnished with a single sprig of fresh mint and some candied orange peel.

Makes 1½ quarts

2 cups / 400 g granulated sugar	1 teaspoon freshly squeezed lemon juice
6 whole star anise	Fresh mint, for garnish (optional)
1½ pounds / 680 g black currants, rinsed (about 4 cups)	Chopped candied orange peel, for garnish (optional)

In a medium saucepan, combine the sugar, 2 cups / 470 ml of water, and the star anise. Bring to a boil over high heat; reduce the heat to medium, and simmer until the sugar completely dissolves, about 5 minutes. Remove the pan from the heat, cover, and let it stand 1 hour. Discard the star anise.

Transfer the currants to a medium pot. Stir in 1½ cups / 350 ml of the anise syrup and place the pot over medium heat. Simmer until the berries have broken down, about 10 minutes. Strain the mixture through a fine-mesh sieve into a bowl, pushing down on the solids with a spatula to extract as much juice as possible. Stir the remaining anise syrup into the strained currant juice. Stir in ⅓ cup / 80 ml of water and the lemon juice. Cover the mixture and refrigerate for at least 2 hours, or until very cold.

Transfer the mixture to an ice-cream machine and churn according to the manufacturer's instructions.

Serve immediately, garnished with mint and candied orange peel, if desired, or transfer the sorbet to a freezer-proof container and freeze it for up to 2 weeks.

RED CURRANT CLAFOUTIS

Clafoutis is a baked dessert that falls somewhere between a custard and cake. It's always dimpled with fruit and in its birthplace, France, that fruit is usually unpitted cherries, which fans say release an almond like fragrance into the batter. This version uses tart red currants instead, which contrast nicely with the rich cream and eggs. You can remove the currants from their branches for easier eating, but you don't have to. Scattering small clusters of berries still clinging to their spindly vines looks beautiful and ensures that you savor dessert slowly, in the traditional (cherry pit–filled) way.

Makes 4 servings

Unsalted butter, as needed	½ cup / 120 ml whole milk
3 large eggs	1 teaspoon pure vanilla extract
⅔ cup / 130 g granulated sugar	½ cup / 70 g all-purpose flour
¼ teaspoon kosher salt	1¼ cups / 190 g fresh red currants, stems removed (optional)
½ cup / 120 ml heavy whipping cream	Confectioners' sugar, for dusting

Preheat the oven to 375°F / 190°C. Butter a 2-quart / 2 L gratin dish (If you don't have one, a 9-inch / 23 cm skillet or cake pan works, too).

In a large bowl, whisk together the eggs, sugar, and salt until the sugar dissolves. Whisk in the cream, milk, and vanilla. Sprinkle the flour over the batter and whisk until combined (it's okay if the batter remains slightly lumpy).

Scatter the currants over the bottom of the prepared dish. Pour the batter over the currants. Transfer the dish to the oven and bake until the edges are puffed and golden and the center is set, about 30 minutes. Remove the dish from the oven and let it cool for at least 10 minutes. Sift confectioners' sugar over the top before serving.

CHOCOLATE ROULADE *with* BLACK CURRANT COULIS

Mary Cleaver is a true pioneer in the farm-to-table food movement. Thirty years ago, when the idea of local food wasn't particularly on anyone's mind, she started The Cleaver Co., a catering business that focused on sourcing sustainable food within a day's drive of New York City. Today she also owns The Green Table, a tasty organic restaurant in Manhattan's Chelsea Market. This is one of her favorite desserts, adapted from a recipe by the famous English chef Dione Lucas. As with all of her recipes, Mary uses only the highest-quality ingredients she can get her hands on, including cream from local pastured cows, chocolate from responsible points of origin, and of course, our fruit.

Makes 8 to 10 servings

BLACK CURRANT COULIS

2 pounds / 910 g black currants, stemmed, rinsed and dried

¾ cup to 1 cup / 150 to 200 g granulated sugar, or as needed

CHOCOLATE ROULADE

Nonstick baking spray, as needed

6 ounces / 170 g bittersweet chocolate, chopped

¼ cup / 60 ml strong brewed coffee, cooled

8 large eggs, separated

¾ cup / 150 g granulated sugar

¼ cup / 20 g unsweetened cocoa powder, divided

2 tablespoons confectioners' sugar

1½ cups / 350 ml heavy whipping cream

2 teaspoons pure vanilla extract

To make the currant coulis, combine the currants, 1 cup / 240 ml of water, and ¾ cup / 150 g of the sugar in a medium, heavy saucepan over low heat. Bring the mixture to a simmer; continue to cook, stirring occasionally, until the currants soften and break down, about 5 minutes. Remove the pan from the heat and pass the currants through a fine-mesh sieve or a food mill fitted with the finest mesh. Taste the purée while it is warm and stir in more sugar, if necessary (you may need to reheat the sauce to dissolve the added sugar; stir in additional water, as needed, to reach the desired consistency).

Preheat the oven to 375°F / 190°C. Arrange an oven rack in the top third of the oven. Spray a 18 x 13-inch (46 x 33 cm) rimmed sheet pan with baking spray and line it with parchment paper, allowing some paper to hang over each side, and spray the parchment as well.

To make the cake, in the top of a double boiler or in a heatproof bowl set over a pot of simmering water, melt the chocolate until smooth. Stir in the coffee.

In the bowl of an electric mixer fitted with the whisk attachment, beat the egg yolks and sugar together until pale and extremely thick; you will know you have gone far enough when the batter falls back into the bowl in a ribbon like pattern when the whisk is lifted. Fold in the chocolate mixture until incorporated. Scrape the mixture into a large bowl. Thoroughly wash and dry the mixing bowl and whisk attachment. Add the egg whites to the clean mixing bowl and whip them in the electric

(continued)

mixer with the whisk attachment until soft peaks form. Gently fold the whites into the chocolate mixture until just combined.

Scrape the batter into the prepared baking sheet, tilting the pan so the batter spreads evenly. Immediately transfer the cake to the oven and bake until the cake is just set, 12 to 15 minutes; the edges will pull slightly away from the pan and a skewer inserted in the center will come out just barely clean. Remove the pan from the oven and let it cool on a wire rack until the cake is just warm to the touch (you want to turn it out before it is completely cool).

Place a sheet of parchment or a clean kitchen cloth larger than the cake on a baking rack, sift 2 tablespoons of the cocoa powder over it, and flip the cake out onto it. Gently peel away and discard the parchment lining from the cake. Using the bottom layer of parchment or the cloth to help you, start at the long edge closest to you and gently roll the cake in the cloth into a log shape (This will help "train" the shape of the cake and prevent cracking once it cools.) Let the cake cool completely on the wire rack on the counter, wrapped around the parchment or cloth.

When the cake is cool and ready to fill, thoroughly wash and dry the mixing bowl and whisk attachment. Add the cream to the clean bowl; whip the cream with the electric mixer to soft peaks. Unroll the cake. Spread the whipped cream over the cake's surface, leaving a 1-inch / 2.5 cm border all around. Re-roll the cake over the filling into the same log shape. (At this point you can slice and serve the cake, or refrigerate it, covered, for up to several hours.)

To serve, transfer the cake to a long platter. In a small bowl, whisk together 2 tablespoons each of cocoa powder and confectioners' sugar. Sift the mixture over the cake's surface. Slice the cake on the diagonal and serve it on plates drizzled with currant sauce.

KIR (OR KIR ROYAL) WITH HOME-BREWED CASSIS

This simple drink, which requires only two ingredients and no shaking or stirring, is a nice change of pace from the current fad of complicated, mixology-inspired cocktails. Traditionally sipped before meals, it combines currant-based crème de cassis with white wine, or, in the case of Kir Royal, Champagne. Try your hand at our home-brewed cassis using fresh currants or substitute store-bought.

Makes 1 serving

2 tablespoons Homemade Crème de Cassis (page 283)
6 ounces / 180 ml chilled white wine or Champagne

Pour the crème de cassis into the bottom of a chilled wineglass . Top with wine or Champagne. Serve immediately.

Gooseberries

HARVEST SEASON: LATE SPRING *to* LATE SUMMER

EVERY SPRING WHEN OUR MARKET TABLES FILL WITH gooseberries, we ready ourselves for plenty of curiosity. Many folks have never even heard of a gooseberry, let alone seen one, held one, or tasted one. It's what I love about our more unusual offerings—they give us the chance to introduce customers to something new and get them excited about experimenting in their home kitchens.

The flavor of gooseberries can be surprising to the uninitiated. Oblong, grape-sized berries, which range in color from golden white to apple green to dark,

Once you start digging around for gooseberry recipes, you might be surprised to find that a whole lot of them are rooted in British cuisine. Gooseberries have long been a part of English food culture, where Brits simmer them into spiced puddings and pies, stuff them into roasted goose, and transform them into gooseberry fool, a classic dish in which the sweetened fruit is folded into billowing whipped cream.

Sweetened and cooked is usually the best treatment for gooseberries. The caramel notes of brown sugar or

JOE'S GROWING TIPS:

- Unlike a lot of other fruits, gooseberries don't need full sun, and even like a little shade (though be careful not to plant them where they'll get no sun at all). Their ideal climate is one that enjoys cool summers, like New England or the northern Pacific coast. They thrive in cool, loamy soil.

- Pruning is important to gooseberries, as they need ample air circulation to prevent mildew. In late winter or early spring, trim the bush of any old, nonproducing branches, and all but six or so new shoots. Keep the plants weed-free at the base, and encourage vertical growth, using string and staking to tie them up, much like tomatoes.

- Gooseberry bushes are thorny. Wear sturdy work gloves when harvesting the berries. Because they tend to ripen at about the same time, you can usually just run your hand along the branches, allowing the fruit to drop into a basket below. The longer they ripen, the sweeter they become, but if the fruit is destined for tart sauces or vinaigrettes, picking them underripe is not a problem. The best way to check for ripeness is to taste them.

plummy burgundy, all share the same musky, lemony flavor, though intensity varies: the green "cookers" are the sourest, while the red can be sweet enough to eat out of hand. A relative of fresh currants, gooseberries have no relation to the husk-covered orange cape gooseberries you also see sometimes at the market, which are related to tomatillos.

honey soothe their sharpness (though white sugar is fine, too), and sweet butter and cream also have a mellowing effect. Cooked into a sauce, gooseberries cut cleanly through oily meat and fish; mackerel in particular is a traditional pairing, though here on the East Coast, bluefish is another option. When the seasons overlap, combine gooseberries with soft, super ripe plums, like sweet golden Shiros, in baked goods or compotes. Elderflower-infused syrups or liqueurs (like St. Germain) are also old standbys, teasing out the fruit's delicate fragrance. Any spirit made from the floral-noted muscat grape, like a sparkling Asti or Beaumes-de-Venise, makes a worthwhile marriage, too.

Give gooseberries a good rinse before "topping and tailing": the process of picking off the stem end and withered blossom. This step can take some time, so if your plan is to cook and strain the berries into a sauce, skip it: you'll be able to strain out the stems at that point. For jellies or jams, look for slightly underripe green berries, which have the most pectin.

SELECTION: Ripe gooseberries have a balloonlike plumpness, with their dense, seed-studded juices stretching the semitranslucent skin drum tight. Look for berries with saturated color, and a smooth or slightly downy complexion. They should have no browning around the stem area.

STORAGE: Although sturdier than other berries, it is still a good idea to pick through for any soft or crushed fruit before storing. You can either refrigerate them in their original container or spread them on a paper towel–lined plate for up to one week. Whole gooseberries freeze exceptionally well (see Freezing Fruit, page 247).

BROILED MACKEREL *and* SMASHED FINGERLINGS
WITH SPICY GOOSEBERRY JAM

The bright kick of gooseberries is a classic with mackerel, cutting cleanly through its richness, but any fatty fish, like wild salmon or bluefish, would work just as well in this dish. If you've never worked with fresh horseradish, be prepared for its pungency—a little bit goes a long way. Grate it into the jam just before serving, since its aroma and flavor starts to drop off pretty quickly once cut. Prepared horseradish won't have the same breadth of flavor but makes a fine substitute, though you may need to add more to taste.

Makes 4 servings

POTATOES

1½ pounds / 680 g fingerling potatoes, scrubbed but unpeeled

¾ cup / 180 ml crème fraîche, divided

Salt and freshly ground black pepper

¼ cup / 10 g chopped chives

SPICY GOOSEBERRY JAM

2 cups / 300 g green gooseberries

¼ cup / 50 g granulated sugar

⅛ teaspoon kosher salt

2 tablespoons freshly grated or prepared horseradish, plus more as needed

¾ teaspoon white wine vinegar

½ teaspoon freshly ground black pepper

MACKEREL

1½ pounds / 680 g mackerel fillets, cut into 4 portions

4 teaspoons extra-virgin olive oil

1 teaspoons salt, plus more as needed

Freshly ground black pepper

To prepare the potatoes, place them in a large pot of salted water. Bring to a boil and cook until tender, 15 to 25 minutes, depending on their size. Drain and immediately transfer them to a large bowl, and smash coarsely with half the crème fraîche and salt and pepper to taste. Fold in the remaining crème fraîche and chives. Cover the bowl with foil to keep warm.

To make the sauce, in a medium saucepan over medium-high heat, combine the berries, sugar, ¼ cup / 60 ml of water, and salt. Bring the mixture to a boil and cook briskly until the berries break down and begin to thicken, about 5 minutes. Stir in the vinegar and pepper. Remove the pot from the heat and cover it to keep it warm.

To cook the fish, preheat the broiler and arrange an oven rack 4 to 5 inches / 10 to 12.5 cm from the heat. Line a rimmed baking sheet with lightly oiled foil. Place the fish skin-side down on the sheet. Drizzle each fillet with 1 teaspoon of the oil and season to taste with salt and pepper. Broil until the fish is golden brown and flakes easily, 3 to 5 minutes.

Just before serving, peel a 2- to 3-inch / 5 to 7.5 cm chunk of fresh horseradish and coarsely grate it into the warm jam. Stir to combine. Serve the fish over the potatoes, with warm jam spooned on top.

PAN-SEARED DUCK BREAST *with* HONEYED GOOSEBERRIES

Duck might sound highbrow, but this is a simple go-to recipe for novice cooks looking to impress. It also serves as a friendly introduction to anyone unfamiliar with gooseberries' tang. Make sure to use the extra-tart green or citrine "cookers" for this sauce, and definitely don't toss the delicious rendered duck fat. Instead, pour the pan drippings into an airtight jar and refrigerate it for up to one month. It's a decadent alternative to olive oil when scrambling eggs, sautéing greens, or roasting potatoes.

Makes 4 servings

DUCK	GOOSEBERRIES
2 (1-pound / 455 g) Moulard Magret duck breasts	1 pint / 300 g fresh gooseberries, tops and tails removed
Kosher salt and freshly ground black pepper	2 tablespoons honey, divided
2 teaspoons fennel seeds	Fine sea salt and freshly ground black pepper
2 teaspoons chopped fresh thyme leaves	
1 teaspoon extra-virgin olive oil	

To prepare the duck, trim off any excess fat from the edges of each breast. Place the breasts skin-side down on a work surface. Score the skin of the duck in a crosshatch pattern, making the slices as deep as possible without cutting into the meat. Season the meat with salt and pepper on each side.

In a mortar and pestle or using the flat of a knife, lightly crush the fennel seeds. In a small bowl, combine the fennel, thyme, and olive oil. Rub the mixture over the duck breast. Let the seasoned duck stand at room temperature, loosely covered with plastic wrap, for 1 hour.

Heat a large skillet over high heat until it is very hot. Place the duck, skin-side down, in the skillet. Reduce the heat to medium-high, and cook for 8 to 10 minutes, continuously spooning off the rendered fat. Flip the duck and cook it to your desired doneness, 4 to 5 minutes longer for medium-rare (140°F / 60°C on an instant-read thermometer). Transfer the breasts to a platter and cover them with foil to keep warm. Drain all but 1 tablespoon of the fat from the pan (reserve all of the other fat for another use).

To make the gooseberries, return the skillet to medium-high heat. Add the berries and 1½ tablespoons of the honey. Simmer until the berries soften to a purée, 5 to 7 minutes. Stir in the remaining ½ tablespoon of the honey, and season to taste with salt and pepper.

Slice the duck breasts thinly against the grain. Arrange the slices on serving plates, spoon the gooseberry sauce over the top, and serve immediately.

RED GOOSEBERRY CURD TRIFLE

Make this fun, spectacular-looking dessert when you want to celebrate a birthday or special milestone. Made by layering slices of cake with fruit and cream, trifle is usually served in a clear bowl so that all of the colorful layers are on view. Red gooseberries turn the curd a soft raspberry color, and because they're so tart, they lend a lemonlike flavor. If you don't have time to make the pound cake, skip it and use a purchased pound cake or angel food cake instead. You will need 8 to 10 cups of cake cubes to pull off three layers.

Makes 12 to 14 servings

GOOSEBERRY CURD

1 pound / 455 g red gooseberries, topped and tailed

1⅓ cups / 270 g granulated sugar

¾ cup / 170 g unsalted butter, cubed

Finely grated zest of 1 lemon

2 tablespoons freshly squeezed lemon juice

⅛ teaspoon kosher salt

5 large eggs

POUND CAKE

1 cup / 225 g unsalted butter

2 cups / 400 g granulated sugar

6 large eggs

2 teaspoons pure vanilla extract

2 cups / 280 g all-purpose flour

¾ teaspoon kosher salt

TO SERVE

3 cups / 710 ml chilled heavy whipping cream

3 tablespoons granulated sugar

1¼ pounds / 570 g fresh strawberries, hulled, divided

To make the curd, in a heavy-bottomed saucepan over medium heat, simmer the berries with ¼ cup / 60 ml of water until the fruit breaks down to a saucy consistency, about 10 minutes. Strain the mixture through a fine-mesh sieve into a medium bowl; you should have about 1 cup / 240 ml of purée.

Rinse and dry the pan and pour in the strained gooseberry purée. Stir in the sugar, butter, lemon zest and juice, and salt. Simmer the mixture, stirring occasionally, over medium heat until smooth. Remove the pan from the heat.

Whisk the eggs in a large bowl until they are completely broken up. Slowly pour the hot gooseberry mixture into the egg mixture, whisking constantly until it is fully incorporated. Scrape the mixture back into the pot and cook it over medium-low heat, stirring constantly, until it thickens, about 5 minutes. Do not let it come to a boil or it may curdle. Strain the mixture through a fine-mesh sieve into a medium bowl and let it cool to room temperature. Once the curd has cooled, place a sheet of plastic wrap on its surface and transfer it to the refrigerator until ready to use.

To make the cake, preheat the oven to 350°F / 180°C. Generously grease and flour a 9 x 5-inch / 23 x 12.5 cm loaf pan.

In the bowl of an electric mixer fitted with the paddle attachment, cream together the butter and sugar until light and fluffy. Beat in the eggs, one at a time, until incorporated, and then beat in the vanilla. In a separate bowl, whisk together the flour

(continued)

and salt. Add the flour mixture to the egg mixture and beat on the slowest speed until just combined. Scrape the batter into the prepared pan and bake until the cake is deep golden brown and a skewer inserted in the center emerges with moist, but not wet, crumbs, 60 to 70 minutes. Remove the pan from the oven and set it on a wire rack to cool completely. Turn the cake out onto a clean work surface and cut it into 1-inch / 2.5 cm cubes.

To assemble the trifle, in an electric mixer fitted with the whisk attachment, beat the cream and sugar until soft peaks form.

Dice 2 cups / 290 g of the strawberries, and thinly slice the remainder.

Spread one third of the cake cubes in the bottom of a large trifle bowl or other large clear glass bowl. Top with one third of the curd, one third of the diced berries and 1 cup / 240 ml of the whipped cream. Repeat until all of the ingredients have been used, ending with a thick layer of whipped cream. Garnish the top of the trifle with the sliced strawberries and serve immediately.

Blackberries

WHENEVER YOU COME ACROSS LOCALLY GROWN BLACK-berries, scoop them up—you're in for a real treat. Incredibly fragile, ripe berries must be picked and sold within a day or so, a feat so difficult for most commercial growers that they pick them underripe instead. If you've ever come home from the supermarket with a plastic container of watery, insipid berries, you know what I mean. By contrast, truly ripe blackberries are suc-

Blackberries are countryside fruits. Once considered a weed, their thorny brambles climb and weave, indiscriminately and sometimes uninvited, up walls and along fences, in fields and forests and roadside thickets. When you come across them, the first thing to do is feast on them whole by the handfuls, possibly sprinkled with a little sugar, until every finger is tinted purple. After that, set to work baking. They are excellent in

JOE'S GROWING TIPS:

- There are two types of blackberries, erect and trailing (also called dewberries), which refers to the growth tendencies of their canes. Erect bushes tolerate colder climates and need less trellis support than trailing berries, which are better suited for southern regions, unless you are diligent about mulching throughout the winter. Be sure to select a hardy variety if you live in a cold climate.

- Pick a sunny spot in the garden for planting, but preferably one that gets a little shade in the afternoon. Though blackberry bushes require moist, well-drained soil, they are flexible: sandy, loamy, and clay earth can all support growth. Pruning is important, both to maintain the plant's shape and to allow for air circulation.

- Like blueberries, blackberries reach full color before they are completely ripened. The ease with which they detach from the stem is your clue; sweet, mature fruit pulls off with no resistance. Drop berries into a wide, shallow container that allows them to spread out. The weight of too many berries on top will crush those on the bottom.

- Do your blackberry picking in the cool of the morning, as warm air softens their skin and makes them more prone to getting squished.

culent, sweet, and edged with light tartness. Like their relative the raspberry (both belong to the genus *Rubus*), blackberries are an aggregate fruit made up of clustering "drupelets": tiny sacs that hold juice and seeds. Over the last hundred years or so, lots of raspberry-blackberry hybrids have cropped up, including the loganberry, boysenberry, and tayberry.

scones, muffins, tarts, and pies, especially when paired with apples, which share the same sweet, spiced wine notes (try stirring a handful of blackberries into applesauce while it simmers). If you find yourself with a windfall of blackberries and no real plans, cook a large batch down to a sauce, strain it, and stash it in the fridge—you'll find yourself pulling it out to drizzle over all kinds of things, from ice cream to cornbread to grilled steak. Comfortable with light, refreshing ingredients like cucumber, melon, and mint, blackberries can also take on the intensity of balsamic vinegar, fruity red wine, and cloves.

When prepping blackberries, the least amount of handling is best. They are easily waterlogged, which dilutes their flavor, so rinse them sparingly—the briefest possible run under a light stream of water will do.

SELECTION: Well-ripened blackberries are plump with a glossy sheen. Usually a slick jet black, they sometimes have a burgundy cast. You might think your carton of berries looks scantily filled, but it's okay; you want them loosely packed, since they are delicate and prone to getting squished. Wild berries are smaller, with more vivid winey undertones. Cultivated varieties are usually larger with a pronounced sweetness.

STORAGE: Because they're so perishable, buy only what you need and try to use them up the same day. If that's not possible, the next best thing is the refrigerator. Transfer them to a paper towel–lined plate, discarding (or eating) any berries that were smashed on the way home. They will last this way for two to three days. You can freeze them, too; they make a particularly good frozen purée (see Freezing Fruit, page 247).

GRILLED SKIRT STEAK *with* BLACKBERRY-SERRANO GLAZE

I always love a good steak, whether we're talking about a juicy sirloin or a thick New York strip, but quick-cooking, full-flavored skirt steak is one worth returning to again and again. The sweet and spicy berry glaze in this recipe is just as foolproof—throw all the ingredients into the blender, marinate the steak the day before, and toss the whole thing on the grill just before supper.

Makes 4 servings

STEAK	GLAZE
1 pound / 455 g skirt steak, cut into 4 pieces	1 cup / 110 g ripe blackberries
1 teaspoon kosher salt	1 cup / 240 ml honey
½ teaspoon freshly ground black pepper	1 cup / 240 ml red wine vinegar
¼ cup / 10 g sliced scallions	1 to 2 serrano chiles, to taste, seeded and coarsely chopped
1½ tablespoons minced fresh oregano	
1 tablespoon extra-virgin olive oil	

To prepare the steak, season the meat liberally with salt and pepper. Place the meat in a large bowl and toss it with the scallions, oregano, and oil. Cover the bowl with plastic wrap and refrigerate for at least 2 hours or overnight. Let the meat come to room temperature for 30 minutes before cooking.

To make the glaze, in a food processor, combine the berries, honey, vinegar, and chiles. Purée the mixture until smooth, and then pour it into a small saucepan over medium heat. Simmer the mixture until it is reduced by two thirds, about 30 minutes. Strain the glaze into a medium bowl through a medium-mesh sieve to eliminate berry seeds. Set it aside to cool at room temperature.

Preheat a grill to medium-high. Shake any excess marinade off the steaks. Transfer the steaks to the grill and cook, covered, for 2 minutes per side. Brush the tops generously with the glaze and cook for 1 minute longer, then flip the steaks, brush the tops with the glaze, and cook for another minute. Spoon any remaining glaze over the steaks before serving.

BLACKBERRY-LEMON ICEBOX PIE

Icebox pie just *sounds* right in the summertime. What could be better at the end of a mercilessly muggy day than opening up your icebox (or newfangled refrigerator) and finding a cold, creamy treat waiting for you? In this pie, the fresh berries are macerated and folded gently into whipped cream so that their delicate, brambly flavor shines through. Don't try to cheat on the cooling step; a nice long chill helps it set thoroughly and slice more easily.

Makes 8 servings

CRUST	FILLING
15 graham crackers, finely crushed (about 1¾ cups / 207 g crumbs)	4 large egg yolks
⅓ cup / 70 g granulated sugar	1½ cups / 350 ml freshly squeezed lemon juice (from about 9 lemons)
Large pinch salt	2 (14-ounce / 410 ml) cans sweetened condensed milk
½ cup / 115 g unsalted butter, melted and cooled	8 ounces / 230 g blackberries, plus more for garnish
	⅓ to ½ cup / 70 to 100 g granulated sugar, or to taste
	¾ cup / 180 ml chilled heavy whipping cream

To prepare the crust, in a large bowl, stir together the graham cracker crumbs, sugar, salt, and melted butter. Press the mixture into the bottom and up the sides of a 9-inch / 23 cm deep-dish pie plate. Chill the crust, uncovered, for 30 minutes in the refrigerator.

Preheat the oven to 375°F / 190°C. Bake the crust until it is firm to the touch and just begins to color around the edges, about 10 minutes. Remove the crust from oven and set it aside to cool at room temperature while you make the filling. Reduce the oven temperature to 325°F / 165°C.

To prepare the filling, in a large bowl, beat the egg yolks with a whisk until they are frothy and thick. Whisk in the lemon juice and condensed milk. Pour the mixture into the prepared crust and bake until custard is slightly set, 30 to 35 minutes. Remove the pan from the oven and let it cool to room temperature. Cover the pan and chill it in the refrigerator for at least 3 hours or overnight.

Place the berries in the bowl of a food processor and give them a taste—if they are sweet, toss the berries with ⅓ cup / 70 g sugar; if they are on the less sweet side, toss them with ½ cup / 100 g of sugar. Let the berries stand at room temperature for 10 minutes, then purée them in the food processor and strain them through a fine-mesh sieve into a medium bowl, pressing on the solids to yield as much purée as possible; you should have about 1 cup / 240 ml of purée. (You can prepare the pie up to this point 1 day ahead).

Before serving, in the bowl of an electric mixer fitted with the whisk attachment, whip the cream to soft peaks. Gently fold in the blackberry purée. Spread the blackberry cream on top of the chilled pie. Garnish with additional berries. Serve immediately, or refrigerate for up to 2 hours before serving.

BLACKBERRY-ORANGE BLOSSOM DOUGHNUTS

These orange-scented, jam-filled doughnuts take a little time, but the payoff is worth it, especially if you've never had homemade doughnuts before. Eat them straight from the fryer, while the blackberry filling is warm and the dough is soft and bready. While the blackberries, orange blossom water, and cinnamon are an incredible match, you can substitute other jams, too, like strawberry or raspberry.

Makes about 1½ dozen 3-inch doughnuts

2¼ teaspoons (1 envelope) active dry yeast	2 large eggs, divided
3¾ cups / 540 g all-purpose flour, divided, plus more as needed	1 to 2 teaspoons orange blossom water, to taste
⅓ cup / 70 g granulated sugar	½ teaspoon kosher salt
½ teaspoon finely grated orange zest	¼ cup / 60 ml Mixed Berry Freezer Jam (page 248) made with blackberries, plus more as needed
½ teaspoon ground cinnamon	Vegetable oil, as needed
5 tablespoons / 70 g unsalted butter, at room temperature	Cinnamon sugar, for dusting

Place 1½ cups / 350 ml of warm water (about 115°F / 45°C) in a medium bowl. Sprinkle the yeast over the water and let it stand until the mixture is slightly foamy, about 5 minutes. Stir in ½ cup / 70 g of the flour. Cover the bowl with plastic wrap and let it stand in a warm place until bubbly, about 20 minutes.

In the bowl of an electric mixer fitted with the paddle attachment, whisk together the sugar, orange zest, and cinnamon. Beat in the butter until the mixture is light and fluffy. Add 1 egg and beat until fully incorporated, at least 1 minute. Separate the second egg and add the yolk to the bowl (refrigerate the white in an airtight container until ready to use). Again, beat the mixture until fully incorporated. Beat in the orange blossom water and salt. With the mixer set on medium-low speed, beat in the yeast mixture and add 2¾ cups / 400 g of flour. Mix until the flour is completely incorporated and the dough begins to wrap around the paddle and pull away from the sides of the bowl. The dough should be very soft and somewhat sticky, but not loose. Add more flour, a tablespoon at a time, if necessary, to achieve the proper consistency.

Lightly grease a large bowl with vegetable oil. Turn the dough out into the oiled bowl, cover the bowl with a kitchen towel, and let the dough rise in a warm place until it has doubled in volume, about 1½ hours. Punch down the dough, cover the bowl with plastic wrap, and refrigerate it for 3 hours or overnight.

Line a baking sheet with parchment and dust it generously with flour. On a lightly floured surface, roll out the dough to a ¼-inch / 6 mm thickness. Using a cookie cutter, cut the dough into 2½-inch / 5.5 cm rounds (cut them as closely together as possible; you should have about 36 rounds). You can also pull together any dough scraps and roll them out once more to cut out additional rounds. Spoon a generous teaspoon of jam onto the center of half of the dough rounds. Remove the egg white from the refrigerator and beat lightly until slightly frothy. Brush the edges of the jam-filled rounds with the egg white. Top with the remaining dough rounds, pressing the edges together to seal. Transfer the doughnuts to the prepared baking sheet; let them rise, uncovered, until slightly puffy, about 30 minutes.

Line a large platter with paper towels. Fill a deep pot with 4 inches / 10 cm of vegetable oil. Heat the oil over medium heat until it reaches a temperature of 370°F / 190°C on a deep-fat or candy thermometer. Using a metal slotted spoon, lower 3 doughnuts into the oil; fry them until deep golden brown, 3 to 4 minutes, turning them occasionally to achieve uniform color. Transfer the fried doughnuts to the prepared platter and dust them with cinnamon sugar. Repeat with the remaining doughnuts.

OAT-MILLET MUFFINS *with* BLACKBERRIES

The popular image of a baker is someone on the roly-poly side, but Molly Killeen of Made By Molly is enviably lean. Part of that might be from hustling to keep up with the customer line at her Brooklyn market stand each Sunday, but she swears it's because after being up to her elbows in cookie dough all day she craves wholesome, fruit- and grain-filled recipes like this one. These moderately-sized muffins bake up quickly and combine the sweet softness of blackberries with a splendid crunch that comes from both the millet inside the muffin and the coarse sugar sprinkled lightly on top.

Makes 1 dozen muffins

Nonstick baking spray	1½ teaspoons kosher salt
⅔ cup / 90 g bread flour	1 teaspoon baking soda
½ cup / 60 g whole wheat flour	2 large eggs
1 cup / 110 g old-fashioned oats, plus more for sprinkling	½ cup / 110 g packed dark brown sugar
¼ cup / 60 g millet	½ cup / 115 g unsalted butter, melted and cooled
2 teaspoons baking powder	½ cup / 120 ml buttermilk
2 teaspoons ground cinnamon	1 cup / 110 g fresh blackberries
	Demerara sugar, for sprinkling

Preheat the oven to 400°F / 205°C. Lightly oil a 12-cup muffin tin with baking spray.

In a large bowl, whisk together the flours, oats, millet, baking powder, cinnamon, salt, and baking soda. In a separate bowl, whisk together the eggs and dark brown sugar; whisk in the butter and buttermilk. Fold the wet ingredients into the bowl of dry ingredients, adding the fruit as you fold.

Divide the batter evenly into the prepared tin. Sprinkle the tops generously with demerara sugar and sparingly with oats. Bake for 5 minutes; rotate the pan 180 degrees and reduce the temperature to 350°F / 180°C. Continue baking until the tops feel slightly firm when pressed with a finger, 7 to 8 minutes longer. Cool in the pan for 5 minutes, and then turn the muffins out onto a wire rack to cool completely.

Blueberries

HARVEST SEASON: EARLY & LATE SUMMER

DUSKY, INDIGO BLUEBERRIES ARE THE QUINTESSENTIAL all-American fruit. They call to mind Fourth of July barbecues, purpled potluck pies, and tall pancake stacks on a Sunday morning. It's not surprising that they are also literally an American fruit, indigenous to North America. Native Americans relied heavily on them, lowbush and highbush. Lowbush plants are wild and grow close to the ground, usually no more than a couple of feet tall. They bear small, currant-sized berries with deep blue-black coloring that hold up beautifully in baked goods like cakes and muffins. Their flavor is richer and woodsier than cultivated highbush berries, which

JOE'S GROWING TIPS:

- Blueberries prefer cold climates where winter temperatures frequently drop below 40°F / 4°C. Some of the best-tasting blueberries are grown in Northern regions where the flux between daytime and nighttime temperatures is greater, but they can grow pretty much anywhere in the United States except the high plains and the deserts of the Southwest. They need plenty of sun as well as abundant, year-round moisture (heavy mulching helps with this). Though they insist on loose, acidic soil—a low pH of 4.5 to 5.0 is ideal—if this doesn't match your soil type, you can still successfully grow blueberries in containers, where it's possible to control pH levels using limestone or sulfur.

- Although blueberries are self-fruiting plants, you should plant several different varieties to allow for cross-pollination if you have the space . Ultimately, you'll enjoy larger yields and a longer growing season.

- Blueberries start out green and steadily make their way to a dusty navy, but by some quirk of nature they appear fully ripened as much as a week before their sugars have fully developed. Once they've turned blue, allow them to stay on the bush an extra week to sweeten them up (but watch out for the birds, who love to nibble on them!). Another indication that they need a few more days is a pale, rose-colored ring around the berry stem.

- Ripe blueberries fall easily from the stem, no tugging needed. Roll your fingertips gently over the branches with a basket or cupped hands waiting beneath. When they're ready the berries will drop eagerly from the bush.

stirring them into cornbreads, drying them over open fires, and using them to flavor meats; today they are still mainly cultivated in Canada and the United States, especially in Northeast regions like my Finger Lakes stomping ground.

There are two main types of blueberry bushes— are larger, with less concentrated juices. Highbush plants can easily top out at 6 feet / 1.8 m. When you picture a blueberry, you probably think of a highbush, as they are more readily available whether you shop at the grocery store or at a farmers' market.

Both types are excellent so long as they are ripe and

fresh. Less messy than other kinds of berries, blueberries make for easy scattering—over oatmeal or ice cream and into salads or waffle batter or kids' lunchboxes (my kids can polish off a whole quart in one sitting). They can be jammed and jellied or baked in almost any way you please, from crumbles to buckles to pies. The wild berries work nicely in a savory risotto, grain salad, or sauce for game meats, like venison. Blueberries have an affinity for tang: think lemon, lime, yogurt, and cream cheese. Fragrant herbs like lavender and lemon thyme also complement their sweetness.

Rinse and drain them well just before using—beyond that, they aren't at all fussy and need no preparation.

SELECTION: Blueberries are best when they're plump, firm (but not hard), and burst open with a satisfying snap when you toss a handful into your mouth. Once they take on a sagging or even slightly shriveled appearance they have begun to lose their lively fruitiness and will taste bland and flat. The frosty silver "bloom" that coats their skin is desirable, indicating freshness.

STORAGE: Because of their taut skin, blueberries have a longer shelf life than other berries. Freshly picked, you can expect them to last up to two weeks in the refrigerator. Tip them out of their basket to sort out any soft ones, then turn them right back in for storage (or if you're particular, you can arrange them on a paper-towel–lined plate as you might more delicate berries, like currants). They are one of the easiest fruits to freeze (see Freezing Fruit, page 247).

BLUEBERRY *and* SORREL SALAD
WITH SWEET ONION VINAIGRETTE

Incorporating fruit into salads is a great opportunity to play with flavors and experiment with whatever looks fresh and interesting at your local farm stand. This combo of ripe blueberries, lemony sorrel, and sweet spring onions is an example of market foraging at its best, proof that when you cook in season, you almost never go wrong.

Makes 4 servings

¼ cup / 30 g thinly sliced spring onion or sweet onion, such as Vidalia

1 tablespoon Champagne vinegar

3 tablespoons buttermilk

2 tablespoons mayonnaise

¼ teaspoon kosher salt

Pinch of sugar

Freshly ground black pepper

5 cups / 120 g fresh spinach leaves

2 cups / 60 g fresh sorrel leaves, cut into thin ribbons

⅔ cup / 90 g fresh blueberries

⅓ cup / 40 g thinly sliced radish

In a small bowl, toss together the onion slices and vinegar; let them stand for 10 minutes at room temperature. In a separate bowl, whisk together the buttermilk, mayonnaise, salt, sugar, and black pepper to taste. Stir in the onions and vinegar, to taste.

In a large bowl, combine the spinach, sorrel, blueberries, and radishes. Toss in the dressing until well combined. Serve immediately.

FINNISH BERRY BROTH

June Russell, the New York City Greenmarket's farm inspector, is a true ally of our local farms and a serious force in the kitchen. She's a walking manual on everything food-related—from obscure heirloom tomatoes to wheat farming statistics to how to make perfect paella for a crowd of fifty. She's also a master of "putting up," or preserving enough fruit during high harvest to last through winter's barren months. Come February when she starts craving a hit of sunshine, her freezer is still rich with berries. That's when she turns to this traditional Finnish soup for an elixir-like fix. It makes for good summer dining on cooler evenings, as a first course or even as a light dessert.

Makes 4 servings

6 cups / 890 g mixed berries, fresh or frozen	½ to ⅔ cup / 100 to 130 g granulated sugar, as needed
3 strips lemon peel	Large pinch kosher salt
2 cardamom pods	2 tablespoons potato flour or cornstarch
1 whole clove	Crème fraîche or buttermilk, for serving

In a small saucepan, combine the berries, lemon peel, cardamom, clove, and 3 cups / 710 ml of water. Bring the mixture to a simmer over medium heat and cook gently for about 20 minutes, until the fruit begins to lighten. Strain the berries through a fine-mesh sieve into a large bowl, pressing gently on the pulp to extract extra juice (you should have 3½ to 4 cups / 830 ml to 1 L of strained purée).

Return the berry broth to the saucepan and place it over medium heat. Stir in ½ cup / 100 g of sugar and bring the mixture to a simmer. In a small bowl, whisk the potato flour with 2 tablespoons of cool water until smooth. Slowly whisk the flour mixture into the hot broth, stirring constantly, until the soup just comes to a boil; reduce the heat to low and simmer for a few minutes until the soup is slightly thickened. Remove the pan from the heat. Ladle the broth into bowls, and serve immediately, topped with a dollop of crème fraîche or a drizzle of buttermilk.

SCALLOP *and* BLUEBERRY CEVICHE

I love ceviche. On a hot summer day, it's nice to have a few recipes up your sleeve that don't require turning on the oven or firing up a grill. Ceviche is that kind of dish. Unlike pan-searing, which can quickly turn scallops rubbery and overcooked, ceviche is a fail-safe curing technique: The acidic lime juice "cooks" the thinly sliced scallop, rendering it tender and sweet. For an impressive presentation, spoon it into chilled martini glasses and serve it with tortilla chips for scooping. You could also substitute diced peaches or nectarines for the blueberries.

Makes 6 servings

1 pound / 455 g sea scallops, sliced ¼-inch / 6 mm thick	Kosher salt and freshly ground black pepper
½ cup / 70 g finely chopped red onion	⅔ cup / 160 ml freshly squeezed lime juice (from about 8 limes)
1 to 2 serrano chiles, seeded and finely chopped	1 cup / 140 g fresh blueberries
3 strips lime peel	¼ cup / 10 g chopped cilantro

In a large, nonreactive bowl, combine the scallops, onion, chiles, lime peel, a large pinch of salt, and a few grinds of black pepper. Pour in the lime juice and toss well. Cover tightly with plastic wrap and refrigerate, tossing occasionally, until the scallops are opaque, at least 2 hours or overnight (up to 16 hours).

Just before serving, toss the blueberries and cilantro into the ceviche. Season to taste with more salt and pepper. Use a slotted spoon to transfer the ceviche to chilled martini glasses or bowls; serve immediately.

LIME-GLAZED BLUEBERRY BUTTERMILK CAKE

Sure to be a big hit at potlucks, family brunches, or any gatherings that call for crowd-pleasers, this light, moist Bundt cake is studded with blueberries and topped with a light lime glaze. You could easily swap out the blueberries for raspberries, blackberries, or a combination of the three.

Makes 8 servings

Nonstick baking spray, as needed	2½ cups / 350 g all-purpose flour
1¾ cups / 350 g granulated sugar	2 teaspoons baking powder
1 tablespoon lime zest	½ teaspoon fine sea salt
1 cup / 225 g unsalted butter, at room temperature	1 cup / 240 ml buttermilk
4 large eggs	2 cups / 280 g fresh blueberries
1 teaspoon pure vanilla extract	½ cup / 60 g confectioners' sugar
	1½ tablespoons freshly squeezed lime juice

Preheat the oven to 350°F / 180°C. Lightly oil a 10-cup / 2.4 L Bundt pan with nonstick baking spray. Dust it with flour.

In the bowl of an electric mixer fitted with the paddle attachment, combine the granulated sugar and zest with your fingertips. Add the butter and beat until light and fluffy, about 3 minutes. Beat in the eggs, one at a time, then beat in the vanilla.

In a separate bowl, whisk together the flour, baking powder, and salt. Add the flour mixture to the butter mixture in three additions, alternating with the buttermilk. With a wooden spoon, gently fold in the blueberries just until incorporated. Scrape the batter into the prepared pan. Bake until the cake is golden and a toothpick inserted in the center emerges clean, about 1 hour.

Remove the pan from the oven and place it on a wire rack to cool for 30 minutes, then invert the cake directly onto the rack and set the rack over a rimmed baking sheet.

In a small bowl, whisk together the confectioners' sugar and lime juice. Pour the mixture evenly over the cake, allowing it to dribble down the sides and sink into the cake. Let the cake cool completely before serving.

MIXED BERRY COBBLER *with* CORNMEAL BISCUIT TOPPING

Just about any fruit has its place in a cobbler. Peaches, apples, plums, berries, rhubarb—even a haphazard mix of them all is bound to taste good when those cooking juices start bubbling hot and sweet beneath a layer of buttery biscuits. Berries really top the list, though. Not only do they meld into a gorgeous swirling, violet jumble, but their sweet-tart flavors meld beautifully, too. Adding cornmeal to the biscuit batter gives the topping extra crispness.

Makes 8 to 10 servings

FILLING	TOPPING
2 pounds / 910 g mixed berries, such as blueberries, raspberries, and sliced strawberries	1 cup / 139 g all-purpose flour, sifted
⅔ cup / 130 g granulated sugar	⅓ cup / 60 g finely ground cornmeal
2 tablespoons freshly squeezed lemon juice	¼ cup packed light brown sugar
3 tablespoons cornstarch	1¾ teaspoons baking powder
	½ teaspoon fine sea salt
	¼ cup / 55 g cold unsalted butter, cut into pieces, plus more for greasing the baking dish
	⅔ cup / 160 ml cold buttermilk

Preheat the oven to 425°F / 220°C. Butter a 13 x 9-inch / 33 x 23 cm baking dish.

To make the filling, in a large bowl, combine the fruit, granulated sugar, lemon juice, and cornstarch. Spread the mixture into the bottom of the prepared pan.

To make the topping, in a large bowl, whisk together the flour, cornmeal, brown sugar, baking powder, and salt. Using a pastry cutter, blend in the butter until the mixture forms coarse crumbs. Stir in the buttermilk until a sticky dough just comes together.

Drop spoonfuls of the biscuit dough on top of the filling. It shouldn't cover the entire surface; the fruit filling should peek through. Bake until the biscuits are browned and the filling is bubbly, about 30 minutes. Serve warm, topped with vanilla ice cream.

BLUEBERRY *and* MASCARPONE TART
WITH CANDIED LEMON

When acclaimed French chef Daniel Boulud opened DBGB, a casual French-brasserie-meets-American-tavern in July 2009, it was blueberry season. Inspired by a childhood memory of combing for wild blueberries during a family vacation in Scandinavia, his pastry chef Mymi Eberhardt set about re-creating her mother's simple holiday snack of blueberries, yogurt, and sugar. In the resulting tart, creamy yogurt is replaced with a mascarpone-slathered pastry shell, and bright lemon zest balances an irresistible mountain of fresh, just-picked berries.

Makes 1 (10-inch) tart

PÂTE BRISÉE

½ cup plus 1 tablespoon / 130 g unsalted butter, at room temperature

1¾ cups / 246 g all-purpose flour

1 cup plus 2 tablespoons / 130 g confectioners' sugar

¼ teaspoon kosher salt

1 large egg, lightly beaten

CANDIED LEMON PEEL

2 lemons

1 cup / 200 g granulated sugar

TART FILLING

2 cups / 450 g mascarpone, divided

¼ cup / 50 g granulated sugar

2 tablespoons all-purpose flour

1 large egg, at room temperature

1 large egg yolk, at room temperature

1½ tablespoons half-and-half

Finely grated zest of 2 lemons, divided

3½ cups / 500 g fresh blueberries

⅔ cup / 160 ml blueberry jam (such as Classic Blueberry Jam, page 253), gently warmed

⅛ teaspoon freshly grated nutmeg, plus more as needed

To make the crust, combine the butter, flour, confectioners' sugar, and salt in the bowl of an electric mixer fitted with the paddle attachment. Mix on medium-low speed until the mixture is crumbly. Beat in the egg until a moist, soft dough forms. Turn the dough out onto a clean work surface and knead once or twice until it comes together. Divide the dough into two equal-sized balls and flatten each into a disk. Wrap each disk in a tight layer of plastic wrap. Chill the dough in the refrigerator for at least an hour (you will only need one dough round; the other can be transferred to a freezer-safe resealable bag and frozen up to 2 months for later use).

Place a 10-inch / 25.5 cm tart pan with a removable bottom on a parchment-lined baking sheet. On a lightly floured work surface, roll the dough out into to a round about ⅛ inch / 3 mm thick. Transfer the dough to the prepared pan, fitting it into the bottom and up the sides (take care not to stretch the dough as you work). Run the rolling pin over the top of the pan to remove any excess dough. Transfer the pan to the refrigerator and chill, covered, for 30 minutes.

Preheat the oven to 350°F / 180°C. Place a parchment round on top of the pie dough and fill it with dried beans, rice, or pie weights. Bake the crust until it is pale golden, 18 to 20 minutes. Remove the pan from the oven and lift out the pie weights and parchment. Set the pan on a wire rack to cool the crust to room temperature.

To make the candied lemon peel, use a paring knife to remove the rind from both lemons. Place the peels in a heavy pot and cover them with cold water. Bring the water to a boil over high heat; drain. Repeat this blanching step two more times with fresh water. Transfer the peels to a bowl.

In the same pot, combine 1 cup / 240 ml of water with the sugar. Bring the mixture to a boil. Add the lemon peels and reduce the heat to low; simmer until the peels are translucent, 60 to 90 minutes. Remove the pot from the heat and set it aside to cool completely. Transfer the peels and syrup to a clean, airtight container and refrigerator until ready to use.

To make the filling, preheat the oven to 300°F / 150°C. In the bowl of an electric mixer fitted with the paddle attachment, beat 1 cup / 240 ml of the mascarpone on low speed. Add the sugar and flour and mix until well combined. Beat in the egg, allowing the mixture to come together, and then beat in the yolk. Scrape down the sides of the bowl with a spatula and beat in the half-and-half and half of the lemon zest. Pour the filling into the prepared crust and transfer the pan to the oven. Bake until the filling is just set, 15 to 25 minutes. Remove the tart from the oven and set it on a wire rack to cool to room temperature, then cover it with plastic wrap and refrigerate until chilled, about 4 hours.

In a large bowl, toss together the berries, jam, remaining lemon zest, and nutmeg. Arrange the mixture on top of the chilled tart in a nice dome shape. Decorate the top of the tart with small scoops of the remaining mascarpone. Remove the lemon rinds from the syrup and cut them into triangular slivers; scatter the rind over the tart. Dust with additional nutmeg.

MUCH DEPENDS ON THE WEATHER

My wife, Kristin, gets a real kick out of how much my dad, my brother Mark, and I are addicted to the weather, constantly checking radars and hourly reports as if we could actually change them. But for us, it's not about figuring out what we're going to wear that day. It's about our livelihood and feeding our family. That's the thing about farming—even when you're not in the field, you're still connected to the land.

Working with Mother Nature isn't always easy. It's frustrating when the skies don't cooperate and a much-anticipated crop is lost. But you keep going, continuing to nurture that bond as you would with any relationship that matters. You duck when she's angry, you move on when you've been hurt, and you feel grateful when she treats you right. My father's famous saying is "Don't worry about what you can't control." Over the years, I've come to understand what he really means: Save your energy for *after* the storm—that's when you'll need it the most.

If you've wondered what keeps a farmer up at night or why your favorite peach was absent from the market one summer, here are some of the obstacles Mother Nature sometimes throws our way.

RAIN: Soft fruits like cherries and plums easily draw in excess moisture. Just a few days of rain leading up to harvest can cause rapid expansion of the flesh, causing their skins to split. Once that happens, a window has been created for decay and mold. Too much rain can also cause mold or softness on delicate raspberries.

HOT, HUMID WEATHER: Just as we are inclined to feel sluggish on muggy days, too much tropical-like humidity wilts our trees and interferes with productivity. A heat-stressed tree can also lead to excessive "fruit drop," an occurrence in which fruit falls from the tree before reaching maturity. Although some fruit drop is nature's way of reducing a heavy load, too much can lead to a smaller-than-usual crop.

FROST OR FREEZING: Ideal winter and spring temperatures are a delicate dance—if the temperatures are too low, they can freeze the dormant fruit tree buds, diminishing or eliminating the upcoming summer's peach or apricot crop in a very short time. But abnormally warm winters can be a problem, too; many of our trees need a long, cold dormant period in which to rest and store up energy for next year's harvest. A fluctuation between warm and cold temperatures isn't good, either; it can cause the trees' trunks to expand, contract, and ultimately crack (a phenomenon called sun scald), leaving an opening for harmful disease.

CRITTERS: Birds, deer, and insects enjoy our fruit as much as we do, causing problems as minor as unwanted snacking and as major as widespread disease. Maintaining a healthy balance between our plants and the wildlife around them is a never-ending struggle that requires constant vigilance.

High
Summer

RASPBERRIES AND
STONE FRUITS

Summer in the Finger Lakes is like a bear emerging from hibernation. After hunkering through a cold winter and damp spring, all the sleepy lakeside villages throw open the shutters and pull out the Adirondack chairs. Just like that—you're in paradise. The eleven long, lean lakes rippling across the region create an idyllic setting for tourists. The hills are lush and green and sailboats, kayaks, and paddleboards float across the cool, clear waters. The lakes also foster an ideal microclimate for wine growing. We boast one of the largest wine regions outside of Napa Valley, with hundreds of vineyards dotting the surrounding area, and wine lovers from all over descend upon us in the summertime to sip and relax.

That said, we are still more or less "undiscovered," which means we enjoy lots of wide-open expanses where kids, dogs, and birds roam freely. I love watching these plains transform from the dull, dusty brown of dormancy into carpets of fresh green. This includes our orchards, which grow increasingly frenetic as summer picks up speed, each crop blending into the next. Within a week of one harvest, you've forgotten what you loved and hated about it; you're too focused on the picking, packing, and selling of the next. The waves of fruit just keep coming and there's no stopping it once we are rolling. Sometimes we lose whole crops to pests, birds, rain, or wind. But there's

no time to mourn. You simply move on to the next. It's a wild cycle that draws all kinds of unique characters to the farm. For most people, it's too heart-wrenching, exhausting, and downright insane, but for the rest of us it's completely addictive.

The first summer fruits are our sweet and tart cherries, which I think of as boom or bust crops. At the same time we're hoping for rain on spring's strawberries, we're also praying that the same rain doesn't fall on our cherries. Cherries easily draw in excess moisture, which can cause rapid expansion and cracking, creating an opening for decay and mold. When this happens we can still salvage the crop—smashed cherries make their way into one of the finest and richest juices in our lineup, the Tart Cherry Stomp (see recipe, page 301)—but dry weather is best, since it allows us to harvest cherries for weeks.

Next come the raspberries and the plums. We wait to pick the berries until they are so ripe they melt in your mouth. This means they are particularly perishable, so we sell most of them in our Geneva farm store and the rest at the farmers' market. The plums, too, must hang on the tree as long as possible, but once they are ready we stay busy harvesting at least three to four varieties at a time (we have dozens, in every color and size imaginable). A favorite here, and one that often confounds us, is the famed Green Gage plum, a sweet European variety that is very temperamental. Even on the eve of harvest,

moisture of any kind can wreak havoc, splitting apart the fruit overnight.

By the time we reach the middle of July, the apricots and peaches have also emerged in quick succession, and the market is an overflowing cornucopia of sweet fruit, beckoning to passersby with vividly rich colors and aromas. This is my favorite time to stand in the market. I love the energy this time of year, the banter between shoppers and farmers, the chance to see old friends, and the genuine enthusiasm for the enormous variety of goods New York growers bring to market. Introducing our fruit to the New York City Greenmarket has really helped us define and diversify our orchards, since constant interaction with our favorite taste testers—our customers—has helped us shape what we do best.

Raspberries

REAL RASPBERRIES ARE A REVELATION. A REAL RASP- berry has to cling to the vine until the sun has coaxed every drop of sugar to its claret-colored surface. They are so soft that rich juices bleed onto your fingertips under the lightest pressure, and the fruit melts on the tongue like a dab of sweet, winey jam. Most are a deep red; others are dark amethyst with an elusive, woodsy allure, or glow honey gold and taste faintly of apricots.

compulsively pluck and sort and pack to get an exquisite berry into your hands.

Like blackberries, dewberries, and salmonberries, raspberries are part of the rose family, which accounts in part for their delicate nature and sweet fragrance. Although loosely called a berry, the fruit is technically a drupelet, a cluster of seeds encased in tiny sacs of juice. When you pick a blackberry from the bush, its central

JOE'S GROWING TIPS:

• Devoted raspberry lovers should consider everbearing varieties, which produce fruit through the summer and into autumn, as opposed to summer varieties that produce one fleeting crop for a few short weeks in July each year.

• Raspberries are especially particular about well-drained soil; although they like moist dirt, they do not like standing water. If possible, plant them in full sun on sloping ground to facilitate drainage.

• A brambly, vivacious plant, raspberries will multiply prolifically if not kept in check. Periodically remove brittle dead canes, trim runners, and cut away any new canes that look less than robust. Trellising the canes can also help tame their growth.

• Only pick raspberries that are fully red and come away easily from their center core. Drop them into a shallow container where they will not pile up too high, which can lead to smashing. If you can, pick berries immediately following a heavy rain and use them up as quickly as possible. If they are left on the plant, they are susceptible to mold, which will spread to green berries. Wear gloves to protect fingers from the sharp tiny stickers that run along the canes.

But it is difficult to get raspberries right. From a grower's standpoint, they are incredibly perishable— their yielding texture makes them prone to crushing and even a light rainfall can quickly lead to mold. This is why the raspberries you encounter at the supermarket will never begin to compare to those you'll find at the local farmers' market. It takes someone with the patience to

core remains intact; when you pick a raspberry the fruit separates from the core, leaving a soft hollow which that the fruit a particular lusciousness.

You can often use raspberries exactly where you would a blackberry. In fact, their concentrated sweetness packs a more intense punch than mellower blackberries, particularly in desserts. They make an unparalleled coulis for ice cream, yogurt, and poached peaches or pears, and they are excellent with anything creamy, from billows of whipped cream to dry, crumbly goat cheese, to light ricotta cheesecakes. They partner wonderfully with cakes; whether it's an airy, lemon-scented sponge or a dense chocolate, both bring out the berries' acidic back notes. You can drop handfuls into crisps, pancakes batters, chilled bowls of sliced melon, and glasses of wine. It's one of the few fruits that don't match well with meat—too much delicacy is lost in the mix. You could, however, mash them with a fruity olive oil and Champagne vinegar to make a sweet-tart dressing for tender young lettuces. Almonds, pistachios, and hazelnuts are the nuts that most flatter raspberries.

If you've picked raspberries yourself, you might consider not rinsing them at all, since they become easily waterlogged, which dilutes their flavor. If this idea horrifies you, then give them a quick rinse under a light stream of water just before using. Some people like the crunchy texture of raspberry seeds, but if they aren't for you, pass the puréed or cooked berries through a fine-mesh sieve or strain it through cheesecloth to sort them out.

SELECTION: Look for berries that are plump and firm with no signs of mold. They should be loosely packed in their cartons, with no sign of crushing or stains on the underside of the box, which will lead to more rapid deterioration.

STORAGE: Sun-warmed raspberries are a treat, but when it comes to storage they must be refrigerated. When y ou get home, remove and discard any extra-soft or over-ripe berries. Arrange the remaining berries in a single layer on a paper towel-lined plate. Place the plate in a cold area of the fridge for two to three days. They are excellent frozen whole or as a purée (see Freezing Fruit, page 247).

TENDER GREENS *with* RASPBERRIES, PISTACHIOS, AND CHIVE BLOSSOMS

This light, colorful salad is a good way to start off a summer meal. Make sure to use the softest, most tender greens your market offers; if you can't find any young, loose leaves, use Boston lettuce instead. It's also delicious served with a crumble of soft, creamy goat cheese on top.

Makes 4 servings

¼ teaspoon kosher salt, plus more as needed

2 to 3 tablespoons Raspberry Vinegar (page 279) or white wine vinegar, to taste

3 tablespoons pistachio oil or extra-virgin olive oil

Freshly ground black pepper

6 cups / 140 g mixed tender greens

1 cup / 110 g fresh raspberries

½ cup / 70 g lightly toasted pistachios

⅓ cup / 40 g thinly shaved fennel

1 small bunch chives with blossoms

In a small bowl, whisk together the salt and 2 tablespoons of the vinegar; whisk in the oil and pepper.

In a large bowl, toss together the greens, raspberries, pistachios, and fennel. Gently toss in the vinaigrette; taste and adjust the seasonings as necessary.

Separate the chive blossoms from the green stems; thinly slice 2 tablespoons of the chive greens (reserve any leftover greens for another use). Sprinkle the chopped chives and blossoms over the salad; serve immediately.

RASPBERRY MOCHA FOOL

This may not be where it got its name, but a fruit fool is definitely the most idiot-proof dessert around. It dates at least to seventeenth-century England, and consists of sweetened, lightly mashed fruit folded into whipped cream. It's often made with fruit on the tart side, like gooseberries, rhubarb, or damson plums, since they complement the sweet cream. Raspberries can really vary in their sweetness, so start by adding a little sugar, then sprinkle in more to taste.

Makes 4 to 6 servings

1 (4-ounce / 110 g) chunk bittersweet chocolate, divided

1 cup / 240 ml heavy whipping cream, divided

2 tablespoons plus 2 teaspoons granulated sugar, divided, plus more as needed

1 teaspoon instant espresso powder

1 teaspoon pure vanilla extract

2 cups / 230 g fresh raspberries

Coarsely chop 3 ounces / 85 g of the chocolate. In a small saucepan combine ⅓ cup / 80 ml of the cream with the chopped chocolate and 2 tablespoons of the sugar. Cook gently over medium-low heat, stirring frequently, until the chocolate melts and the sugar is dissolved. Remove the pan from the heat and whisk in the espresso, the vanilla, and the remaining ⅔ cup / 160 ml of cream. Transfer the mixture to the bowl of an electric mixer, cover with plastic wrap, and transfer the bowl to the refrigerator to chill thoroughly.

In a small bowl, lightly mash together the raspberries and the remaining 2 teaspoons of sugar. Let the mixture stand at room temperature for 15 minutes. Taste the fruit and sprinkle in more sugar if necessary.

Just before serving, use an electric mixer fitted with the whisk attachment to whip the chilled mocha cream to soft peaks. Fold in all but ½ cup / 60 g of the berries. Spoon the cream into individual ramekins or small bowls and top each with a spoonful of the reserved raspberries. Using a vegetable peeler, shave some of the remaining chocolate over each serving.

RASPBERRY MADELEINES

Madeleines are light, three-bite sponge cakes that make an addictive treat during afternoon or morning coffee breaks. Originally from France, they are baked in a special shell-shaped mold. Adding raspberries isn't even a little bit traditional, but the subtle brightness of raspberries gives these a nice lift. These cakes are at their best the same day you bake them.

Makes one dozen cakes

5 tablespoons / 70 g unsalted butter, at room temperature, divided

½ cup plus 2 tablespoons / 85 g all-purpose flour, divided, plus more for dusting

3 ounces / 85 g raspberries (about ½ cup)

2 large eggs, at room temperature

⅓ cup / 70 g granulated sugar

½ teaspoon finely grated lemon zest

¼ teaspoon baking powder

¼ teaspoon kosher salt

Confectioners' sugar, as needed

Preheat the oven to 375°F / 190°C and position a rack in the center position. Grease a 12-cup madeleine pan generously with 1 tablespoon of the butter (make sure to get into the tin's ridges) and dust with flour, tapping out any excess. In a small saucepan, melt the remaining 4 tablespoons / 55 g of butter; remove the pan from the heat and let the butter cool.

In a small bowl, lightly mash the berries. Stir in 2 tablespoons of the flour.

In the bowl of an electric mixer fitted with the whisk attachment, beat the eggs, sugar, and lemon zest until the mixture is pale and thick and has tripled in volume, about 5 minutes. In a small bowl, whisk together the remaining ½ cup / 65 g of flour, the baking powder, and the salt. With the mixer running at medium-low speed, add the dry ingredients, a little at a time, until just incorporated. Using a spatula, fold in the melted butter in three additions. Gently fold in the berries.

Drop large spoonfuls of the batter into the center of each madeleine mold. Do not spread the batter evenly over the tin, but leave them in a mound; they will spread as they bake. Bake until the edges of the cakes are golden brown and the centers spring back lightly when pressed, 10 to 12 minutes.

Rap the pan lightly on a counter to release the cakes. Transfer the cakes to a wire rack to cool completely. Dust with confectioners' sugar and serve. Eat within a day.

VANILLA CREAM CHEESE CUPCAKES *with* BLACK RASPBERRY BUTTERCREAM

When Agatha Kulaga and Erin Patinkin met at a book club a few years ago, they never imagined that they would someday own Ovenly, one of Brooklyn's most popular bakeries. Here, they've turned their talents to the sweetness of fruit for these moist, light vanilla cupcakes slathered generously with berry-rich, lilac-hued buttercream. They love taking advantage of summer's fleeting crop of black raspberries, but red raspberries or blackberries are fine, too.

Makes 2 dozen cupcakes

VANILLA CREAM CHEESE CUPCAKES	BLACK RASPBERRY BUTTERCREAM
4 cups / 570 g all-purpose flour	¾ cup / 90 g ripe black raspberries, plus 24 more, for garnish
4 teaspoons baking powder	
1 teaspoon kosher salt	¾ teaspoon finely grated lemon zest
1 (8-ounce / 230 g) package cream cheese, at room temperature	¾ cup / 170 g unsalted butter, cubed and at room temperature
1 cup / 225 g unsalted butter, at room temperature	6 cups / 680 g confectioners' sugar, divided
2½ cups / 500 g granulated sugar	3 to 6 tablespoons /45 ml to 90 ml heavy whipping cream, as needed
¼ cup / 60 ml pure vanilla extract	
4 large eggs, at room temperature	
½ cup / 120 ml canola oil	
½ cup / 120 ml whole milk	

To make the cupcakes, preheat the oven to 350°F / 180°C. Fill two 12-cup cupcake pans with paper liners.

In a large bowl, whisk together the flour, baking powder, and salt; set aside.

In the bowl of an electric mixer fitted with the paddle attachment, beat the cream cheese, butter, sugar, and vanilla until light and fluffy, 3 to 4 minutes. Beat in the eggs one at a time, mixing for 30 seconds between each addition; beat in the oil. Gradually beat in the flour mixture in 3 additions, alternating with the milk, and ending with the flour mixture. Do not overmix.

Divide the batter among the cupcake liners (they should be about two-thirds full). Bake until a toothpick inserted in the center of a cupcake emerges clean, 20 to 23 minutes. Transfer the cupcakes to a wire rack to cool completely before frosting.

To make the buttercream, place the black raspberries and lemon zest in the bowl of a food processor and purée until smooth. Strain the pulp through a fine-mesh strainer into a medium bowl, pressing down on the solids with a spatula to extract as much purée as possible. Discard the seeds and set the purée aside.

In the clean bowl of an electric mixer fitted with the paddle attachment, cream the butter with 1½ / 300 g cups of the sugar and 2 tablespoons of the cream on low speed until combined. Beat in the remaining sugar and the raspberry purée until incorporated. Increase the mixer speed to medium-high and beat until the mixture is very light and fluffy, 3 to 4 minutes, Beat in additional cream, as needed, to achieve the desired consistency.

Frost each cupcake generously with the buttercream and garnish each with a raspberry before serving.

RASPBERRY-COCONUT THUMBPRINT COOKIES

The granola-like texture and wholesome ingredient list makes these baked treats feel slightly more virtuous than your average cookie, worthy of kids' lunch bags and even an on-the-go breakfast snack. If you have a dairy-free loved one in your life you can make these with coconut or olive oil to great results, but melted butter yields the richest flavor and the most golden-brown color.

Makes about 2 ½ dozen cookies

5 ounces / 140 g fresh raspberries (about 1 cup)	2 cups / 230 g rolled oats
½ cup / 100 g granulated sugar	½ teaspoon ground cinnamon
¼ teaspoon freshly squeezed lemon juice	½ teaspoon fine sea salt
2 cups / 160 g shredded unsweetened coconut	1 cup / 240 ml melted unsalted butter, coconut oil, or olive oil
2 cups / 240 g whole wheat pastry flour	1 cup / 240 ml pure maple syrup

In a small, heavy-bottomed saucepan over medium heat, combine the raspberries and sugar. Bring to a boil, stirring frequently, until the mixture is thick and glossy, and most of the large bubbles have subsided, 5 to 10 minutes. Remove the pan from the heat and stir in the lemon juice. Transfer the mixture to a small bowl and let it cool completely at room temperature.

Preheat the oven to 350°F / 180°C. Line 2 rimmed baking sheets with parchment paper.

In a large bowl, whisk together the coconut, flour, oats, cinnamon, and salt. Whisk in the butter and maple syrup.

Roll the dough into 1½-inch / 4 cm balls and place them on the prepared baking sheets, about 1 inch / 2.5 cm apart. Flatten each ball lightly with the palm of your hand, then make a small indentation in the center of the dough with your thumb. Fill each indentation with a small spoonful of jam.

Transfer the pans to the oven and bake until golden brown (if using butter) or pale golden (if using coconut or olive oil), 15 to 20 minutes. Remove the pans from the oven and transfer the cookies to wire racks to cool completely. Store the cookies in an airtight container at room temperature for up to 1 week.

RASPBERRY LIME RICKEY

Lime rickeys, once a New York City fountain-drink staple, are traditionally made with lime, seltzer, and cherry syrup. This homemade version uses fresh raspberries instead, which break down quickly into a syrupy purée and match just as well with the lime juice. Before they became popular as after-school sodas, a "rickey" usually meant an unsweetened cocktail made with whiskey, lime juice, and seltzer. If you feel like combining the best of both worlds, feel free to add a shot of bourbon or gin to yours.

Makes 2 to 3 servings

6 ounces / 170 g fresh raspberries
½ cup / 100 g granulated sugar
½ cup / 120 ml freshly squeezed lime juice, as needed
1 to 2 cups / 240 to 470 ml plain seltzer

In a small saucepan over medium-high heat, combine the raspberries, sugar, and ½ cup / 120 ml of water. Bring the mixture to a boil; reduce the heat to medium-low and simmer, stirring often, for 5 minutes.

Remove the pan from the heat and let it cool completely at room temperature. Strain the syrup through a fine-mesh sieve into a bowl; press down on the solids with the back of a wooden spoon or spatula to extract as much juice as possible from the berries (you should have about 1 cup / 240 ml of syrup).

For each serving, fill a tall glass with ice. Stir in 2 tablespoons of lime juice and ⅓ cup / 80 ml of the syrup. Top off each glass with seltzer. Add additional lime juice, to taste.

Cherries

HARVEST SEASON: EARLY SUMMER to MIDSUMMER

LIKE EVENING FIREFLIES AND THE SMELL OF BARBECUE, the first cherries at market signal that summer has officially arrived. The earliest of the stone fruits to reach harvest, cherries mark the shift from the bright, delicate flavors of spring's berries and rhubarb to summer fruits' succulent juiciness. We grow a mix of cherries at the orchard: plump maroon Oxhearts, full of dark, sticky sweetness; yellow and crimson–flushed Queen Annes, which boast sweet, cream-colored flesh; and two

anything else for pies and jams. Their tang also mates well with rich meats like duck, ham, and cured sausages. Although they are almost always sweetened and cooked, you can sometimes enjoy them out of hand if they're nice and ripe. Sweet cherries, on the other hand, make a reliably addictive snack; they're crisp, juicy, and easy to pop in your mouth (keep a bowl nearby for pits). They also hold up terrifically in salads, whether combined with peaches in a fruit salad or tossed with greens,

JOE'S GROWING TIPS:

- Cherries are averse to long, hot summers and need a good winter chill to save up energy for spring, so cooler temperate climates are best. Sour cherries like a dry, gravelly loam, while sweet cherries can tolerate a slightly heavier clay loam. Most sweet cherry trees require a second tree to aid in pollination; sour cherry trees are often self-fertile.

- Like other stone fruit trees, cherry trees prefer to be planted in a spot where they can bask in sun by day but cool air can drain away from them in the evening. A sloped hillside provides good circulation and usually good water drainage, too.

- Excessive watering can crack or rot the fruit, especially once it is nearly ripe. Because cherries bear fruit so early in the season, average winter and spring precipitation is usually enough to maintain steady moisture levels. Prune the tree on dry days, removing any dead or crossing branches to maintain an open, spreading shape.

- Pick cherries only when they are fully ripe and well colored. Pluck both fruit and stem from the branches; attached stems help preserve the cherries' life.

sours—Montmorency, a full, soft sour cherry with a luminous ruby hue, and Balaton, a slightly sweeter sour cherry with darker flesh and more firmness.

Sweet and sour cherries serve different purposes in the kitchen. Sour cherries are softer and more delicate than sweet cherries, and lend tart character to soups, crisps, compotes, and cakes. Many cooks won't use

crumbly goat cheese, and balsamic vinaigrette. Even a simple pitcher of ice water is made more refreshing when you drop in a handful of pitted sweet cherries. Sweet cherries are excellent churned into ice cream, especially one that uses tangy buttermilk, yogurt, or crème fraîche as its base. White cherries are commercially used in the production of maraschino cherries; try them in homemade versions, too (see recipe, page 281).

All cherries harmonize with vanilla bean, deeply warm spices like cloves or nutmeg, dark chocolate, or a glug of brandy. As with other stone fruits such as apricots and plums, cherries belong to the genus *prunus*, a relative of the almond; when left unpitted in cooking, cherries' stones provide a delicate almond aroma.

Rinse cherries briefly under cold water just before using, then remove the stems (this mitigates waterlogging). Kitchen gadgets can be a waste of money, but when it comes to cherry pitters: get one. Some even include a handy splashguard to contain splattering juices. You can also cut the fruit in half with a paring knife, and squeeze out the pit with your fingertips.

SELECTION: Choose full, glossy fruit with good color. White cherries will never develop more than a reddish blush, but the creamy gold background should be richly colored. Avoid any cherries that appear bruised, wrinkled, or dull. If possible, purchase cherries with the stems still attached; the freshest stems will still be green, not brown.

STORAGE: Place cherries in a perforated bag and store them in the coldest part of the fridge, away from any foods that have strong odors, since cherries readily absorb surrounding scents. They should keep this way for 4 to 5 days. They freeze well whole or pitted; frozen fruit works well in baking (see Freezing Fruit, page 247).

DARK CHOCOLATE CHUNK-CHERRY MUFFINS

When it comes to breakfast treats, Molly Killeen at Made By Molly knows best. She's been doing it for over 15 years and spent more than a decade as the pastry chef at the celebrated NYC bakery Amy's Bread. The addition of fresh sour cherries takes this already excellent chocolate muffin to the level of magic. The fruit creates soft pockets that zing against the dark chocolate crumb and toothy chocolate chunks. You could dress them up with a scoop of ice cream for dessert, but these are true breakfast muffins, to be enjoyed with a morning coffee. Use the best quality cocoa powder you can find (Valrhona is a great choice).

Makes 1½ dozen muffins

½ cup / 115 g unsalted, European-style butter, melted

½ cup / 120 ml vegetable oil

⅔ cup / 70 g unsweetened Dutch-processed cocoa powder

⅔ cup / 140 g semisweet chocolate chunks or chips, divided

4 large egg whites

1 cup / 200 g granulated sugar

1⅓ cup / 320 ml buttermilk

⅔ cup / 160 ml sour cream

¼ cup / 60 ml molasses

2 teaspoons pure vanilla extract

1⅓ cups / 190 g bread flour

1½ teaspoons baking powder

1 teaspoon baking soda

1½ teaspoons kosher salt

2 cups / 310 g pitted sour cherries

Preheat the oven to 350°F / 180°C. Lightly grease 18 cups of two standard-size muffin tins or fill them with paper liners.

In a small saucepan over low heat, melt the butter with the oil, cocoa powder, and ⅓ cup / 70 g of the chocolate chunks, stirring constantly until the mixture is smooth. Remove the pan from the heat and set it aside to cool slightly.

In a large bowl, whisk together the egg whites and sugar until foamy. Whisk in the buttermilk, sour cream, molasses, and vanilla. In a separate bowl, sift together the flour, baking powder, baking soda, and salt; whisk the mixture well to combine. Whisk the chocolate mixture into the egg mixture, and then fold the wet ingredients gently into the dry ingredients. Add the remaining ⅓ cup / 70 g chocolate chunks as you fold. Do not overmix.

Divide the batter evenly amongs the prepared muffin tins; tuck a small handful of cherries gently into the batter of each cup (this helps prevent the fruit from sinking during baking). Transfer the tins to the oven and bake for 10 minutes, then rotate the pan 180 degrees and continue to bake until the tops of the muffins feel slightly firm when pressed with a finger, 10 to 15 minutes more. They will dome slightly while baking, then settle into a dense cake as they cool. If the tops of the muffins seem to be browning too much for your liking, reduce the oven temperature to 325°F / 165°C. Remove the tins from the oven and cool the muffins in their pans on a wire rack until completely cool before turning them out.

DUTCH BABY PANCAKE *with* WARM CHERRY COMPOTE

A short stack drizzled with maple syrup is a breakfast classic, but sometimes it's nice to switch things up. This warm cherry compote is the kind of dish you'll polish off standing at the stove before you even have a chance to serve it. Dutch baby, a puffy, baked German pancake, is an impressive sight, but this sauce is just as addictive spooned over waffles or French toast.

Makes 4 to 6 servings

COMPOTE	DUTCH BABY
1 pound / 455 g sweet cherries, pitted and halved	4 large eggs
⅓ cup / 70 g granulated sugar	¾ cup / 180 ml whole milk
2 teaspoons freshly squeezed lime juice	¾ cup / 110 g all-purpose flour
⅛ teaspoon freshly grated nutmeg	1 teaspoon pure vanilla extract
	Pinch fine sea salt
	¼ cup / 55 g unsalted butter

To make the compote, in a medium pot over medium heat, combine the cherries, sugar, and 2 teaspoons of water. Simmer until the cherries are soft and the sauce thickens slightly, 10 to 15 minutes, then whisk in the lime juice and nutmeg. Cover the pot and keep the compote warm over low heat.

Preheat the oven to 475°F / 245°C.

To make the Dutch baby, in a medium bowl, whisk together the eggs, milk, flour, vanilla, and salt until few lumps remain. Place the butter in a 9-inch / 23 cm cast-iron skillet and transfer the skillet to the oven. Wait until the butter is melted and bubbling—about 7 minutes—then remove the skillet from the oven and pour in the batter. Return the skillet to the oven and bake until the pancake is puffed and golden, 15 to 20 minutes.

Remove the skillet from the oven and cut the Dutch baby into slices. Serve immediately, topped with the cherry compote.

SMOKED DUCK *and* CHERRY CONFIT TOASTS

Sweet or sour cherries are a great way to highlight the richness of game meats, such as duck and venison. The smoked duck is perfect here, but really any smoked meat or cured sausage would make a nice substitute. You can easily make the confit ahead of time and store it for about a week or so in the fridge until it's time for a quick weeknight dinner or an easy appetizer for company. If using sour cherries, increase the sugar to taste and omit the vinegar.

Makes 4 to 6 servings

2 tablespoons unsalted butter	Pinch fine sea salt
1 small shallot, peeled and thinly sliced (½ cup / 80 g)	8 (½-inch / 1.3 cm-thick) slices good-quality rye bread
½ teaspoon finely chopped rosemary	Extra-virgin olive oil, as needed
12 ounces / 340 g sweet cherries, pitted (2 cups)	2 tablespoons whole-grain mustard
1 tablespoon granulated sugar	1 pound / 455 g smoked duck breast, thinly sliced
2 tablespoons brandy	1 cup / 50 g torn arugula leaves
¼ teaspoon sherry vinegar, plus more to taste	

Melt the butter in a medium skillet over medium heat. Add the shallot and cook until they are soft and golden brown, about 10 minutes. Stir in the rosemary and cook for 30 seconds. Add the cherries and sugar and cook, stirring frequently, until cherries are caramelized, about 5 minutes. Stir in 2 tablespoons of water. Cook, breaking up the cherries with a spoon, until the mixture bubbles and begins to thicken. Add the brandy and cook until cherries are soft and saucy. Remove the skillet from the heat and stir in the vinegar and salt. Set the compote aside to cool.

Preheat the broiler. Arrange the bread slices on a baking sheet and drizzle the tops with oil. Place the bread under the broiler until it is lightly toasted, 1 to 2 minutes per side. Slather one side of each toasted bread slice with mustard. Top each toast with sliced duck, a spoonful of compote, and a small handful of arugula. Serve immediately.

DRUNKEN CHERRY-KIRSCH MILK SHAKES

Serve this spiked milk shake as a cooling cocktail or a dessert—it falls somewhere in between. Kirsch, a fruit brandy distilled from sour Morello cherries, is the perfect spirit to use here, but Grand Marnier or rum would be good, too. You can also leave out the alcohol altogether for a kid-appropriate treat.

Makes 2 servings

1 cup / 170 g frozen pitted sweet cherries	1 cup / 240 ml vanilla ice cream
½ cup / 120 ml milk	1 to 1½ ounces / 30 to 45 ml Kirsch, to taste
1 teaspoon pure vanilla extract	

In a blender, combine the cherries, milk, and vanilla; pulse until the cherries are coarsely chopped. Add the ice cream and Kirsch and blend just until the mixture is smooth and frothy. Pour into frosted glasses and serve.

TRIPLE-CHERRY LATTICE PIE

Some say that the only kind of cherry to use for pie is a sour one. While it's true that bright sour varieties shine exceptionally when tucked into buttery pastries, you'll be rewarded with deeper, more complex flavor if you use a mix of sour and sweet. Just make sure to use ripe, freshly picked fruit. The lattice crust may seem impossibly intricate when you look at it, but don't worry—once you get the first few steps down, you'll be a pro.

Makes 8 servings

DOUBLE PIE CRUST

2½ cups / 350 g all-purpose flour

¾ teaspoon kosher salt

1 cup plus 2 tablespoons / 255 g cold unsalted butter, cut into cubes

2 teaspoons granulated sugar

5 to 8 tablespoons ice water, as needed

FILLING

2 cups / 310 g pitted sour cherries

1 cup / 170 g pitted Queen Anne cherries

1 cup / 170 g pitted sweet Bing cherries

2½ tablespoons cornstarch

¾ cup / 150 g granulated sugar

⅛ teaspoon kosher salt

1 teaspoon freshly squeezed lemon juice

½ teaspoon pure vanilla extract

1 large egg yolk

2 teaspoons heavy whipping cream

To make the crust, in a large bowl, whisk together the flour and salt. Using a pastry cutter, work in the butter until the mixture forms coarse crumbs. Mix in the water, a tablespoon or two at a time until the dough just holds together when squeezed; it should be moist, but not wet. To avoid a tough crust, handle the dough as little as possible. Divide the dough into 2 equal-sized balls. Flatten the balls into disks and wrap each tightly with plastic wrap. Chill the disks for at least 1 hour or up to two days.

Preheat the oven to 425°F / 220°C and place a foil-lined rimmed baking sheet on the lowest rack.

To make the filling, in a large bowl, combine the cherries, cornstarch, sugar, salt, lemon juice, and vanilla. Let the mixture stand at room temperature for 15 minutes.

On a clean, lightly floured surface, roll 1 disk of dough to a 12-inch / 30.5 cm circle (keep the other disk in the refrigerator). Transfer the round to the bottom of a 9-inch / 23 cm metal pie pan; allow excess dough to hang over edges. Cover the bottom crust loosely with plastic wrap and refrigerate while you roll out the second disk of dough to a 12-inch / 30.5 cm circle (this will be the lattice).

Scrape the filling into the bottom crust. Using a sharp knife or pastry jagger, cut the second crust into ¾-inch / 2 cm-wide strips. Take half of the strips and lay them vertically across the pie, spaced evenly. Fold back every other strip halfway and insert a new strip across the center of the pie, perpendicular to the other strips. Drop the folded strips over the new strip.

(continued)

Fold back the vertical strips that were not folded the first time slightly less than halfway; insert another cross strip perpendicular to the vertical strips. Drop the folded strips over the newly inserted one. Continue this pattern from the center to the outer edge of the pie, making sure to space the strips evenly as you work. Repeat the process on the other half of the pie, again working from the center to the edge.

Once all the strips have been used and the lattice is in place, brush the undersides of the strips' ends with water and gently press them to the edge of the bottom crust to adhere. Trim the crust with a ½-inch / 1.3 cm overhang from the rim of the pie plate. Roll the overhanging dough over the edge of the lattice top and crimp decoratively. In a small bowl, whisk together the yolk and cream; use a pastry brush to lightly coat the crust with the mixture.

Transfer the pie to the preheated pan in the oven. Bake for 20 minutes. Reduce the oven temperature to 375°F / 190°C and move the pie to the center rack. Continue baking until the crust is golden brown and the juices are bubbling thickly, 45 to 55 minutes more. If the crust starts turning dark before the filling has thickened, tent the top of the pie loosely with foil. Remove the pie from the oven and set it on a wire rack to cool completely (at least 2 to 3 hours to avoid a runny filling) before slicing.

Note: If you'd rather skip an intricate lattice crust in favor of something easier, here are two ways to cheat: Instead of basket-weaving the dough strips over and under each other, you can simply lay half the strips one way across the pie, then crisscross the remaining strips right on top, allowing equal space between each strip of dough. Or press cookie-cutter shapes out of the rolled-out dough and arrange them with their edges touching over the filling.

Apricots

I'M PROUD OF ALL OF OUR FRUITS, BUT I AM ESPECIALLY proud of our apricots—they speak more about Red Jacket Orchards than almost anything we do. It's rare to find apricots growing in regional fruit markets. They are terribly temperamental, stubborn, and susceptible to frost. But three decades ago my father and grandfather planted

It's likely that you've run into some pretty terrible apricots in your lifetime. Many people have never even eaten a good fresh apricot, which is a shame. There is an ocean of difference between a bad apricot and a good one. Bad ones can be dry, mealy, and a little bit tart. A dead-ripe apricot, one that has fully matured on the tree

JOE'S GROWING TIPS:

- Apricots only grow well in particular areas: they're more finicky than other fruit trees. They usually bloom early, so a prematurely warm day followed by a frost can damage their flowers and buds; on the other hand, scorching summer weather can damage the fruit and trunks. Temperate climates with chilly winters are best. Plant trees in well-drained soil where they will receive full sun.

- In the early years of an apricot tree's life, pruning is needed to establish a shape that allows for good sunlight penetration. After that, prune primarily to keep the centers open, allowing the sun to hit the older branches, from which new buds develop. The trees can be pruned anytime after the bud swell (typically in March) until just after the blossom period.

- As with peaches and plums, apricot trees sometimes need thinning of small, unripened fruit to prevent excess strain on the branches and to allow remaining fruit to grow more robustly. Try to leave at least 3 inches / 7.5 cm between fruit, taking care to separate any clusters of fruit, which can lead to malformation or rot.

- Cracked fruit sometimes results from hot, humid weather and provides an entry for bacteria. When thinning the tree of fruit, try to leave some under budding leaves that will eventually provide shade from sunburn.

- Leave fruit on the tree until it is fully colored and soft but not squishy. Apricots ripen over a period of several weeks, so you will need to harvest them periodically to get optimum fruit each time. They are easily removed from the tree with a twist of the wrist.

some apricot trees anyway. Through perseverance, ingenuity, and a stubbornness known only to farmers, they found a way to make them thrive. Over the years, our specialized Red Jacket varieties have won praise from *Gourmet* magazine, the *New York Times*, and lots of happy customers.

(like ours) is so soft that you can pull apart the velvety halves with your fingers, give a gentle squeeze, and watch pearls of delicious, sweet apricot nectar percolate up. Its skin is a saturated sunset orange with lightly freckled scarlet cheeks.

Like peaches, plums, and cherries, apricots are of the *Prunus* genus. They usually arrive at the market sometime in mid-July, just after cherries and just ahead of peaches and nectarines. Make sure to eat plenty out of hand or at least raw in fruit salads, sliced over frozen yogurt, or diced into pilafs and light green salads in place of their dried counterparts. Their honeyed juices cook into vibrant jams, chutneys, and cobblers and make first-rate palate-cleansing sorbets and granitas. At the orchard, we press the rich juice into our popular Apricot Stomp (see recipe, page 299), a refreshing summertime alternative to lemonade. Most Middle Eastern flavors work well with apricots, including mint, rosewater, orange blossom, pistachios, golden raisins, cardamom, and lamb (although pork is another terrific companion). Almonds, a close relative, make the most perfect match of all; in fact, if you crack open an apricot pit, you will find an almond-scented stone buried inside. Steep a handful of these milky white kernels in cream, sauces, and spirits to infuse a subtle nutty aroma. Like other fruit seeds, such as apple and peach, apricot kernels contain trace amounts of prussic acid which, when consumed in large quantities, can have a toxic effect. If desired, you can roast the whole puts in a 350°F / 180°C oven for 15 minutes before cracking them. This not only destroys the kernel's toxin-creating enzyme, but makes them easier to open.

Wash apricots just before using. If desired, peel them as you would peaches (see page 125), although the skin is usually thin enough that it's not really necessary, and with a truly ripe apricot it can be a messy job. Once cut, they begin to brown quickly; prevent discoloration with a sprinkle of lemon juice.

SELECTION: Ripe apricots (and you should only purchase them ripe) are highly aromatic and should have smooth undamaged skin free of cracks and bruises. Their color is rich and golden, different from the washed-out yellow-green of underripe fruit. They should have a good amount of give with some firmness when squeezed in the palm of your hand.

STORAGE: Refrigerated apricots last up to two weeks; store them in the crisper drawer. They freeze well sliced or whole (see Freezing Fruit, page 247).

APRICOT-ALMOND SCONES

The bright back-notes of apricots harmonize beautifully in baked goods like scones and quick breads, cutting nicely through the rich, buttery crumb. You can always throw some into any simple muffin or pancake batter without worrying that the final result will be anything but improved. Split these scones while warm and slather on your favorite homemade jam.

Makes 6 scones

¾ cup / 180 ml heavy whipping cream, plus more as needed

1 large egg

1 teaspoon pure vanilla extract

2 cups / 280 g all-purpose flour, plus more as needed

¼ cup / 50 g granulated sugar

1¾ teaspoons baking powder

½ teaspoon fine sea salt

⅛ teaspoon grated nutmeg

6 tablespoons / 85 g cold unsalted butter, cubed

8 ounces / 230 g ripe apricots, pitted and diced (1 cup)

¾ cup / 60 g coarsely chopped toasted almonds

Demarara sugar, as needed

Preheat the oven to 400°F / 205°C. Line a large baking sheet with parchment paper.

In a medium bowl, whisk together ¾ cup /180 ml cream, egg, and vanilla. In a separate bowl, whisk together the flour, sugar, baking powder, salt, and nutmeg. Using 2 forks or a pastry cutter, cut the butter into the dry ingredients until the mixture forms coarse crumbs. Stir in the apricots and almonds. Using a wooden spoon, stir in the wet ingredients. Add additional cream, a tablespoon at a time, if needed, until the dough just comes together. Alternatively, you can use a food processor: In a medium bowl, whisk together ¾ cup / 180 ml cream, egg, and vanilla. In the food processor, pulse together the flour, sugar, baking powder, salt, and nutmeg. Add the butter and pulse until the mixture forms coarse crumbs. Pulse in the wet ingredient mixture until just combined. Add additional cream, a tablespoon at a time, if needed to bring the dough together. Turn the dough out onto a lightly floured surface and quickly knead in the apricots and almonds, handling the dough as little as possible.

Turn the dough out onto a lightly floured surface and pat it into a ¾-inch / 2 cm-thick circle. Cut the dough into 6 equal wedges and arrange them on the prepared baking sheet about 1 inch / 2.5 cm apart. Brush the tops of the scones with cream and sprinkle with Demarara sugar. Transfer the baking sheet to the oven and bake the scones until golden brown, 16 to 20 minutes. Remove the baking sheet from the oven and let the scones cool slightly before serving.

APRICOT-QUINOA TABBOULEH

Riffing on the classic Middle Eastern dish, this quick summer salad substitutes striking red quinoa for the bulgur and juicy apricots in place of tomatoes. Like any good tabbouleh, it is also lush with fresh herbs. Boiling and draining the quinoa like pasta instead of steaming it like rice prevents it from getting soggy.

Makes 6 servings

1 cup / 230 g red or white quinoa	12 ounces / 340 g ripe apricots, pitted and chopped (about 2½ cups)
2 teaspoons freshly squeezed lemon juice, plus more as needed	1 cup / 60 g coarsely chopped fresh parsley
½ teaspoon kosher salt	1 cup / 60 g coarsely chopped fresh mint
½ cup/ 120 ml extra-virgin olive oil	½ cup / 30 g thinly sliced scallions, white and light green parts
Pinch red chili flakes	

Bring a large pot of salted water to a boil. Add the quinoa and cook until the center of each grain takes on an opaque appearance, 10 to 12 minutes. Drain the quinoa and set it aside to cool.

In a small bowl, whisk together the lemon, salt, oil, and chili flakes. In a large bowl, combine the quinoa, apricots, parsley, mint, and scallions; gently fold in the dressing. Serve immediately, or refrigerate in an airtight container up to 4 hours.

CHARRED PORK CHOPS *with* APRICOT-ROSEMARY SAUCE

When it's time to harvest apricots, the bounty is often plentiful but short-lived. You can eat them my favorite way, standing over the kitchen sink, or you can use them in cooking. Their sweet-tart flavor works well against rich and smoky pork. With the rosemary growing just feet from the grill, this sauce was a natural pairing. It would also be delicious over grilled lamb chops, served with a simple, cardamom-scented pilaf.

Makes 4 servings

1 tablespoon extra-virgin olive oil, plus more as needed	1 pound / 455 g ripe apricots, pitted and diced (2½ to 3 cups)
¼ cup / 40 g finely chopped red onion	2 tablespoons Apricot Stomp (page 299), or freshly squeezed orange juice
Kosher salt, as needed	1 to 3 tablespoons good-quality honey, as needed
2 garlic cloves, finely chopped	Freshly ground black pepper
1 tablespoon minced, peeled fresh ginger	4 (8-ounce / 230 g) center-cut, bone-in pork chops, 1-inch / 2.5-cm thick
1 teaspoon finely chopped rosemary	

Heat 1 tablespoon of oil in a heavy-bottomed saucepan over medium heat. Add the onion and a pinch of salt. Cook, covered, until the onion is soft and translucent, 5 to 10 minutes. Uncover and stir in the garlic, ginger, and rosemary; sauté for 2 minutes.

Stir in the apricots, juice, 2 tablespoons of water, and 1 tablespoon of the honey. Simmer until the fruit breaks down to a chunky-smooth consistency. Season to taste with salt and pepper. Stir in more honey, if desired. Cover the pot and keep the sauce warm over low heat.

Preheat a grill to medium-high. Season the pork chops generously with salt and pepper and brush them with oil, then transfer them to the grill and cook, covered, until undersides are golden brown, about 5 minutes. Turn the pork chops and continue to cook until their interior is no longer bright pink (145°F / 63°C on an instant-read thermometer), about 5 minutes more. Remove the pork chops from the grill and let them rest on a platter for 5 minutes. Serve the pork chops with the warm apricot sauce spooned over top.

RUSTIC APRICOT *and* RASPBERRY CROSTATA

If you can roll out pie crust, you can make crostata: a free-form tart that doesn't require any fussy crimped edges or lattice tops. You just fold the dough up over the fruit filling. In fact, the less carefully you do this, the more perfectly "rustic" the results. Make sure you bake it on a rimmed baking sheet lined with parchment to catch any bubbling juices that escape from the pastry.

Makes 8 servings

PASTRY DOUGH	APRICOT-RASPBERRY FILLING
1½ cups / 200 g all-purpose flour	1 to 1¼ pounds / 455 to 560 g fresh apricots, pitted and sliced (3½ cups)
1 tablespoon granulated sugar	
¼ teaspoon fine sea salt	1½ cups / 170 g raspberries
½ cup / 115 g unsalted butter, cold and cut into cubes	⅔ cup / 70 g packed light brown sugar
	3 tablespoons cornstarch
2 to 4 tablespoons ice water, as needed	1 teaspoon pure vanilla extract
	½ teaspoon ground cinnamon
	¼ teaspoon fine sea salt
	2 tablespoons heavy whipping cream
	Demerara sugar, for sprinkling

To make the pastry dough, in the bowl of a food processor, pulse together the flour, sugar, and salt. Add the butter and pulse until the mixture forms coarse crumbs. Pulse in the ice water, a tablespoon at a time, until the dough holds together when pressed. It should be moist, but not wet. Form the dough into a ball and flatten it into a disk. Wrap the disk tightly with plastic wrap and refrigerate for 1 hour.

Preheat the oven to 425°F / 220°C. Line a large rimmed baking sheet with parchment.

On a lightly floured surface, roll out the dough to a 12-inch / 30.5 cm circle. Transfer the dough circle to the prepared baking sheet, cover the sheet with plastic wrap, and refrigerate the dough until ready to use.

In a large bowl, gently toss together the fruit, brown sugar, cornstarch, vanilla, cinnamon, and salt. Mound the filling in the center of the dough, leaving a 2-inch / 5 cm border all around. Fold the crust up and around the filling. Brush the crust with the cream and sprinkle with demerara sugar. Bake until the crust is golden brown and the filling is bubbling, 45 to 50 minutes. Remove the baking sheet from the oven and let the crostata cool for at least 15 minutes before serving.

APRICOT PIT PANNA COTTA *with* APRICOT GRANITA

We love that like Dan Barber and his restaurants Blue Hill and Blue Hill at Stone Barns, this dish is all about respect for ingredients—not one bit of our fruit goes to waste. This recipe taps into a secret we love sharing at the market: crack open an apricot pit, and you will find a small, milky kernel nestled inside that contributes a delicate, almond like flavor to custards, jams, syrups, and this panna cotta. It's a great way to use up pits from a canning project, or you can start a collection in an airtight container in your freezer until you've accumulated enough.

Makes 10 servings

APRICOT GRANITA	PANNA COTTA
10 ounces / 280 g apricots, pitted and coarsely chopped (pits reserved)	3 cups / 340 g apricot pits
4 teaspoons superfine sugar	4 cups / 950 ml heavy whipping cream
½ teaspoon freshly squeezed lemon juice	2 (¼-ounce / 7 g) envelopes unflavored gelatin powder
	1 (14-ounce / 400 g) can sweetened condensed milk
	6 ounces small apricots, pitted and sliced, for serving

To make the granita, blend the apricots until very smooth in a food processor. Scrape into a liquid cup measure; you should have about 1 cup / 240 ml of purée. In a small pot, bring ¼ cup / 600 ml of water to a boil.

In a small bowl, stir together the superfine sugar with 4 teaspoons of the boiling water until the sugar dissolves. In a wide, shallow, freezer-safe container, stir together the purée, ½ cup / 120 ml of cold water, the sugar syrup, and the lemon juice. Cover with foil and transfer to the freezer. Freeze, breaking up any icy chunks with a fork every 30 minutes, until the mixture is frozen into flaky crystals, about 3 hours (you can make this up to 1 day ahead; store, covered, in the freezer).

To make the panna cotta, place the apricot pits in a single layer on a large dish towel. Cover with a second dish towel. Using a kitchen mallet or hammer, crush the pits to expose their almond like kernels. Scrape the shells and kernels into a medium pot. Cover with the cream. Bring the mixture to a simmer over medium heat. Cook gently for 5 minutes.

While the cream is heating, place 6 tablespoons of cold water in a large bowl. Sprinkle the gelatin over the surface of the water. Let stand for 5 to 10 minutes.

Stirring constantly, slowly pour the apricot pit mixture into the gelatin. Stir until the gelatin completely dissolves. Stir in the condensed milk until combined. Strain the mixture through a fine-mesh sieve; discard the apricot pits.

Ladle the cream mixture into ten 4-ounce / 115 g ramekins; let them cool to room temperature, then cover the ramekins with plastic wrap and refrigerate until completely set, at least 8 hours.

To serve, dip the bottoms of each ramekin in a small bowl of hot water to loosen. Run a small offset spatula around the outer edge of each panna cotta; overturn them onto individual serving plates. Top each panna cotta with a very small scoop of granita and fresh apricot slices. Serve immediately.

Peaches and Nectarines

HARVEST SEASON: MIDSUMMER to EARLY FALL for PEACHES;
MID- to LATE SUMMER for NECTARINES

THE WORDS MOST OFTEN USED TO DESCRIBE THE BEST qualities of fruit—succulent, sublime, juicy, fragrant—can be liberally applied to fresh, ripe peaches and nectarines. You measure good ones by the mess they leave behind. I love watching the surprise on customers' faces when they bite into a peach at the peak of summer harvest. You need napkins (lots of them) to catch the tidal wave of sweet syrup running down your chin.

have a mild lemony top note that's not always present in peaches. Both have golden or creamy white skin with rosy cheeks and yellow or white flesh. You can use them interchangeably in cooking, and any practical information about one applies to the other.

The fruit can be freestone (the fruit separates easily from the pit) or clingstone (the pit must be removed with a knife). You might come across both at your local

JOE'S GROWING TIPS:

• Peaches and nectarines generally prefer warm, sunny Mediterranean-like climates, but hardier, Northern-appropriate varieties exist, too. They need sandy loamy soil with a neutral pH level. Good drainage is essential. A site that warms slowly in the spring and is less susceptible to winter freezes is best, such as next to a body of water or on the southern slope of a hill.

• Annual pruning ensures the sun can reach the center branches, which helps stimulate new fruit growth. Come early spring, cut out any branches that have died over the winter and thin branches that are growing inwards or downwards. Concentrate on creating an open, spreading shape, and don't be bashful. Peach trees should be pruned more generously than any other tree.

• It's exhilarating to see a tree bearing fruit, but too much can weigh it down and weaken its limbs, causing potential injury. Midway through the season, take time to thin the tree of small, undeveloped fruit. Aim to leave 8 inches between remaining fruit for good growth and sizing.

• To allow fruit to develop maximum sugars, wait until the background coloring turns a deep, rich gold. Twist the fruit sideways, removing it from the branch; hard, direct tugging can bruise the fruit.

Peaches and nectarines are so closely related (like plums, cherries, and apricots, both are of the genus *Prunus*) that stories have been told of peaches growing on nectarine trees and vice versa. The differences are small: peaches are covered in fine fuzz, while nectarines are smooth-skinned, and nectarines generally

market, but freestone fruit is more commonly sold to consumers, just because it's easier to eat and prepare. Clingstone fruit, which can be frustrating to slice, is best for canning and preserving.

A peach's culinary weapon is in its easygoing sweetness. Success is guaranteed with basic shortcake, ice cream, and jam recipes, or you can embellish with complementary flavorings like lemon verbena, lavender, mint, or maple. The fruit makes stellar pies, but because they're so juicy you must either use ample thickener or, for open-faced tarts, nestle them in custard. Quickly sautéing sliced fruit prior to baking can also help concentrate the juices. Any other stone fruit or sweet berry makes a great pairing, and a peach's melting texture purées beautifully into chilled soups, blended drinks, and sauces. They swim happily in alcohol, whether poached in wine, dropped into sparkling wine, or mingled with bourbon in baked goods. Delicate white peaches agree with rosewater's floral notes, cardamom's mild warmth, and soft, tender lettuces.

You can also contrast the honeyed notes against savory foods—smoky bacon, grilled pork chops or chicken, spicy arugula, and hardier herbs like rosemary or thyme can all stand up to the fruit. Peaches take nicely to delicate seafood like crab or shrimp and milky-soft cheeses, such as mozzarella, ricotta, or mascarpone. Nuts like almonds, pecans, or pistachios work well in almost any dish, sweet or savory.

For eating out of hand, the fruit only needs a rinse under cool water. When cooking, peaches are usually be peeled (thin-skinned nectarines don't really need it). You can use a vegetable peeler or try this less messy technique: cut a shallow X in the bottom of each peach with a paring knife, then drop them in a pot of boiling water for 20 seconds or so. Transfer the fruit immediately to a bowl of ice water. You will see the skin shrink from the flesh; pull the skin away with your fingers.

Slicing peaches and nectarines depends on the pit. Slice around the perimeter of freestone fruit, following its raised seam. Twist the fruit halves and pull them apart. The stone will pop out easily. Clingstone can be more difficult; cut the flesh in quarters, then use a paring knife to slice each quarter away from the stone. If not using immediately, toss peach slices with lemon juice or drop them into acidulated water to prevent browning.

SELECTION: Underripe peaches and nectarines grow softer and more fragrant on the countertop, but they won't get any sweeter, so look for fully tree-ripened fruit. This means nothing hard, green, or lacking fragrance. Ripe peaches have a distinct peachy perfume, and the flesh will give slightly under pressure. Testing the flesh with a prodding thumb can bruise your farmer's peaches; instead cradle the fruit in your palm and squeeze very gently, looking for the slightest give. Skin color provides another clue: mature fruit has a honey gold, almost orange background. A red blush is attractive, but it only indicates the fruit's variety, not ripeness.

STORAGE: Refrigerated peaches keep for up to one week, but you sacrifice some flavor; to help restore it, bring the fruit to room temperature before eating. Fruit left on the counter is sweetest, but it will only last a few days. If your fruit is underripe, leave it in a paper bag on the counter for a day or so until it softens. Eat or discard bruised fruit as soon as possible, to prevent spoilage of the surrounding fruit. You can freeze peeled, sliced peaches (See Freezing Fruit, page 247).

DOUGHNUT PEACHES *with* SHEEP'S MILK YOGURT AND HONEY-ALMOND GRANOLA

Squat, pastel-colored doughnut peaches are one of our most popular varieties. Super juicy and a bit sweeter than other peaches, fitting neatly into the palm of your hand, they're a fantastic three-bite snack at the park, beach, or while waiting in line at the farmers' market. Their syrupy, gushing juices form an instant sauce, one that's especially nice over a tangy sheep's milk yogurt. This granola serves more than you need here; stash any extra in an airtight jar in your pantry for up to three weeks.

Makes 4 servings

GRANOLA	YOGURT PARFAIT
1½ cups / 170 g rolled oats	2 cups / 470 ml plain sheep's milk yogurt
¾ cup / 60 g chopped raw almonds	8 doughnut peaches, pitted and diced
½ cup chopped / 60 g raw cashews	(2 cups / 680 g)
½ cup / 30 g unsweetened coconut flakes	
⅓ cup / 80 ml honey, plus more for drizzling	
¼ cup / 60 ml vegetable oil	
2 tablespoons packed light brown sugar	
¼ teaspoon ground cinnamon	
¼ teaspoon ground cardamom	
4 ounces / 110 g mixed dried fruit, chopped (½ cup)	

To make the granola, preheat the oven to 300°F / 150°C. In a large bowl, combine the oats, nuts, coconut, honey, vegetable oil, sugar, cinnamon, and cardamom. Spread the mixture on a large, rimmed baking sheet. Transfer the baking sheet to the oven and bake, stirring every 10 minutes, until the mixture is dry and rattles around on the pan when it is shaken, 30 to 40 minutes. Remove the baking sheet from the oven and let the granola cool to room temperature. Stir in the dried fruit.

Spoon a small amount of granola into each of 4 parfait glasses. If you don't have parfait glasses, any squat glass or small glass bowl will do. It should be clear, however, so that the layers will be visible. Spoon ¼ cup / 60 ml of yogurt into each glass, followed by another sprinkling of granola, and a layer of diced peaches. Repeat the layering, ending with a final sprinkle of granola. Drizzle honey over the top of each parfait and serve immediately.

JUICY PEACH, TOMATO, *and* BASIL SALAD

Chef Adam Shepard of Brooklyn's Lunetta has a great motto when it comes to sourcing ingredients: "Don't buy food from strangers." His market-driven menu, full of Mediterranean-inspired small plates, gives him lots of opportunities to get to know his local producers. This salad's lemon syrup dressing plays off of the sweet-tart notes naturally present in both ripe tomatoes and peaches. Season the salad aggressively and don't worry if lots of juices collect in the bottom of the bowl—just serve it with good, crusty bread for sopping.

Makes 4 servings

½ cup / 100 g granulated sugar	¼ teaspoon salt, plus more as needed
½ cup / 120 ml freshly squeezed lemon juice (from 4 lemons)	2 tablespoons extra-virgin olive oil, plus more as needed
3 firm, brightly-flavored tomatoes	8 fresh basil leaves, torn into pieces
2 medium ripe peaches	Freshly ground black pepper

In a small saucepan over medium-high heat, bring the sugar, ½ cup / 120 ml of water and the lemon juice to a boil. Reduce the heat to medium-low and simmer until the syrup reaches a consistency slightly looser than honey and turns a rich golden color, 15 to 25 minutes. Remove the pan from the heat and set it aside to cool at room temperature; once fully cooled it should have the consistency of honey and will have reduced to about ¼ cup / 60 ml.

Meanwhile, core and pit the tomatoes and peaches; cut each into slender wedges (about 8 per piece of fruit). Combine the peaches, tomatoes, and salt in a large bowl. Stir in the oil and some of the syrup. How much syrup you need depends on the sweetness of the fruit; begin with a tablespoon and add more as needed. Toss in the basil and season to taste with black pepper and additional salt. Let the salad stand for 5 minutes before serving.

GRILLED RADICCHIO AND NECTARINE SALAD
with BLUE CHEESE VINAIGRETTE

Grilled leafy vegetables might seem like an unusual preparation, but radicchio was made for the barbecue. The sturdy leaves have no problem standing up to high heat, and they take on an amazing smokiness that tempers radicchio's characteristic bitterness. Factor in sweet nectarines and the salty tang of blue cheese and you've got a winner.

Makes 4 to 6 servings

2 small heads radicchio, quartered lengthwise

6 tablespoons extra-virgin olive oil, divided

¾ teaspoon kosher salt, plus more as needed

1 serrano chile, seeded and finely chopped

1 tablespoon freshly squeezed lemon juice, plus more as needed

3 ounces / 85 g firm blue cheese, such as Cabrales or Stilton, crumbled (about ¾ cup)

2 cups / 60 g arugula

3 medium nectarines, pitted and finely diced (1½ cups)

Preheat the grill to high. In a small bowl, toss the radicchio with 3 tablespoons of the oil and sprinkle with salt. Transfer the radicchio to the grill and cook uncovered, turning occasionally, until lightly charred but not blackened, about 2 minutes. Remove the radicchio from the grill and let it cool, and then slice it thinly and place it in a large bowl.

In a small bowl, whisk together the chile, lemon juice, ¾ teaspoon of salt, and the remaining 3 tablespoons of oil. Crumble in the cheese and stir gently.

Add the arugula and nectarines to the radicchio in the large bowl. Toss gently with the dressing. Taste and add more salt if necessary; serve immediately.

GRILLED SHRIMP, PROSCIUTTO, *and* PEACH SKEWERS

I live for the grill. For me, making a meal in the great outdoors harkens to our ancient, primitive roots. When you're cooking for a crowd in the summertime, these grilled skewers are the solution. They look good, come together quickly, and have that irresistible sweet and salty thing going for them. Keep them coming as stand-and-eat appetizers at a casual backyard barbecue or plate them on a bed of peppery greens for a light, sit-down meal.

Makes 6 to 8 servings

1 pound / 455 g large shrimp, peeled and deveined

2 teaspoons extra-virgin olive oil

¼ teaspoon kosher salt

¼ teaspoon chili flakes

2 rosemary sprigs

4 ounces / 110 g thinly sliced prosciutto, cut lengthwise into ½-inch / 1.3 cm-thick strips

1 pound / 455 g firm but ripe peaches (about 2), pitted and cut into 2-inch / 5 cm chunks

½ cup / 14 g fresh basil, chopped, for serving

6 to 8 handfuls fresh arugula, for serving

If you are using bamboo skewers, soak 10 skewers in cold water for at least 20 minutes before using, to prevent them from catching fire on the grill.

Pat the shrimp dry with paper towels and transfer them to a large bowl. Toss the shrimp with the oil, salt, and chili flakes. Using the side of a knife, gently bruise the rosemary and drop it into the bowl. Cover the mixture with plastic wrap and let it stand for 20 minutes at room temperature.

Wrap each shrimp with a strip of prosciutto. Thread the prosciutto-wrapped shrimp onto the skewers, piercing the head and tail. Alternate the shrimp with the peaches.

Preheat a grill to medium-high. Transfer the skewers to the grill and cook, covered, until the shrimp are just opaque and the peaches are slightly caramelized, 2 to 3 minutes per side. Sprinkle the skewers with basil and serve immediately on beds of arugula.

CHICKEN SALAD *with* NECTARINES AND WALNUTS

This recipe is a terrific way to use up leftover chicken after a dinner party or holiday meal. You can also easily double it for a big batch that will get you through several days of easy meals. Unlike gamier meats like lamb or duck, mild chicken doesn't overwhelm nectarines' fresh sweetness. Walnuts provide texture and crunch. It's also a great salad for brown-bagging, sandwiched between slices of crusty, country-style bread.

Makes 2 to 4 servings

⅓ cup / 30 g walnut halves

¼ cup / 60 ml mayonnaise

2 tablespoons walnut or olive oil

1 tablespoon white wine vinegar

¼ teaspoon kosher salt, plus more as needed

Freshly ground black

2 cups / 340 g diced roasted chicken, preferably a mix of white and dark meat

1½ cups / 340 g pitted and diced nectarines (1 to 2 medium)

2 tablespoons thinly sliced scallion, white and light green parts

2 tablespoons finely chopped flat-leaf parsley

1 tablespoon finely chopped fresh tarragon

4 large Boston lettuce leaves, for serving

Preheat the oven to 350°F / 180°C. Spread the walnuts on a rimmed baking sheet and toast them in the oven until fragrant and lightly colored, 10 to 15 minutes. Remove the baking sheet from the oven, let the nuts cool, and then chop them coarsely and place them in a large bowl.

In a small bowl, whisk together the mayonnaise, oil, vinegar, salt, and pepper to taste.

Add the chicken, nectarines, scallion, parsley, and tarragon to the walnuts in the large bowl and toss to combine. Fold in the mayonnaise mixture. Taste the salad and add more salt and pepper if necessary. Spoon the salad onto the lettuce leaves and serve immediately.

CARAMELIZED NECTARINE SPLIT SUNDAE
with HOMEMADE MARASCHINO CHERRIES

Banana splits are classic, but this version, which nestles the ice cream between warm, syrupy nectarines, is even better. The hazelnuts and slightly boozy cherries are excellent grown-up sundae toppings, but feel free to load up on your own favorites, like chocolate sauce or pecans.

Makes 4 servings

4 small, perfectly ripe nectarines, split and pitted

⅓ cup plus 1 tablespoon / 80 g granulated sugar, divided

2 tablespoons brandy

¾ cup / 180 ml heavy whipping cream, divided

1 tablespoon unsalted butter

Small pinch of coarse sea salt, such as fleur de sel

Vanilla ice cream, for serving

Toasted chopped hazelnuts, for serving

Homemade Maraschino cherries (page 281), for serving

In a small bowl, toss the fruit with ⅓ cup / 67 g of the sugar. Heat a large skillet over medium-high heat until hot. Add the nectarines, cut-side down, and cook, without moving, until the undersides are well caramelized, 3 to 4 minutes. Flip the nectarines and cook, without moving, 3 to 4 minutes longer. Remove the pan from the heat and pour in the brandy; then return the pan to the heat and simmer until the liquid is almost completely evaporated. Stir in ¼ cup / 60 ml of the cream and the butter. Simmer, stirring gently, for 2 minutes, or until the sauce has thickened. Sprinkle in the salt. Remove the pan from the heat and let the sauce cool to slightly warmer than room temperature.

In the bowl of an electric mixer fitted with the whisk attachment, whip the remaining ½ cup / 120 ml of the cream with the remaining 1 tablespoon of the sugar until it forms soft peaks.

Scoop the ice cream into 4 serving bowls. Nestle a nectarine wedge on each side of the scoops. Top each serving with a drizzle of caramel sauce and a dollop of whipped cream. Sprinkle with nuts and top with cherries.

WINE-POACHED NECTARINE TART

If there's one thing Sara Kate Gillingham has a lot of, it's great recipes. A cookbook writer and founding editor of thekitchn.com, (the culinary arm of the popular design blog Apartment Therapy), she's logged many thousands of cooking hours and nearly as many at the farmers' market shopping for ingredients at our stand. This tart is almost two desserts in one—nectarines poached in a sweet, spiced wine syrup, and a flaky, fruit-topped tart. For a simple dessert, serve the poached nectarines by themselves, chilled and drizzled with syrup, or spend a little extra time to make the entire, guest-worthy tart.

Makes one 9-inch tart

TART PASTRY	NECTARINE TOPPING
1¼ cups / 180 g all-purpose flour	2 cups / 470 ml white dessert wine, such as Muscat or Sauternes
2 tablespoons granulated sugar	1 cup / 200 g granulated sugar
¼ teaspoon kosher salt	2 cinnamon sticks
7 tablespoons / 100 g unsalted butter, cut into very small pieces and chilled	3 whole star anise
2 to 4 tablespoons ice water, as needed	5 firm but ripe nectarines or peaches
	½ cup / 120 ml heavy whipping cream
	¼ cup / 30 g confectioners' sugar
	1 teaspoon pure vanilla extract

To make the crust, in a large bowl, whisk together the flour, sugar, and salt. Using a pastry cutter or your fingers, cut or rub the butter into the dry ingredients until the mixture resembles a coarse meal (work quickly to keep the butter cold). Mix in the water with a fork, 1 tablespoon at a time, until the dough just comes together; it should be moist, but not damp or wet. Gather the dough into a large ball and flatten it into a disk with the palm of your hand. Wrap the disk tightly in plastic wrap and chill it in the refrigerator for 1 hour.

On a lightly floured surface, roll the dough to a ¼-inch / 6 mm-thick round (about 11 inches / 28 cm in diameter). Transfer the dough to a 9-inch / 23 cm fluted tart pan with a removable bottom, pressing it lightly but snugly into the bottom and up the edges of the pan, allowing excess dough to hang over the edges. Run a rolling pin over the top of the pan to trim off any excess. Pierce the bottom of the crust several times with a fork, cover it with plastic wrap, and then transfer it to the refrigerator to chill for 30 minutes.

Preheat the oven to 400°F / 205°C and arrange a rack in the center position. Line the chilled tart shell with foil or parchment and fill it with pie weights, dried beans, or rice. Bake until the shell is set and golden, about 12 minutes. Carefully remove the weights and foil or parchment; continue to bake until the pastry is golden brown, 10 to 15 minutes more. If the edges begin to brown too quickly, cover them with a ring of foil. Remove the pan from the oven and let it cool completely on a wire rack before filling.

(continued)

To make the filling, combine the wine, sugar, cinnamon, and star anise in a medium pot. Using a paring knife, cut a small X in the bottom of each nectarine and lower them into the pot. Add water to just cover the nectarines (about 2 cups / 470 ml). Bring the liquid to a gentle boil over medium-high heat. Cover the pot and reduce the heat to low. Simmer very gently (do not let the mixture come to a boil) until the nectarines are tender when pierced with the tip of a knife, 5 to 10 minutes. Carefully remove the nectarines with a slotted spoon and transfer them to a bowl of ice water until completely cool. Drain the nectarines and pat them dry; peel the skin away with your fingertips and thinly slice the fruit into wedges, discarding the pits.

Remove the pot from the heat and strain the poaching liquid through a fine-mesh sieve, reserving 1½ cups / 350 ml. Pour the reserved liquid into a wide skillet over medium-low heat and bring it to a simmer. Cook the liquid until it reduces to a syrup thick enough to coat the back of a spoon, 10 to 15 minutes. Remove the skillet from the heat and set it aside to cool.

Just before serving, in the bowl of an electric mixer fitted with the whisk attachment, whip together the cream and confectioners' sugar until stiff peaks form. Beat in the vanilla.

Brush a thin layer of nectarine syrup on the bottom of the cooled tart crust. Spread the whipped cream over the syrup. Arrange the nectarine slices on top, fanning them in concentric circles with the small ends facing the center. Carefully brush the nectarine slices generously with the remaining syrup. Serve immediately.

LEMON VERBENA–NECTARINE ICED TEA

This mellow, fruity iced tea goes down smoothly, without any of the bitterness sometimes associated with caffeinated brews. Pouring hot water over the nectarines softens them slightly and helps release their sweet aroma into the tea. You could also make this tea with dried chamomile blossoms. Drop in fresh raspberries or a mint sprig for extra color when serving.

Makes 4 servings

2 cups / 30 g fresh lemon verbena leaves (or 1 loosely packed cup / 10 g dried leaves)
2 ripe nectarines, peeled, pitted, and finely diced (1 cup)
¼ cup to ⅓ cup / 60 to 80 ml honey, as needed

Tie the leaves in a square of cheesecloth and place the sachet in a large bowl with the nectarines. Pour 4 cups / 1 L of boiling water over the fruit and herbs. Steep the tea for 5 minutes. Remove the cheesecloth, squeezing to extract any additional flavor, and discard it. Let the nectarine mixture cool completely to room temperature.

Transfer the steeping mixture to a blender and add the honey (do this in batches if necessary). Purée until smooth. Pour the tea into a pitcher and whisk in more honey to taste. Transfer the pitcher to the refrigerator and let it chill until very cold. Serve over ice.

PEACH-BOURBON GELATO *with* PRALINE SWIRL

Growing up, lots of us made ice cream the old-fashioned way, using a hand-cranked machine insulated with a layer of ice and rock salt. Everyone took turns churning the custard because after a few minutes your arm was ready to fall right off. These days, the electric ice-cream maker might be the equipment of choice, but this gelato, fragrant with orchard peaches and spiked with bourbon, retains that homespun appeal—without all the hard work!

Makes about 1½ quarts / 1.5 liters

PRALINES	GELATO
3 tablespoons granulated sugar	1½ pounds / 680 g ripe peaches, peeled, pitted, and sliced (3½ cups)
2 tablespoons packed dark brown sugar	¾ cup / 150 g granulated sugar, divided
¼ teaspoon fine sea salt	2⅓ cups / 550 ml whole milk
¼ teaspoon grated nutmeg	1 cup / 240 ml heavy whipping cream
⅔ cup / 90 g whole pecans	⅛ teaspoon fine sea salt
1 large egg white, whisked with ½ teaspoon water	6 large egg yolks
	2 tablespoons bourbon
	1 teaspoon freshly squeezed lemon juice

To make the pralines, preheat the oven to 300°F / 150°C.

In a small bowl, stir together the sugars, salt, and nutmeg. In a separate bowl, toss the nuts with the egg white, then sprinkle in the sugar mixture and toss to combine. Spread the nuts on a Silpat-lined baking sheet (or a baking sheet lines with lightly greased aluminum foil). Bake, tossing occasionally, until the nuts are fragrant and golden, about 20 minutes. Remove the baking sheet from the oven and transfer the nuts immediately to a bowl to cool. When they are cool enough to handle, finely chop the nuts (they can be made up to 1 week ahead and stored in an airtight container at room temperature).

To make the gelato, in a small saucepan, combine the peaches, ¼ cup / 50 g of the granulated sugar, and 1 tablespoon of water. Simmer the mixture over medium-low heat until the peaches are soft and the sugar melts, about 5 minutes; cool. Press the mixture through a food mill into a medium bowl.

In a medium saucepan, simmer together the milk, cream, the remaining ½ cup / 100 g sugar, and the salt over medium-low heat. In a small bowl, whisk together the egg yolks. Whisking constantly, slowly pour the hot cream into the beaten yolks. Pour the mixture back into the saucepan and cook over medium-low heat, stirring constantly, until custard is thick enough to coat the back of a spoon. Strain the custard through a fine-mesh sieve into a medium bowl. Whisk in the peach purée, bourbon, and lemon juice. Cover the bowl with plastic wrap and transfer it to the refrigerator for at least 3 hours or overnight.

The next day, freeze the custard in an ice-cream machine according to the manufacturer's directions. Add the chopped pralines during the last 5 minutes of churning. Serve immediately or freeze the gelato in an airtight container for up to 1 week.

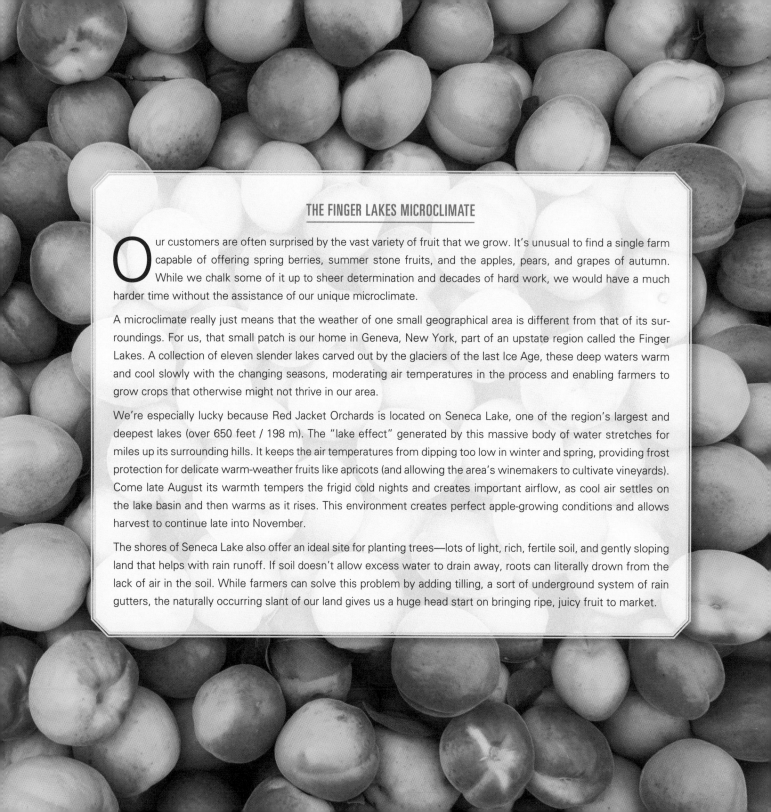

THE FINGER LAKES MICROCLIMATE

Our customers are often surprised by the vast variety of fruit that we grow. It's unusual to find a single farm capable of offering spring berries, summer stone fruits, and the apples, pears, and grapes of autumn. While we chalk some of it up to sheer determination and decades of hard work, we would have a much harder time without the assistance of our unique microclimate.

A microclimate really just means that the weather of one small geographical area is different from that of its surroundings. For us, that small patch is our home in Geneva, New York, part of an upstate region called the Finger Lakes. A collection of eleven slender lakes carved out by the glaciers of the last Ice Age, these deep waters warm and cool slowly with the changing seasons, moderating air temperatures in the process and enabling farmers to grow crops that otherwise might not thrive in our area.

We're especially lucky because Red Jacket Orchards is located on Seneca Lake, one of the region's largest and deepest lakes (over 650 feet / 198 m). The "lake effect" generated by this massive body of water stretches for miles up its surrounding hills. It keeps the air temperatures from dipping too low in winter and spring, providing frost protection for delicate warm-weather fruits like apricots (and allowing the area's winemakers to cultivate vineyards). Come late August its warmth tempers the frigid cold nights and creates important airflow, as cool air settles on the lake basin and then warms as it rises. This environment creates perfect apple-growing conditions and allows harvest to continue late into November.

The shores of Seneca Lake also offer an ideal site for planting trees—lots of light, rich, fertile soil, and gently sloping land that helps with rain runoff. If soil doesn't allow excess water to drain away, roots can literally drown from the lack of air in the soil. While farmers can solve this problem by adding tilling, a sort of underground system of rain gutters, the naturally occurring slant of our land gives us a huge head start on bringing ripe, juicy fruit to market.

WILD GINGER PEACH PIE

Just like our farm, Four & Twenty Blackbirds in Park Slope, Brooklyn, is a family-run business, owned by sisters Emily and Melissa Elsen. The shop changes its offerings with the seasons and their pies are some of the best out there, with crisp buttery crusts and fillings that strike just the right balance between traditional and innovative. This pie is a great example. A homey, straightforward peach pie with two unusual touches—the addition of wild ginger and angostura bitters—it's a tasty way to keep summer fruit on its toes. Wild ginger is a low-growing rhizome with a subtle taste and aroma similar to common gingerroot. If you're unable to find or forage your own, regular store-bought fresh ginger is a fine substitute.

Makes one 9-inch pie

Double Pie Crust (page 111), disks chilled

2½ to 3 pounds / 1.2 to 1.4 kg fresh peaches, peeled (see instructions, page 125)

2 tablespoons freshly squeezed lemon juice

½ cup / 100 g packed light brown sugar

¼ cup / 50 g granulated sugar

3 tablespoons cornstarch

2 teaspoons finely minced wild or regular fresh ginger

¼ teaspoon ground allspice

½ teaspoon kosher salt, plus more as needed

Dash of angostura bitters

1 large egg

Demerara sugar, for sprinkling

On a lightly floured surface, roll out each disk of dough into a 12-inch / 30.5 cm circle. Fit one circle into the bottom of a 9-inch / 23 cm pie plate, allowing the edges of the crust to hang over the rim of the plate. Place the other circle on a rimmed baking sheet. Cover both loosely with plastic wrap, transfer them to the refrigerator, and chill for at least 30 minutes or until ready to use.

Preheat the oven to 425°F / 220°C; arrange 2 oven racks in the bottom and center positions. Place a rimmed baking sheet on the bottom rack.

Cut the peaches into ½-inch / 1.3 cm-thick slices. Transfer the fruit to a large bowl and sprinkle with the lemon juice. Toss in the sugars, cornstarch, ginger, allspice, salt, and bitters; toss to combine.

Pour the filling into the chilled pie shell, leaving behind the excess juices in the bottom of the bowl. Arrange the top crust over the fruit. Pinch and crimp the 2 crust edges together to seal. Transfer the pie to the refrigerator and chill for 15 minutes.

Whisk the egg with 1 teaspoon of water and a pinch of salt. Brush the top of the pastry with the egg wash and sprinkle with the demerara sugar to your liking. Place the pie on the rimmed baking sheet on the lowest rack of the oven. Bake until the pastry is set and beginning to brown, 20 to 25 minutes. Reduce the oven temperature to 375°F / 190°C and move the pie to the center rack. Continue to bake until the pastry is a deep golden brown and the juices are bubbling throughout, 30 to 35 minutes longer. Remove the baking sheet and pie from the oven and place it on a wire rack to cool completely, 2 to 3 hours. Serve the pie slightly warm or at room temperature. The pie will keep refrigerated for 3 days or at room temperature for 2 days.

PEACH MINT JULEP

A twist on the classic derby cocktail, this is one for back porch drinking on a lazy Sunday. Bourbon's notes of caramel, butter, and spice mate naturally with Disaronno, an amber-colored amaretto that gets its nutty almond aroma from an infusion of apricot kernel. Take care not to over-muddle the fruit and mint or you risk overwhelming all the subtle flavors at play. Just a few turns of the wrist should do.

Makes 1 serving

¼ cup / 60 g finely chopped peeled ripe peach
5 fresh mint leaves
1 teaspoon granulated sugar, or more to taste
2 ounces / 60 ml bourbon
1 ounce / 30 ml amaretto

Place the peach, mint leaves, and sugar in the bottom of a sturdy cocktail glass. Using a cocktail muddler, lightly crush the mixture until it smells minty. Fill the glass with ice. Pour in the bourbon and amaretto. Stir quickly and serve immediately.

Plums

HARVEST SEASON: MIDSUMMER & LATE FALL

AS ANYONE WHO KNOWS MY DAD CAN TELL YOU, HE is fanatical about plums (Chef Daniel Humm even dubbed him "Mr. Plum" in his book *I Love New York*). Plums have thrived in the Finger Lakes for hundreds of years, and they were so popular in the early twentieth century that there's even a point along Seneca Lake—

It's a big job. There are enough plum varieties in the world to please every palate. More than twenty-five of them grow in our orchards, which sounds like a lot until you realize that thousands more exist. It is an incredibly diverse fruit. A plum can be wide and heart-shaped, small enough to hide in a fist, or elegantly ovate.

JOE'S GROWING TIPS:

- A lot of novice orchardists start with plum trees because they are fairly hardy. They prefer temperate zones where winters are chilly (although they are susceptible to frost damage) and the summers are moderate to hot. They thrive in full sun and loamy soil (especially when it has a higher lyme content) and don't need much watering, except in the early years and during extreme dry spells.

- If possible, plant your plum tree in the fall, which gives it time to become stronger before the growing season begins. Dig a hole large enough to accommodate the roots. To prevent sunburn on the young bark, wrap burlap around the lower trunk. Expect the tree to bear fruit between its third and fifth year.

- In late spring, prune the trees of dead or crossing branches, and work to create an open, spreading shape where light can easily reach the center. Their shallow roots like to be clear of weeds; mulch the area at the base of the tree each spring to discourage competing growth.

- Like peach trees, plum trees' branches become fragile when weighed down with too much fruit (this is particularly true of Japanese varieties). Halfway through the growing season, thin the tree of small, unripe fruit, aiming to remove enough so that no one piece of fruit touches another.

- Pick plums destined for canning while somewhat firm and tart, as soon as you see their powdery bloom. For all other fruit, don't judge by its color, but pick once it yields to light pressure of the fingertips. Plums should come off easily with a gentle, sideways twist.

known as Plum Point—where the steamships used to pull ashore, drop the plank, and load in the fresh orchard fruit. Plums are near to our family's heart, and my dad, a true aficionado, has made it his mission to re-establish the area's plum industry.

The skin can be gold, crimson, purple, or chartreuse; it might be so singularly colored that it appears almost translucent, or mottled with an overlaying hue. The flesh can be scarlet, yellow, or pale green, with a flavor that ranges from sharp to herbaceous to lusciously sweet.

Sometimes a plum tastes of all these flavors at once.

Like apricots, peaches, and cherries, plums are members of the genus *Prunus*, and they come in two main families: Japanese and European. Japanese varieties, like Santa Rosa, Shiro, and Satsuma are typically a reddish purple or yellow and are known for their juicy sweetness, round and excellent for eating out of hand. We pick these first, usually around mid-July. European varieties, which arrive later but last until late fall, tend to be elongated in shape and less juicy. These are often the tart, dense-fleshed fruit you turn to for baking and canning; varieties include Italian, Empress, Damson, and Reine Claude. Their skin leans toward cool purplish-black or green.

Deciding which plum to use where is a matter of personal taste and experimentation. The tart, firmer fruits are made for jamming and jelly-making and are nice in cakes and muffins, where the fruits' brightness provides pleasant contrast. You can also cook them into a sweetly piquant sauce or glaze for slow-cooked briskets, pork ribs, or lamb loin. These less juicy varieties are best for tarts or pies, too, since they're less apt to turn a crust soggy. With juicier varieties, it's best to roast or bake them in a hot oven with spices like cloves and nutmeg, splashed with orange juice or brandy; the juices bubble into a concentrated, caramelized syrup.

The ripest of plums can have a deep, almost brooding quality that pairs well with flavors like basil, lavender, coriander, ginger, and hot chiles; it also takes to black currants and blackberries, and of course, other stone fruits. If you have a motley assortment of plums, chop them for a colorful salsa for grilled fish or chicken, or throw them into a grain salad with fresh herbs and chopped walnuts or almonds. Plums' skin can be somewhat tart and tannic, so avoid pairing it with anything that contains a bitter edge, such as molasses.

Rinse fresh plums under cool running water. You can peel them if you'd like—some dislike the skin's sharp flavor—but if you plan to cook them, be aware that without skin the soft flesh melts quickly into a sauce. Like peaches and nectarines, plums can be freestone (with a pit that easily separates) or clingstone (needing the aid of a knife). To split freestone fruit, cut around the fruit along its raised ridge; twist the halves and pop out the pit. To remove the pit from clingstone fruit, cut around the fruit into quarters, and then use a paring knife to slice each quarter away from the stone.

SELECTION: Choose plums with a supple firmness. They should give willingly when cradled in your palm; anything hard is underripe. Their skin should be vibrantly colored, not dull, bruised, or damaged. A powdery "bloom" is a good sign, indicating that the fruit has not been overly handled. Though not as fragrant as peaches or apricots, plums should have a fresh, honeyed scent.

STORAGE: Ripe plums will keep for up to two weeks in the refrigerator, but they will taste sweetest at room temperature. They will ripen very quickly if you leave them on the counter. If your plums are really firm, leave them out in a paper bag for a few days; refrigerating underripe fruits can turn the flesh brown and mealy.

PLUM VARIETIES

(Each variety is organized in order of arrival to market.)

VARIETY	APPEARANCE	FLAVOR	BEST FOR
Japanese			
Golden Sugar Plum (Early Golden)	Round and circular with golden skin and an occasional red cheek	sweet flesh; great plum flavor	First plum of the season; excellent for fresh eating
Oblynia	Medium-large; red skin with yellow flesh	Juicy and sugary flesh	Excellent for fresh eating; good for cooking
Owishi Washi	Medium-large; red skin and flesh	Juicy, sweet	Excellent for fresh eating; good for cooking
Methley	Medium to small with reddish-purple skin; crimson flesh	Distinctive flavor with finely textured flesh; juicy and sweet	Excellent for fresh eating, salsas, salads, jellies, and sauces
Shiro	Medium-sized with translucent golden, pink-blushed skin and a white bloom	Juicy and sweet	Excellent for fresh eating, roasting, and baking; the early plums make great jams and preserves
Santa Rosa	Ruby red with faint freckling; gold flesh	Firm flesh; rich, classically sweet, and tangy	Excellent for fresh eating, cakes, ice creams, and canning
Satsuma	Heirloom variety. Medium to large in size; glowing red skin and deep red flesh. Small pit	Firm, meaty, juicy sweet, and lively	Excellent for fresh eating, pies, canning, and preserving
Simka	Purple, almost burgundy skin; pale yellow-white flesh	Subtly sweet and aromatic; fruity	Excellent for fresh eating; great for cooking or baking
Fortune	Large with dark red skin and yellow flesh	Sweet, aromatic; best when fully ripened	Excellent for fresh eating; good for baking

European			
Oullins Gage	Greenish-gold gage plum, medium- to large-sized and oblong; yellow flesh	More sweet than tart; tender, succulent texture; exceptional quality	Excellent for fresh eating; great for cooking, especially tarts and kuchens
Castleton	Dark blue to purple skin; ovate shape	Sweet-tart	Excellent for fresh eating; good for canning and cooking.
Mount Royal	Round and medium- to large-sized; bluish black skin with golden flesh	Meaty, tender, and juicy; outstanding balanced flavor when tree-ripened	Excellent for fresh eating; excellent for preserves and cooking; can be dried for prunes
Bluebyrd	Plump, elongated shape; deep blue skin; amber-colored flesh	Very sweet flavor	Excellent for fresh eating; good for cooking
Empress	Very large, kiwi-sized; indigo-purple skin and yellow flesh	Firm, fine texture; sweet and subtly tart, especially if not fully ripened	Best for canning and baking; holds up well to high heat as in roasting or grilling
Italian	Smaller size; dark-purple skin and green-gold flesh	Slightly sweet with tart, almost lemony notes; softer fruit has more sugar and sweetness	Excellent for fresh eating, canning, and baking; flesh is excellent for drying into prunes
Yellow Egg	Large heirloom variety with golden skin and flesh; oval shape	Firm, juicy; honey-sweet and rich when ripe	Excellent for fresh eating and baking; good for canning
Green Gage	Heirloom variety also called Reine Claude; small to medium oval shape; luminous green-gold skin and amber flesh	Full-bodied, rich, confectionary flavor with tender and smooth texture	Finest dessert plum; superior for jams, compotes, preserves, and baking
Damson	Small to medium and oval shaped; bluish purple skin and yellow flesh	Juicy, spicy, and slightly astringent; firm-textured	Best choice for jams, jellies, chutneys, tarts; tarts, and wine
President	Large, round to oval shape; blue-black skin with yellow flesh	Fine-textured; sweet-tart flavor	Good for all-purpose use

SALMON *with* PLUM, CUCUMBER, AND MINT SALAD

Not only is this salad a beauty to behold, it's explosively flavorful, too. The syrupy, slightly tannic flavors of the plum really come alive when tossed with zingy rice vinegar and an abundance of clean, fresh mint. Although pan-roasted salmon has a melt-in-your-mouth quality that contrasts nicely with the bright fruit, you could throw the fish on the grill instead; the smokiness would also add a nice layer of complexity.

Makes 4 servings

4 (6- to 8-ounce / 170 to 230 g) skin-on wild salmon fillets	1 cup / 130 g diced Kirby cucumbers
Kosher salt and freshly ground black pepper	¼ cup /10 g thinly sliced scallion, white and light green parts
Zest of 2 limes	¼ cup / 10 g fresh mint leaves, torn into pieces
2½ tablespoons grapeseed oil, divided	1 tablespoon seasoned rice vinegar, plus more as needed
1 pound / 455 g ripe mixed plums, pitted and diced	

Season the salmon liberally with salt and pepper. Rub the lime zest into the flesh.

Heat a large skillet over high heat. Add 1 tablespoon of the oil to the pan. Add the fish, flesh-side down and sear, without moving, until the underside is golden, 3 to 4 minutes. Turn and continue cooking to your desired doneness, 3 to 4 more minutes for medium-rare.

While the salmon cooks, prepare the salad: In a large bowl, combine the plums, cucumbers, scallion, and mint. Toss in the 1 tablespoon of vinegar, the remaining 1½ tablespoons of oil, and salt and pepper to taste. Taste the salad and add more vinegar, if desired.

Place each salmon fillet on an individual plate and top with a few spoonfuls of the salad; serve any remaining salad alongside.

GRILLED SPARE RIBS *with* PLUM-GINGER GLAZE

Rich, fatty pork ribs have a natural affinity for plums, especially when the fruit has melted into a sticky, honeyed glaze fragrant with spice. Similar to a Chinese plum sauce typically served with duck, this sauce is great with a mix of plums; if possible use some that are luminously ripe alongside a few firmer ones. The mature fruit provides musky sweetness, while the less ripe plums lend welcome sour notes. Just keep cooking until they've all collapsed. Serve the ribs atop a heap of aromatic jasmine rice and sautéed bok choy, with an ice-cold beer to wash it all down.

Makes 4 servings

2 (2¼-pound / 1 kg) racks spare ribs, trimmed, membranes removed	⅓ cup / 80 g packed dark brown sugar, plus more as needed
1½ tablespoons freshly ground black pepper	2 tablespoons soy sauce
3 tablespoons kosher salt, plus more as needed	1½ tablespoons rice wine vinegar
2 tablespoons peanut oil	2 tablespoons grated fresh ginger
2 garlic cloves, crushed	1 teaspoon ground allspice
2½ pounds / 1.2 kg mixed plums, pitted and coarsely chopped	Toasted sesame seeds, for serving

Season the ribs with the pepper and 3 tablespoons of the salt. Wrap each rack tightly with foil and divide the racks between two large baking sheets; let them stand at room temperature while you prepare the sauce.

In a large, heavy-bottomed saucepan, heat the peanut oil over medium heat. Add the garlic and cook for 1 minute. Stir in the plums, sugar, soy sauce, vinegar, ginger, allspice, and a pinch of salt. Simmer over medium heat until the mixture is thick, jammy, and bubbling, about 30 minutes. Taste and adjust the seasonings as necessary. Press the mixture through a food mill into a medium bowl.

Preheat the oven to 325°F / 165°C. Position baking racks in the top and bottom thirds of the oven. Transfer the ribs on their baking sheets to the oven racks and bake until the ribs are tender, about 2 hours. Remove the baking sheets from the oven, unwrap the ribs, and pour off any excess fat.

Preheat the grill to medium-high. Brush the ribs generously with the glaze. Grill, covered, until the ribs are lightly charred, about 5 minutes per side. Brush with additional glaze, sprinkle with sesame seeds, and serve immediately.

EMILY NICHOLSON'S PLUM KUCHEN

My fondest memories growing up on the farm lead directly to my grandparents' kitchen table, where we shared almost every lunch. A welcome break from the never-ending physical work in the orchards, it was a chance to talk about our day, discuss farm decisions, and brush up on our debating skills with my grandfather. The best part of it all was my grandmother—her gracefulness, her sharp wit, and her cooking! Every meal finished with fruit. Usually it was just fresh from the orchards, but sometimes there were the treats, like her kuchen. I love this dish because it's simple, not too sweet, and wonderfully fruit-forward. She would spread the dough very thinly on a well-greased pan, the fill the top entirely with fruit. Most often she made it with apples because we had those year-round, but she would use peaches or apricots in summer and plums in fall. I love the tart edge and rich dark flavor of this variation.

Makes 6 to 8 servings

1 cup / 140 g all-purpose flour	¼ cup / 60 ml whole milk
¼ cup plus 2 teaspoons / 50 g granulated sugar	1 large egg
2 teaspoons baking powder	3 cups / 600 g pitted sliced plums
Pinch fine sea salt	¼ cup packed light brown sugar
6 tablespoons / 85 g butter, cold and cut into cubes, divided	½ teaspoon ground cinnamon
	¼ teaspoon grated nutmeg

Preheat the oven to 400°F / 205°C. Lightly grease a 9-inch / 23 cm square baking pan.

In a large bowl, whisk together the flour, granulated sugar, baking powder, and salt. Using your fingers, work in 2 tablespoons of the butter until it is well distributed; mixture will have a mealy consistency. Whisk in the milk and egg.

Tightly nestle the plums in the bottom of the prepared pan. Sprinkle with brown sugar, cinnamon, and nutmeg. Dot all over with the remaining butter. Pour the batter over the fruit. Transfer the pan to the oven and bake until golden and bubbling, 20 to 25 minutes. Remove the pan from the oven and let the kuchen cool slightly before serving.

STONE FRUIT-MASCARPONE GRATIN

This dish is easy summer eating. When stone fruit hits its peak mid-summer and the market is teeming with syrupy plums, peaches, and nectarines, it's time to pull out this recipe. Roast the fruit and assemble everything before dinner. You can slip it in the oven to broil while someone clears the table for dessert. The warm, sweet fruit partners beautifully with the caramelized, slightly bitter notes of the molten sugar and cream topping.

Makes 4 servings

---

1 pound / 455 g mixed plums, nectarines, and peaches, pitted and sliced

1 tablespoon melted unsalted butter

⅛ teaspoon fine sea salt

1 cup / 230 g mascarpone

3 tablespoons superfine sugar

Preheat the oven to 450°F / 230°C. In a large bowl, toss the fruit with the butter and salt, then spread the mixture on a large baking sheet and transfer the baking sheet to the oven. Roast the fruit, tossing occasionally, until the slices are tender and golden around the edges, about 25 minutes. Remove the baking sheet from the oven and set it aside to cool completely.

Preheat the broiler. Spread mascarpone into the bottom of a gratin dish. Scatter the cooled roasted fruit over top. Sprinkle the sugar over the fruit. Run the gratin under the broiler, watching carefully to prevent it from burning, until the sugar melts and the fruit is lightly charred, 1 to 2 minutes. Serve immediately.

GRILLING FRUIT

Come summer, most of us spend a lot of nights firing up the grill, even building entire meals around smoke-in-fused foods—grilled chicken alongside lightly charred corn on the cob next to slabs of seared zucchini and eggplant. But a dessert of grilled fruit can actually become the best part of dinner. Heat's role in cooking is to bring out a food's inherent flavor—the hotter the flame, the more quickly natural sugars are drawn to a food's surface, where they caramelize on contact with the heat source. When you marry a high-heat cooking method like grilling with the plentiful sugars of fresh fruit, you quickly appreciate their compatibility.

Sweet, ripe fruit really needs nothing more than a clean grill grate (it's important to brush away any remnants of meat, fish, or vegetable char). Juicy, medium-sized summer fruit seems to work best: try peaches, nectarines, plums, and apricots. Pears are nice on fall nights when it's warm enough to eat outside. Halve the fruit (do not peel), remove any pits or seeds, and place them, cut-side down, onto a well-heated grill. Don't move them around. Just wait until the undersides are well caramelized. How long this takes depends on the sugar content of the fruit, but a few minutes is usually plenty. Carefully flip the fruit and repeat on the other side. There is no need to check for tenderness.

You can also tinker with more elaborate preparations: brush the cut surfaces with honey, brandy or melted butter (or combine all three); sprinkle with cardamom or a pinch of black pepper; anoint with the barest drizzle of balsamic vinegar or a splash of fruit juice (Black Currant-Apple works well with any fruit: page 297). Once off the grill, let them sit for a short minute, just long enough for the molten, sugary edges to cool and candy. Slice and serve the grilled fruit over ice cream or on a platter, showered with torn mint leaves or toasted coconut.

PERFECT FRUIT PIES

I f you've ever struggled with some of the pitfalls of fruit pies—runny fillings, soggy crusts, not enough sugar—you may have found yourself wondering where the old expression "easy as pie" ever came from. But making pie actually *is* easy. You have one big goal: to create a full-bodied filling that captures fruit's sweet juices within a crisp, flaky crust. Getting there is simply in the details, and they are all things that can be learned. Once you've discovered some tried-and-true tricks of expert pie bakers and learned to apply them consistently, you will get a beautiful pie every time. Easy.

Perfect Pie Crust

A good pie crust is the essential base of a worthwhile pie-eating experience. It's the first thing anyone notices about a pie, and it's the first part of the pie you taste. If the crust appears pale and doughy, or crumbly and cracked, your confidence in that particular pie is going to immediately waver. Even if you can get past its looks, the texture is likely to disappoint, too.

The best way to learn how to make good pie crust is to do it by hand. You can achieve excellent and fast results in a food processor, but wait until you've gotten good at reading pie dough before you try. Once you've handled the dough enough to know when it's reached the proper consistency, the process will feel fairly intuitive. That's when you're ready to move on to kitchen appliances. Start with the double-crust recipe on page 111.

The Role of Moisture

Moisture (usually water) is both the best friend and the enemy of pie crust. Too little and your crust will be crumbly and hard to roll out. It might crack while baking, allowing your delicious juicy filling to seep into the bottom of the pan or up and over the sides. Too much moisture and you're likely to "overwork" the dough, creating an unfortunately tough crust.

Overworked dough is the most common mistake among inexperienced pie bakers. Water activates gluten, the strands of protein naturally present in flour. This is good. Gluten gives pie structure and keeps your crust from becoming total mush. But if you add too much water, the dough will turn stretchy and elastic, almost like bread dough (that's one reason bread dough is kneaded, to activate that gluten).

How much water is the right amount depends on a couple of factors, including the humidity in the air and the type of flour you are using. That's why you almost always see crust recipes offer a range of how much water to add. It's not an exact science. Some cooks also add a small spoonful of vinegar to their crust, which inhibits the formation of gluten. You can do that, but adding water slowly is a more reliable path to success.

Once you've whisked together the flour and salt, work in the butter (with your fingertips or a pastry cutter) until it's evenly distributed in coarse, pea-sized nubs. Now dribble in about half the water your recipe calls for. Using a light hand or a pastry cutter, work it loosely into the flour until the mixture feels uniformly moistened. Continue adding water, 1 tablespoon at a time, until it reaches the right consistency: it should look a little crumbly and not at all stretchy; moist, but not damp, and definitely not wet. If you squeeze a handful of the crumbs together in your fist, they will stick together firmly in a ball that you can break apart with little resistance.

Chilling Dough

Resist the temptation to skip chilling your dough. Chilling allows the gluten time to relax, preventing shrinkage during baking. It also resolidifies the dough's butter, which is important. Those solid nuggets of fat are what lifts the crust during baking, giving it a desirable flakiness. Pie crust needs at least 1 hour of chill time, and if you have 2 hours or more to spare, even better. Wrapped in plastic wrap, pie dough keeps in the refrigerator for up to three days.

In general, it's good to keep everything nice and cold when you're making crust. Always start with cold butter (you may sometimes even see instructions to stick it in the freezer) and ice water—not just cold water—for moistening. If you have time, you can even prechill the flour. All of these steps help keep the dough adequately cool so that the butter doesn't melt and the dough doesn't get too wet or too warm.

Rolling the Dough

The last step to getting the pie crust right is rolling it out. Do this before you even start on your filling. You can fit the bottom crust into your pie tin and place your top crust on a plate or small baking sheet. Cover them with plastic and let them firm up a bit in the refrigerator while you prepare the filling.

Start with a lightly floured board. Use just enough flour to keep the dough from sticking; too much makes the dough dry and tough. The objective in rolling out pie crust is to handle the dough as little as possible. Running the pin back and forth over the pastry over-kneads it, making it stretchy. Instead, start with your pin in the center of the dough and roll upwards to the outside edge. Return the pin to the center and roll downwards to the outside edge. Repeat on the right and left sides of the dough; continue this pattern until you've reached the suggested pastry thickness and diameter.

Freezing Pie Crust

Pie crust freezes beautifully and is a great way to save on kitchen time down the road. You can do it two ways: Wrap the flattened disks of dough in a layer of plastic wrap followed by a layer of foil and freeze; defrost in the refrigerator before using. Alternatively, you can roll out the crust, transfer it to a pie plate, crimp it, and freeze the whole thing in a freezer bag (make sure your pie plate is freezer safe). The shell can go straight from freezer to oven, but you will need to factor in an additional 10 to 15 minutes of baking time. Frozen pie crust keeps for up to two months.

Assembling and Baking the Pie

Once you've got a well-made crust you're halfway there. All that's left is the filling and baking of the pie. Make sure you start with the right pan: Opt for heavy aluminum or glass pie plates. Lightweight aluminum or pretty ceramic pie plates conduct heat less efficiently and won't give you the crisp crust you're seeking.

Fruit Filling

A good filling depends on two main factors: sugar and thickener. Since levels of sweetness and acidity in fruit vary, how much sugar to add depends a lot on what type of fruit you're using. A good rule of thumb is to start with ¾ cup / 150 g of sugar for every 5 cups / 850 g of sweet fruit like peaches, and as much as 1½ cups / 300 g for every 5 cups / 850 g of more tart fruits, like gooseberries or rhubarb. You should always let your palate be your guide and add more sugar if a recipe needs it, but you will need to increase the amount of thickener since sugar releases extra moisture in baking. When it comes to thickeners, you can choose from several options, depending on what kind of fruit you are using and the desired consistency of your filling (see Thickening Pies, page 159).

Fresh fruit needs a short marinating period to allow the natural juices time to gather; this also strengthens the fruit's cell walls and helps it maintain its shape during cooking. Toss the fruit with the sugar, thickener, salt, and lemon juice, if using (it often provides a nice counterpoint to the sweet fruit). Let the mixture stand at room temperature for about 15 minutes and no longer than half an hour or it will release too many juices and inhibit the thickening process. This is also true when you add the filling to your crust. Wait to do this until your oven is completely preheated and you're ready for baking. Fill the pie, seal the top crust, and place it in the oven immediately. Allowing the filled pie to stand can yield a soggy bottom crust.

You can very successfully substitute frozen fruit in pies. Use unsweetened fruit only, and substitute the same volume of frozen fruit as you would for fresh. You can also use the same amount of thickener; if the fruit seems particularly icy, add an extra teaspoon or so of starch. Unlike fresh fruit, frozen fruit should be transferred to the pie shell and baked as soon as you've mixed it with the remaining ingredients to prevent it from releasing too much liquid. The pie will probably need additional baking time, usually 20 to 30 minutes.

Baking the Pie

When it comes to baking a fruit pie, especially one that is double-crusted, a hot, thoroughly preheated oven is vital. For a crisp bottom crust, begin the pie on a rack in the lower third of the oven, close to the oven's hot floor. Many recipes start fruit pies at a high temperature to firm up the crust and then reduce the temperature to tenderize the filling; move the pie to a middle rack around the same time that you adjust the temperature. Rotate the pie 180 degrees halfway through to ensure even baking. If, after baking several pies on a lower rack, you find that the crust still isn't browning as much as you'd like, place a baking sheet on the lower rack while the oven preheats. Bake the pie on the hot sheet; the crust will begin browning more quickly.

Double-crusted pies need a place for steam to exit. Lattice pies have natural vents between the strips of dough, but you should make several slashes in the center of all other top crusts before baking. To achieve that magazine-worthy shiny surface, brush the crust with milk, cream, or egg. You can also sprinkle the top with demerara sugar, which provides a pleasant, crunchy contrast to the soft fruit. If you do choose to apply a glaze, the crust will likely begin to brown about halfway through baking. If it seems to be coloring too quickly, loosely tent the top of the pie with foil to slow it down.

Because the crust often turns golden before the filling is finished, home cooks sometimes panic and pull the pie out before it's fully baked. Pie thickeners must reach a boiling point before they begin to set the pie. It's easy to see if a pie thickener has done its job. The juices in the center will bubble thickly like syrup and should be clear, not cloudy (the exception to this is a flour-thickened pie, which might be slightly less shiny). If the juices are still thin the pie isn't ready—plain and simple. Keep baking, tenting the pie with foil if necessary to prevent overbrowning. As the juices begin to bubble, they are likely to spill out over the edges of the pan. Have a foil-lined, rimmed baking sheet ready on the rack directly below the pie to catch any errant juices.

Cool fruit pies thoroughly, for at least 3 hours. This gives the filling time to set, making it easier to slice. Cool pies in the pan on a wire rack. Elevating the pie in this way encourages air circulation beneath the pan and maintains that crisp bottom crust you worked so hard to achieve. Fruit pies are at their best the day they are baked, but once cooled they will keep on the counter, covered, for up to two days.

Thickening Pies

All pies need thickeners to give the fruit juices body and prevent them from oozing out of the sliced pie. The most common thickeners are flour, cornstarch, and tapioca. All are starches that swell once heated, absorbing any surrounding water in the process. As the starch molecules reach a boiling point, they separate, creating a network of delicate bonds with the water. You'll know this has happened when your filling takes on a glossy, transparent appearance. Avoid baking your pie too much past this point. The longer those fragile bonds cook, the more likely they are to burst and break down, reducing your filling to a thin mess. Deciding which starch to use depends on personal preference and what result you are looking for.

FLOUR: Flour is an easy thickener to reach for, since most of us always have some in the pantry, but it can sometimes give fillings a gummy consistency and cloudy appearance. The exception to this is apple pie, which takes to flour better than any other thickener. Flour has less thickening power than cornstarch and tapioca, so you need to use about twice as much.

Use about 6 tablespoons of flour for every 5 cups / 850 g of fresh fruit. Apples only need about 3 tablespoons. Avoid using with juicy berries, which turn gooey with flour thickeners.

QUICK-COOKING TAPIOCA: These little white beads are made from the cassava root. They are flavorless and produce a superior gloss in pies, particularly beautiful in colorful berry pies. They also hold up well when thawed, making them the choice for any pie you intend to freeze. Although the beads soften during baking they don't dissolve completely; if you're fussy about looks, don't use them in open or lattice-topped crusts, as keen diners might spot them. You can also try grinding them in a coffee or spice grinder for better dissolving powers, or look for tapioca starch. Though less easy to find, tapioca starch comes in a powdered form that dissolves completely.

Use about 3 tablespoons of tapioca for every 5 cups / 850 g of fresh fruit. Apples only need about 1½ table-spoons. Juicy berries need 4 to 5 tablespoons.

CORNSTARCH: Cornstarch is nearly flavorless, though not completely. Some find it too starchy tasting, while others think its subtle sweetness enhances a pie's flavor. It produces smooth, silky fillings and doesn't break down when reheated. The downside is that its texture is compromised when pies are frozen and it thickens poorly with high-acid fruits like cherries, plums, and rhubarb.

Use about 3 tablespoons of cornstarch for every 5 cups / 850 g of fresh fruit. Apples only need about 1½ tablespoons, while juicy berries need 4 to 5 tablespoons.

Fruit with Fruit:
Delicious Combinations

Using a single type of fruit in a pie highlights its inherent qualities and produces true, fruit-forward flavor. But combining compatible fruits can draw out the best characteristics of each in surprising harmony. Stick to two (and no more than three) fruit combinations per pie. These combinations can also be applied to other baked goods and desserts. Here are some good ones to try:

APPLES: Rhubarb, black currants, sweet and sour cherries, pears, strawberries, raspberries, quince, blackberries

APRICOTS: Black currants, raspberries, blackberries, peaches, nectarines, plums

BLACKBERRIES: Apples, rhubarb, strawberries, blueberries, raspberries, peaches, nectarines

BLUEBERRIES: Peaches, nectarines, apricots, strawberries, blackberries, raspberries

CHERRIES: Pears, currants, apples, peaches, nectarines

CONCORD GRAPES: Pears, apples

CURRANTS: Cherries, apricots, apples, pears

GOOSEBERRIES: Strawberries, rhubarb

PEACHES/NECTARINES: Blueberries, raspberries, strawberries, black currants, apricots, plums

PEARS: Raspberries, currants, apple, quince, grapes

PLUMS: Peaches, nectarines, apricots, raspberries

QUINCE: Apples, pears, raspberries

RASPBERRIES: Peaches, nectarines, apricots, apples, blueberries, blackberries

RHUBARB: Gooseberries, strawberries, apples, blackberries, raspberries

STRAWBERRIES: Rhubarb, gooseberries, apples, blackberries, blueberries, raspberries, peaches, nectarines, apricots

APPLES, PEARS, CONCORD GRAPES, AND QUINCE

SOME YEARS, SUMMER STUMBLES UNEXPECTEDLY INTO AUTUMN. I WAKE UP TO FIND THE BLUE SKIES HAVE PACKED UP, LEAVING BEHIND A BRISK, GRAY HORIZON OF SWIRLING LEAVES. OTHER TIMES IT LINGERS, STUBBORNLY REFUSING TO RELINQUISH ITS SUNNY HOLD. WE'VE EXPERIENCED EVERY POSSIBLE SWING OF THIS CAPRICIOUS SEASON, BUT WHEN WE'RE LUCKY, THE TRANSITION HAPPENS ALMOST IMPERCEPTIBLY, WITH WARM DAYS GRADUALLY FOLLOWED BY INCREASINGLY COOLER, LONGER EVENINGS. THIS IS THE DELICATE BALANCE WE HOPE FOR MOST, SINCE IT PROVIDES THE TEMPERATURE GRADIENTS THAT TRULY "FINISH" FALL FRUIT, BRUSHING THEM WITH COLOR AND DEVELOPING THEIR EXCEPTIONALLY COMPLEX FLAVORS.

Ultimately, whatever the weather brings, autumn remains my favorite season at the orchard, the period when we steel ourselves for the "Great Gathering." Our farm may be lush with berries and stone fruits in the summer, but fall is when our orchards are at peak production, bearing apples, pears, prune plums, quince, and grapes, not to mention the makings of some great sweet apple cider. With so much harvesting to be done, autumn feels particularly purposeful, each shortening day a reminder that time is dwindling and winter's freeze is not far off. After months of steady farming, we now have six short weeks to harvest up to 40 million apples, pears, prune plums, grapes,

and quince. We're in the fields by sunrise, maximizing every daylight hour until the harvest moon appears in the early evening sky, hanging so low and large you can almost step into its orange glow.

Our orchards surround Seneca Lake and the hills of Geneva, or what I like to call the "Silicon Valley of fruit growing." Home to Cornell University's prestigious Agricultural Experiment Station, Geneva is the birthplace of many famed apple varieties, including the perennially popular Jonagolds, Macouns, Cortlands, and Empires, as well as newer varieties like Snapdragon and Ruby Frost. Our relationship with Cornell affords us access to research and technology that improves and expands our offerings. The first apples to arrive at market are the early bearing Paula Reds and Ginger Golds in August. These tart-sweet eating apples usher in September's larger crop of fan favorites, like McIntoshes, Cortlands, Macouns, Galas, and sweet, crunchy Honeycrisps, one of the few apples I've seen that can turn indifferent buyers into raving fanatics. Before long, classic Empire, Golden Delicious, and Jonagold apples are ready, just in time for cool-weather pies, crisps, and baked apples. Some of our most prized varieties take the longest to mature and won't reach harvest until November, including spicy Braeburns, tart Granny Smiths, rustic Staymans, and our beloved Fuji, a sweet variety that is the key ingredient in our fresh Fuji Apple Juice (page 305).

Customers associate pears with the later fall months, but we start picking most varieties long before, usually starting at the end of August. Pears are finicky fruits when it comes to harvest. If left on the tree until ripe, they develop a gritty, mealy texture, so we must pick the fruit on the firm side and cure them in cold storage to encourage proper ripening. Asian varieties can hang longer on the branch until almost completely tree-ripened. Agricultural experts are working hard to breed new varieties that will introduce the possibility of "ever-ready" tree-ripened strains (with melting flesh) in the next five to ten years.

The fruit that really gets customers clamoring are the grapes, which we begin to harvest around the first week of September. First come the Fredonia grapes, followed by the Concords and finally, the delicate-tasting Niagaras. My family experimented with lots of different grape varieties over the years to find those with the best flavor, and these three were our clear winners. All of these varieties have pips that require seeding or spitting, but the outstanding quality more than makes up for it. For several weeks, our pickers hit the vineyards—carefully snipping bunches from the vines, then cautiously transferring the delicate fruit to trays so that they can make it to market unscathed.

Autumn's best weeks at market are at this time, midway through the season when it all finally overlaps. Majestic purples bump up against mossy greens and rusty reds, and crisp apples are sliced for sampling alongside juicy pears. Customers sip cider, simultaneously swapping summer stories and holiday baking tips. As our season winds down, everyone else's seems to be gearing up, for school, work, and renewed responsibilities. It's the last push of the year, the beautiful, bountiful transition between harvest season's whirling momentum and winter's stillness. For now, just one extra layer is enough to ward off the increasing chill, but soon we'll be unpacking our coats and putting the trees to rest for another season.

Apples

HARVEST SEASON: LATE SUMMER to LATE AUTUMN;
AVAILABLE YEAR-ROUND

APPLES ARE READILY AVAILABLE ALL YEAR LONG. IN supermarkets and many farmers' markets, you can always find varieties that are delicious and, even better, locally grown. Its sheer accessibility means it doesn't always market transitions from the riotous vibrancy of summer produce to the rustic crimsons and russets of this fall fruit. Now an apple is exactly what you want, whether it's a crisp, tart Macoun, a spicy, pink-streaked Gala, or

JOE'S GROWING TIPS:

- Apples grow best in temperate zones, where the summers are hot and the winters offer a long, cold dormant period (most apples can withstand winter temperatures down to -30°F / -34°C). They are happiest in well-drained, sandy to heavy clay loam, but can tolerate most soil so long as it's not too dry or too muddy.

- Apple trees produce quickly and enduringly. A single tree can usually bear fruit within the second year and continue faithfully for another fifty years. Annually prune any crossing center branches or dark, brittle deadwood. Leave older branches that contain fruiting "spurs," the bud-lined twigs from which the fruit grows. One spur can bear fruit for many years.

- The roots of apple trees are long and spread slightly beyond the reach of the mature branches. To prevent competition between trees, allow ample space between them when planting. However, if you desire smaller trees, purchase trees that are on dwarf or semidwarf rootstocks. These smaller trees will devote more of their energies to making fruit instead of making wood, and they can be planted as close as 4 to 9 feet / 1.2 to 2.7 m apart. Dwarf trees will provide the best-quality fruit but will require stakes or trellises to support them once the cropping starts.

- As apples ripen, the starch turns to sugar. In our world, we test for ripeness using special flesh pressure testers along with sugar and starch indicators. A casual apple grower's best way for determining when fruit is ready is to know the fruit's approximate date of harvest and then sample the occasional fruit just before that timing. To pick apples, grasp them firmly in one hand and lift the fruit up and sideways with a twist. Be careful not to break off or damage the fruiting spur, from which the fruit grows. If possible, pick with the stem and leaf intact, which helps maintain freshness. Although apples are sturdier than other fruit, they bruise easily, so handle them with care. Like all fruit, apples are living organisms; once harvested, they are best kept in a cool environment where their respiration rate is slowed, thus extending their "peak flavor" status.

inspire the same frenzy as the arrival of sweet, thumb-sized strawberries or summer's first plums, apricots, or peaches.

But all that changes when apple season *really* begins, during the late summer harvest. This is when the an aromatic, tangy Northern Spy.

Much of what distinguishes an apple is how it's grown. Soil, geography, and weather—what the French call "terroir"—all work together to produce fruit that strikes a harmonious balance of sugar and acid. Our rich glacial soils and the unique Seneca Lake microclimate (which also fosters a striking difference between day and nighttime temperatures) create ideal apple-growing conditions, enabling us to bring over thirty varieties to market each year.

What to do with so many apples? You can't go wrong with the classics, tucking slices into pies, crisps, and pandowdy, simmering them into sauce, or stuffing and baking the fruit whole. There's apple kuchen, one of my grandmother's most treasured annual traditions, which remains a family favorite to this day. Apples are also easily preserved. Their high levels of pectin, a natural thickener, make them ideal for jellies, jams, chutneys and butters, though they can be dried, vinegared, brandied, and juiced, too. In fact, many of our apples are destined for our juicer; pairing naturally with fruits like rhubarb and berries, apples constitute the base of all our cold-pressed juices.

Partner the most aromatic apples with a hunk of sharp cheese (an aged Cheddar or Parmesan is perfect); meats like poultry, pork, or sausage; and full-flavored mackerel or herring. Apples also do well with herbaceous ingredients like fennel (the seed or bulb), sage, and lemon thyme; even cilantro pairs surprisingly well. Dried raisins, dates, and currants mate nicely in sweet or savory preparations, as do toasted nuts and spices like cinnamon, nutmeg, and cloves. Rich maple or brown sugars or molasses offsets the fruit's brighter notes.

As the harvest season gives way to winter, you may find apples preserved in a waxy coating. A rinse under warm water dissolves it. The skin can be left on or is easily removed with a vegetable peeler, depending on how you plan to use the fruit. Cut out and discard the bitter seeds and woody core. Apples brown easily, so drop slices in acidulated water or sprinkle them with lemon juice if not using immediately.

SELECTION: Apples should be heavy for their size, richly colored, and very firm. Although you want to avoid bruised, soft, or cracked fruit, light scratching or "scald" (dry patches) are fine and don't affect flavor. It's worth considering your plans when picking out an apple, since they vary greatly in crispness, flavor, and behavior in cooking. In general, sweet-tart apples with a dry, firm texture are best for baking; tart, slightly underripe fruit is a good choice for jams; and sauce apples should have complex flavor and a softer texture that breaks down easily. Snacking apples depend a great deal on preference (See Apple Varieties chart, pags 170–171).

STORAGE: It's fine to store apples on the counter, but they will ripen up to ten times more quickly than refrigerated apples, which have a nice, long storage life of several weeks. An ideal climate is cold and moist; a perforated bag in your crisper drawer works nicely. Because apples produce ethylene, a gas that hastens deterioration, store them away from perishable foods, like broccoli, cucumbers, and greens. You can freeze apples, too (see Freezing Fruit, page 247).

APPLE VARIETIES

VARIETY	APPEARANCE	TEXTURE	FLAVOR	BEST FOR
Baldwin	Red and green background	Very crisp and firm	Tart and tangy	All-purpose, keep well; great for cider pressing
Braeburn	Red on yellow background	Crisp and firm	Sweet-tart, and spicy	Baking or snacking; keeps well in storage
Cortland	Red skin with patches of yellow-green; snow white flesh	Tender and juicy	Sweet and slightly tart	Slow to brown, it's great raw in salads; also good for sauces
Crispin/Mutsu	Greenish yellow with red-orange blush; coarse flesh	Very crisp	Spicy, tart, and sweet	Delicious for eating, great for baking
Empire	Maroon with yellow blush; creamy white flesh	Crisp	Well-balanced sweet and tart	All-purpose; kid-friendly
Fuji	Bright red-pink and large	Very firm, holds up well to cooking	Syrupy sweet	Excellent for eating, baking, and juicing; keeps well in storage
Gala	Pinkish stripes on yellow background	Crisp	Aromatic and sweet	Snacking, salads
Ginger Gold	Greenish gold; white flesh	Crisp and firm, holds up well to cooking	Rich and succulent	All-purpose: slow to brown
Golden Delicious	Pale yellow	Crisp and juicy	Sweet, mellow	Baking, snacking, salads, apple butter
Golden Supreme	Greenish gold to golden brown; cream flesh	Firm, juicy	Sweet	Drying, baking, cider
Granny Smith	Spring green with occasional blushed cheeks	Crisp, hard, and juicy	Tart	Snacking, salads, baking

Honey Crisp	Two-toned red and yellow skin; coarse, cream-colored flesh	Exceptionally crisp and juicy	Honey sweet with hints of tartness	Supreme snacking, good for sauces and baking
Ida Red	Red with hints of yellow; yellow, faintly pink flesh	Firm and juicy, holds up well to cooking	Sweetly tart	Baking (especially pies), sauces, eating, freezing
Jonagold	Gold with blushing orange stripes; creamy flesh	Crisp and juicy, holds up well to cooking	Sweet, balanced with tart	Great for baking and snacking
Lady	Pint-sized, red cheeks with green background	Firm, tender	Subtly sweet-tart	Ornamental, great around the holidays; good keeping and eating
McIntosh	Red cheek with green background	Tender	Sweet and tangy	Eating; pies and sauces; quick-cooking
Macoun	Dark red	Tender and juicy	Sweet, aromatic, berry-like	Excellent for sauces and cheese plates
Newtown Pippin	Greenish yellow with russeting near stem; pale yellow flesh	Extra crisp and juicy	Slightly tart	Best for baking and ciders, as they brown quickly
Northern Spy	Thin green skin, flushed with red	Crisp, juicy	Tart and tangy with a rich acidity	The standard for excellent pies; also great for juices and cider
Red Delicious	Deep red with white striping	Crisp	Mildly sweet	Snacking, salads
Rome	Red flecked with white; greenish white flesh	Firm, holds up well to cooking	Mild and tart	Great for sautéing, sauces, baking, freezing
Stayman	High red or malted red with patches of russeting	Snappy bite	Distinctly sweet-tart, winey flavor	Pies and general baking; partners well with savory

SMOKED TROUT, APPLE, and PURSLANE SALAD

Smoked trout has a meaty quality completely different from that of delicate fresh trout. Its intensity is nicely tempered with something bright. Here, that means a tangy apple (Stayman, Ida Red, or Northern Spy are all good choices) and a tangle of lemony purslane. From mid summer until the weather turns brisk, the market spills over with this robust green, but if you can't find any check your backyard—those who don't know better consider it a weed. Serve this salad alone or heaped on top of thickly sliced brown bread.

Makes 6 to 8 servings

¼ cup / 60 ml crème fraîche	3 tablespoons finely chopped dill
2 tablespoons Champagne or white wine vinegar	Salt and freshly ground black pepper
2 tablespoons minced shallot	8 ounces / 230 g whole smoked trout
1 tablespoon Dijon mustard	12 cups / 310 g loosely packed purslane or watercress, torn into bite-sized pieces
3 tablespoons extra-virgin olive oil	1 large sweet-tart apple, cored and diced

In a small bowl, whisk together the crème fraîche, vinegar, shallot, and mustard. Whisk in the oil and dill, and season to taste with salt and pepper.

Peel the skin from the trout and pull the fillets from the center bone. Run your fingers along the fish, locating and removing any pin bones. Break the fish into large chunks.

In a large bowl, toss together the purslane, trout, and apple. Pour in the dressing and toss to combine.

KALE, APPLE, and KOHLRABI SLAW

Kale and kohlrabi grow beautifully in cool weather, and you'll spot them at the market around the time apples arrive. Like many of nature's seasonal mates, the three make a harmonious trio. Fresh and clean-tasting, this salad is still hearty enough to transition to fall. It's also adaptable: Try raw fennel in place of the kohlrabi or dried figs instead of the currants. Tossing the kale with the warm vinaigrette renders it just tender enough to enjoy uncooked.

Makes 6 to 8 servings

1 bunch curly kale (8 ounces / 230 g), stems removed and leaves thinly sliced

1 medium bulb kohlrabi, peeled and cut into ⅛-inch / 3 mm-thick matchsticks

½ small red onion, thinly sliced

½ cup / 60 g pine nuts

2 teaspoons fennel seeds

½ cup / 120 ml extra-virgin olive oil

Pinch chili flakes

¼ cup / 60 ml cider vinegar

1 teaspoon kosher salt, plus more as needed

1 sweet-tart apple, cored and cut into ⅛-inch / 3 mm-thick matchsticks

½ cup / 60 g dried currants

In a large bowl, combine the kale, kohlrabi, and onion.

In a small, dry skillet over medium heat, toast the pine nuts until golden, 2 to 3 minutes. Remove the skillet from the heat and add the toasted nuts to the kale mixture. Add the fennel seeds to the skillet and toast until just fragrant, about 1 minute. Transfer the seeds to a mortar and pestle and crush lightly. Return the fennel seeds to the skillet and add the oil. Heat the oil over medium-low heat until it is warm and the seeds turn pale golden in color. Stir in the chili flakes and cook for 30 seconds. Stir in the vinegar and salt and let the mixture heat through for 1 minute.

Pour the dressing over the salad, add the apple and currants, and toss well. Serve immediately.

APPLE, GRUYÈRE, AND
PORK PRESSED SANDWICHES *with* GRILLED ONIONS

This is a Sunday lunch kind of sandwich. You take a little leftover pork from Friday or Saturday night's dinner, some fixings from the fridge, a few fresh apples, and you suddenly have a hot and seriously substantial meal. Nutty Gruyère cheese is great here, but another salty, meltable cheese such as aged Cheddar or Gouda works, too.

Makes 4 servings

1 small red onion, peeled and sliced into ¼-inch / 6 mm rings	2 teaspoons Dijon mustard
1 teaspoon finely chopped fresh sage	4 slices (½-inch / 1.3 cm-thick) slices country-style bread
2 teaspoons extra-virgin olive oil	10 ounces / 285 g leftover roast pork, thinly sliced
Pinch of fine sea salt	1 large tart apple, such as Granny Smith, quartered, cored, and thinly sliced
Freshly ground black pepper	2 ounces / 60 g Gruyère cheese, grated (½ cup)
¼ cup / 60 ml mayonnaise	

Toss the onion slices with the sage, the oil, the salt, and pepper to taste. Heat a cast-iron grill pan over high heat. Grill the onions until tender, about 10 minutes. Remove the pan from the heat, let the onions cool, and chop them coarsely. In a medium bowl, combine the chopped onion with the mayonnaise and mustard. Wipe out the grill pan.

Spread one side of each slice of bread with the onion mixture. Layer pork and apples on half of the onion-covered slices. Sprinkle with cheese and top with the remaining bread slices. Drizzle the tops and bottoms of the sandwiches with olive oil.

Return the grill pan to medium heat. Cook the sandwiches, pressing down occasionally with a spatula, until the bread is crisp and the cheese is melted, 2 to 3 minutes per side. Serve immediately.

SPICED APPLE-CHESTNUT SOUP

Cookbook author and *New York Times* columnist Melissa Clark never misses a Saturday shopping trip to the farmers' market. She's been known to turn up on chilly days when even the farmers are too snowbound to make it. This recipe is inspired by two of her prized late-autumn ingredients—crisp apples and earthy, sweet chestnuts (plus a dousing of apple brandy for good measure). Rather than roasting and peeling your own chestnuts, save yourself the hassle and buy the prepared kind that come in a vacuum-sealed bag or jar.

Makes 4 to 6 servings

¼ cup / 70 g finely chopped, pitted dates	1 medium carrot, peeled and diced
3 tablespoons apple brandy, such as Calvados, divided	1 medium leek, halved lengthwise and thinly sliced crosswise
3 tablespoons unsalted butter, divided	1 large sweet-tart baking apple (see Apple Varieties chart, pages 170–171), peeled, cored, and chopped
1 tablespoon honey	
¾ teaspoons kosher salt, divided	2½ cups / 590 ml chicken stock
¼ teaspoon freshly ground black pepper, divided	3 sprigs fresh thyme
¼ teaspoon ground cinnamon	2 sprigs fresh rosemary
⅛ teaspoon freshly ground cloves	½ cup / 120 ml heavy whipping cream
1 (14-ounce / 415-ml) jar whole roasted chestnuts	Toasted slivered almonds, for garnish
1 celery stalk, diced	Freshly grated nutmeg, for garnish

Place the dates in a small bowl and add boiling water to cover. Let stand for 5 minutes; drain and discard the liquid. Return the dates to the bowl and add 1 tablespoon of the brandy. Cover the bowl with plastic wrap and set aside at room temperature.

In a large skillet, melt 2 tablespoons of the butter over medium-high heat. Stir in the honey, ¼ teaspoon of the salt, ⅛ teaspoon of the black pepper, the cinnamon, and the cloves. Add the chestnuts and cook, stirring occasionally to coat the chestnuts with the butter mixture, until the chestnuts are golden and caramelized, 3 to 4 minutes. Stir in the remaining 2 tablespoons of brandy and cook, scraping up any browned bits from the bottom of the skillet, until the liquid is mostly evaporated. Remove the skillet from the heat and set it aside.

In a large pot, melt the remaining tablespoon of butter over medium-high heat. Stir in the celery, carrot, and leek; cook, stirring, until the vegetables have softened, about 5 minutes.

Stir the chestnuts, apples, stock, and remaining ½ teaspoon of salt and ⅛ teaspoon of pepper into the pot. Tie the thyme and rosemary sprigs together with kitchen twine and add them to the pot. Bring the mixture to boil; reduce the heat to medium-low and simmer, uncovered, until the vegetables are very tender, 25 to 30 minutes. Remove and discard the herbs.

Purée the soup in batches in a food processor or blender (or use an immersion blender), and return it to the pot. Stir in the cream and warm the soup through over low heat.

Ladle the hot soup into warm bowls, top each serving with a sprinkling of dates and almonds and a few grates of nutmeg.

JOE'S BRAISED SAUERBRATEN
WITH RED CABBAGE *and* APPLES

Sauerbraten is a traditional German dish that involves tenderizing a tough cut of meat like brisket in a spiced vinegar brine before cooking. It's a technique that works like a charm: Sauerbraten always emerges meltingly soft and juicy. This recipe belonged to my Grandma Emily, whose parents came from Germany in the 1890s. Eventually, she passed the recipe along to my father, who has been making it at family holidays for years. We all love the addictive sharpness of the vinegar, but you can tinker with the proportions (just substitute more water or even some wine) if you crave a mellower flavor. The sweet sautéed apples and cabbage provide nice contrast to the sauerbraten's bite. At our house, we always soak up extra gravy with Emily's potato dumplings (mashed potatoes combined with egg, flour, and nutmeg, then shaped into balls and simmered in water until they float to the top), but plain boiled potatoes or buttered noodles make a nice accompaniment, too.

Makes 6 to 8 servings

BEEF	RED CABBAGE AND APPLES
4 pounds / 1.8 kg beef bottom round	2 tablespoons unsalted butter
2 cups / 470 ml cider vinegar	½ teaspoon caraway seeds
1 large yellow onion, diced	1 small yellow onion, finely chopped
1 slice rye bread, cut into ½-inch / 1.3 cm chunks (1 cup)	½ medium head red cabbage, cored and thinly sliced
1 teaspoon kosher salt	2 tart-sweet apples, peeled, cored, and thinly sliced
1 teaspoon caraway seeds	1 tablespoon cider vinegar
10 whole peppercorns	2 teaspoons granulated sugar
3 whole cloves	Kosher salt and freshly ground black pepper
¼ cup / 40 g all-purpose flour	
⅔ cup / 160 ml whole milk	

In the bottom of a large Dutch oven, combine the vinegar, 3 cups / 710 ml of water, and the onion, bread, salt, caraway seeds, peppercorns, and cloves. Add the beef. Cover and refrigerate for at least 8 hours or overnight, turning the beef every few hours.

Preheat the oven to 350°F / 180°C. Place the pot on the stovetop and bring the liquid to a simmer over medium-high heat; cook gently, uncovered, for 30 minutes. Cover and transfer the pot to the oven to continue cooking until the meat is very tender, 1½ to 2 hours.

Transfer the meat to a large platter. Spoon 4 tablespoons of fat from the surface of the pot juices and reserve; strain the remaining liquid through a fine-mesh sieve into a medium heat-proof bowl. Return the pot to medium-high heat. Whisk in the reserved fat and the flour. Cook for 2 minutes, until the mixture begins to turn golden. Slowly whisk in 2 cups / 470 ml of

(continued)

the strained juices and the milk; simmer until the gravy is thick and bubbling, and thin it with additional pan juices, if desired. Taste the gravy and add more salt and pepper as necessary.

While the meat braises, prepare the cabbage and apples: Melt the butter in a very large skillet over medium heat. Add the caraway seeds and cook for 1 minute until fragrant, then toss in the onion and a pinch of salt. Cook, stirring constantly, until the onion is very soft, about 5 minutes. Toss in the cabbage and another pinch of salt. Cover and cook the vegetables for 10 minutes. Stir in the apple, vinegar, and sugar. Cover and cook until both the cabbage and apple are very tender, about 10 minutes more. Season with salt and pepper to taste.

Thinly slice the meat and spoon the gravy liberally over the top. Serve with the sautéed cabbage and apples and your favorite hearty side.

CIDER-BRAISED PORK BELLY *with* ROASTED CAULIFLOWER PURÉE

Recent (and self-proclaimed "permanent") transplants to the Finger Lakes, Rune and Giulietta Hilt fell in love with the area while visiting and decided to make a new life in our quiet town. Bringing with them Giulietta's Italian grandmother Carmelinda (who reminds me of my own grandmother), mother Susan, and Susan's husband Dennis, they opened Red Dove Tavern, a comfortable farm-to-table restaurant in downtown Geneva. In the process, the family transcended local culinary expectations and extended true friendships to our community of growers, cooks, and artists. In typical Hilt-family fashion, this recipe celebrates the Finger Lakes, relying on locally raised pork, local Riesling, and, of course, our Red Jacket Orchard cider. At the restaurant, they usually serve this dish sprinkled with corn shoots, a deliciously sweet, milky microgreen, but a hit of parsley works, too.

Makes 4 to 6 servings as a first course

PORK BELLY	ROASTED CAULIFLOWER PURÉE
2 (1-pound / 455 g) pieces fresh pork belly, skin removed	1 (1-pound / 455 g) head cauliflower, trimmed and cut into florets (6 cups)
2 teaspoons kosher salt	2 tablespoon extra-virgin olive oil
1 teaspoon freshly ground black pepper	½ teaspoon kosher salt, plus more as needed
2 cups / 470 ml Red Jacket apple cider, or other favorite cider, plus more as needed	1 cup / 240 ml heavy whipping cream, warmed
2 cups / 470 ml medium-dry Riesling, plus more as needed	2 tablespoons unsalted butter, at room temperature, plus more as needed
2 whole bay leaves	Freshly ground black pepper
	Chopped parsley, for serving

To prepare the pork belly, preheat the oven to 325°F / 165°C. Season the pork belly with the salt and pepper. Place the pork in a 13 x 9-inch / 33 x 23 cm baking dish; it should be deep enough to almost submerge the pork belly in cider and wine. Pour in the cider and wine and drop in the bay leaves; the pork should be three quarters of the way covered by liquid; if not, add additional wine and cider in equal proportions. Cover the dish with a tight-fitting lid or aluminum foil. Transfer the dish to the oven to cook until the meat is melt-in-your-mouth tender, 2 to 2½ hours. Remove the dish from the oven and let the pork cool to room temperature in its braising liquid; cover with plastic wrap and refrigerate overnight.

To make the cauliflower purée, preheat the oven to 400°F / 205°C. Toss the cauliflower with the oil and salt. Spread the florets in a single layer on a large rimmed baking sheet. Roast, tossing occasionally, until the cauliflower is golden brown, 20 to 30 minutes.

Remove the baking sheet from the oven and transfer the hot cauliflower to a food processor or blender. Add the cream and 2 tablespoons of the butter and blend until the mixture is smooth and uniform in color. Taste and blend in another tablespoon of butter if desired; season to taste with salt and pepper. Transfer the purée to a bowl and cover it with foil to keep warm.

While the cauliflower roasts, remove the pork from the refrigerator. Discard most of the excess fat that has collected on the

(continued)

surface of the pan. Strain 2 cups / 470 ml of the remaining liquid into a large saucepan; simmer the liquid over medium-high heat until it is reduced by half, about 10 minutes. Cover the pot and keep it warm over low heat.

Cut the pork pieces into 2-inch / 5 cm squares. Place a large skillet over high heat until it is very hot. Arrange the pork pieces in the skillet and cook, turning once, until both sides are crisp and hot, 2 to 3 minutes per side.

Spoon some warm cauliflower purée in the center of each plate; top with the crisp pork belly and drizzle with the warm braising juices. Garnish with parsley and serve.

FALL APPLE CRUSH COCKTAIL

Brother and sister duo Tyler and Kari Morris have built a business around preserving the true essence of fruit. Morris Kitchen makes small-batch artisan syrups using only a couple of ingredients, but each is carefully curated for potency, with syrup flavors including preserved lemon, ginger, rhubarb, and our personal favorite at the orchard, the Boiled Apple Cider, made using our trees' fruit. Just as great for drizzling over dessert as they are for whisking into cocktails, the Morris family syrups are worth seeking out, but if you can't find them look for an apple cider molasses at your local farmers' market instead.

Makes 1 serving

2 ounces / 60 ml bourbon

½ ounce / 15 ml Morris Kitchen Boiled Apple Cider Syrup, or other apple cider molasses

½ ounce / 15 ml freshly squeezed lemon juice

1 ounce / 30 ml seltzer

Apple slice, for garnish

Fill a cocktail shaker three quarters of the way with ice and top with bourbon, syrup, and lemon juice. Shake well. Strain into a rocks glass. Top with a splash of seltzer and a large ice cube. Garnish with an apple slice.

ALMOND-CRUSTED CARAMEL LADY APPLES

Caramel apple cravings usually kick in just before Halloween, around the same time toothy jack o' lanterns convene on front stoops everywhere. But between the gooey caramel and the hefty apple, polishing off a whole one can be tough. This recipe uses pint-sized lady apples instead, an especially perfect portion for kids. Putting them together is a fun family activity: just watch little hands carefully when working with the hot caramel syrup.

Makes about 1½ dozen apples

6 tablespoons plus 2 teaspoons / 95 g unsalted butter, divided, plus more for greasing

1¼ cups / 130 g blanched finely chopped almonds

⅛ teaspoon fine sea salt, plus more as needed

18 (³⁄₁₆-inch / 4.8 mm-thick) wooden dowels

18 lady apples

1½ cups / 300 g packed dark brown sugar

¾ cup / 180 ml dark corn syrup

10 ounces / 300 ml sweetened condensed milk

Melt 2 teaspoons of the butter in a medium skillet over medium heat. Add the almonds and cook, stirring often, until they are golden brown, about 2 minutes. Remove the skillet from the heat; transfer the almonds to a wide, shallow bowl and sprinkle them lightly with a pinch of salt.

Line a rimmed baking sheet with buttered waxed paper. Insert the sticks vertically through the apples where the stem meets the fruit, and arrange the apples on the prepared baking sheet.

In a medium, heavy-bottomed pot, melt the remaining 6 tablespoons of butter. Add the sugar, corn syrup, and ⅛ teaspoon of salt. Cook over medium heat until the caramel comes to a boil; stir in the milk. Cook until the mixture reaches a temperature of 248°F / 120°C on a candy thermometer. Remove the pot from the heat.

Working quickly, dip each apple in the caramel mixture to coat evenly (allow excess caramel to drip back into the pot), then roll each apple in almonds. Return the apples to the prepared baking sheet to cool completely before serving.

SPICED MOLASSES BAKED APPLES

Baked apples are a homey, cold weather dessert, simple enough that you can make them any night of the week. Try this rich, molasses-glazed version at the height of apple season, when the fruit is fresh, firm, and unwaxed. The basting juices will stick to naked apple skin more easily. Unsulfured molasses lends deeper, purer sugar cane flavor than its sulfured counterpart.

Makes 4 servings

4 large Golden Delicious apples	¼ teaspoon freshly grated nutmeg
¼ cup / 30 g chopped toasted pecans	⅛ teaspoon ground cloves
2 tablespoons dried cherries	⅛ teaspoon salt
2 tablespoons cold unsalted butter, cut into cubes	¼ cup / 60 ml unsulfured molasses
1 tablespoon packed dark brown sugar	3 tablespoons dark spiced rum

Preheat the oven to 375°F / 190°C and lightly grease an 8-inch / 20.5 cm-square baking pan. Cut out the woody core and seeds of the apples, leaving ½ inch / 1.3 cm of the bottoms intact. Using a vegetable peeler, remove a strip of peel from around the equator of each apple (this will prevent the skin from bursting during baking).

In a small bowl, combine the pecans, cherries, butter, sugar, spices, and salt. Stuff a small amount of this mixture into the center of each apple; transfer the apples to the prepared pan.

In a small bowl, whisk together the molasses and rum. Drizzle the mixture over and around the apples. Transfer the pan to the oven and bake, basting often with the pan sauces, until the apples are tender and golden, 35 to 40 minutes. Remove the pan from the oven, and let the apples cool slightly before serving.

TART APPLE-CALVADOS SORBET

This creamy sorbet makes a wonderful light dessert or palate cleanser between courses. The secret ingredient—celery—will keep people guessing, with a subtle herbaceous quality that rounds out the sorbet's flavor. A sprinkling of apple brandy at the end enhances the fruit's inherent spicy, wine-like qualities.

Makes 1 generous pint / 470 ml

3 pounds / 1.4 kg Granny Smith apples (about 6)
1 cup / 200 g granulated sugar
2 medium celery stalks, finely chopped

2 tablespoons freshly squeezed lemon juice, plus more to taste
Apple brandy, such as Calvados, as needed

Quarter and core the apples (they do not need to be peeled); cut them into large chunks. In a large pot, combine the apples, sugar, and just enough water to cover the fruit (about 4 cups / 1 L). Bring the liquid to a simmer and cook, stirring frequently, until the apples are just tender, about 10 minutes.

In a food processor or blender, purée the fruit, cooking liquids, and chopped celery in batches until smooth. Strain the mixture into a medium bowl through a fine-mesh sieve lined with cheesecloth. Press gently on the mixture to extract as much juice as possible without clouding the strained juice with pulp. You should have about 4 cups / 1 L of juice.

Return the strained juice to the pot and simmer over medium-high heat until it is reduced to 3 cups / 710 ml, 20 to 30 minutes. Stir in the lemon juice. Remove the pot from the heat and let the mixture cool completely at room temperature, then cover the pot and transfer it to the refrigerator for at least 3 hours or overnight.

Transfer the chilled mixture to an ice-cream maker and churn according to the manufacturer's instructions. To serve, spoon dollops of sorbet into small dishes and drizzle with a small spoonful of brandy.

DANISH APPLE DUMPLINGS

Nothing says "farmhouse cooking" quite like a cast-iron skillet. Its sturdy, practical heft pretty much begs for a hot scramble of eggs, sizzling bacon, and these tasty dumplings. You'll need a special, dimpled cast-iron skillet (an abelskiver pan) to make this dish, but it's inexpensive, easily found at kitchen stores, and worth the investment: served piping hot, abelskivers are breakfast perfection, with the fluffy insides of a pancake and the crisp, sugared crusts of a doughnut.

Makes about 1 dozen dumplings

1¼ cups / 180 g all-purpose flour	1 cup / 240 ml whole milk
3 tablespoons granulated sugar	3 tablespoons melted, cooled butter, plus more for cooking
2¼ teaspoons baking powder	
½ teaspoon fine sea salt	1 medium apple, peeled, cored, and finely diced
¼ teaspoon ground cardamom	⅓ cup / 40 g confectioners' sugar, for sprinkling
1 egg, lightly beaten	½ teaspoon ground cinnamon

In a large bowl, sift together the flour, sugar, baking powder, salt, and cardamom.

In a separate bowl, whisk together the egg, milk, and melted butter. Fold the egg mixture gently into the flour mixture. Fold in the apple.

In a small bowl, whisk together confectioners' sugar and cinnamon.

Heat a cast-iron abelskiver pan over medium heat until a drop of water sizzles in the pan. Brush the divets with melted butter. Fill each cup two-thirds full with batter. Cook for 30 seconds until a thin skin develops on the underside of each dumpling, then turn each dumpling gently with a spoon and let the batter flow from the top of the dumpling into the bottom of the divet. Allow the underside of the dumpling to form a skin and repeat, turning every 30 seconds, or until the dumplings are evenly golden brown and cooked through. Remove the dumplings from the pan with a skewer and dust them with cinnamon sugar. Serve immediately.

CLASSIC APPLE TARTE TATIN

From the moment they opened their first restaurant, Diner, under the Brooklyn Bridge in 1998, Mark Firth and Andrew Tarlow made a whole-hearted commitment to supporting local farms. They opened Marlow & Sons, a cozy nook of a restaurant, right next door in 2004. If you make it to New York City, both places are worth the train ride to Williamsburg, Brooklyn; you won't be disappointed. This tasty rustic tart—a French classic—is typical of Marlow & Sons' European sensibility. It came to us courtesy of the restaurant's Executive Pastry Chef, Ashley Whitmore.

Makes 1 (12-inch / 31-cm) tart

PUFF PASTRY	APPLES
4 cups / 560 g all-purpose flour	2½ to 3 pounds / 1.1 to 1.4 kg firm baking apples, such as Fuji
2½ teaspoons kosher salt	10 tablespoons / 140 g unsalted butter
3/14 cups / 740 g unsalted butter, cubed and chilled	1¼ cups / 250 g granulated sugar
½ to 1 cup / 120 to 240 ml cold water	1½ teaspoons vanilla extract
	Juice of ½ lemon

To make the puff pastry, in an electric mixer fitted with the paddle attachment, mix together the flour, salt, and butter on low speed. Mix for about 30 seconds, until part of the butter starts to mix into the flour. Trickle in the cold water quickly, mixing for about 15 seconds. Start with ½ cup /120 ml of water if it's a wet or humid day and use all of the water if it's a dry day or if the dough still seems very dry.

Pour the shaggy dough onto an 18 x 12-inch / 45.5 cm x 30.5 cm sheet of parchment paper. Gently press the dough mass into a rectangle measuring 14 x 8 inches / 35.5 x 20.5 cm, using a bowl scraper to keep a neat, straight edge. The dough may be loose at first, but with the turns will come together. Using the parchment to help, fold one third of the dough over toward the center of the rectangle, as though folding a letter. Fold the opposite side over that. Rotate the dough 90 degrees. This is the first turn.

Evenly press out the dough into a large, flat rectangle again, and repeat the folding process two more times, switching to a rolling pin once the dough comes together. Keep the rectangle neat with clean, square edges. This completes the first three turns. Cover the dough and transfer it to the refrigerator to rest for 30 minutes.

Remove the dough from the refrigerator and repeat the rolling and folding three more times; be mindful of keeping the stacked rectangular shape. When forming the rectangle, use a rolling pin to roll evenly across the length of the dough so that the layers will be evenly distributed on top of one another. Cover the dough and refrigerate for another 30 minutes.

Remove the dough from the refrigerator and use a rolling pin to roll it out evenly until ¼ inch / 6 mm thick. Cover the dough and let it rest for 10 minutes in a cool area. (Roll between layers of parchment and refrigerate if it's the only cool place you can find.) Using a sharp knife, cut out two 12-inch / 30.5 cm circles. Pull the leftover scraps together, just overlapping the edges and press them together with a rolling pin to form another 12-inch / 30.5 cm round, trimming as necessary. Prep

1 dough round: Using a sharp knife, score the pastry with a 1 x 1-inch / 2.5 x 2.5 cm X in the center, cutting all the way through the dough. Make a few more 1-inch / 2.5 cm-long lines parallel to the edges of the pastry round. This will allow the pastry to rise evenly, the steam will escape neatly, and you will be able to check for doneness of the inner layers of pastry. Cover the prepared dough round and refrigerate until ready to use. (You will only need one round. Roll the remaining 2 rounds between layers of parchment and wrap tightly in plastic wrap; freeze for up to 6 months.)

To prepare the tart, preheat the oven to 400°F / 200°C. Arrange a wire rack on the bottom shelf of the oven. Peel and core the apples. Cut them into 1-inch / 2.5 cm-thick wedges.

In a clean 12-inch / 30.5 cm cast-iron pan, melt together the butter and sugar. Cook over medium-high heat until the mixture begins to brown slightly, about 10 minutes. Gently swirl the pan if the browning is uneven. Cook until the sugar turns to a blond caramel color.

Remove the pan from the heat. Starting at the outside edge of the pan, nestle in the apple slices in concentric circles. Pack in as many as you can fit, as they'll cook down a lot.

Return the pan to medium heat and bring the caramel back to bubbling. Cook until the bubbling is nice and even and the caramel darkens slightly, about 5 minutes. (Do not cook the fruit too long as it will spend additional time in the oven.) Remove the pan from the heat and tuck in as many extra apple slices as you can. Don't worry about being too neat. Drizzle the vanilla extract and the lemon juice over the fruit. Drape the pastry over the apples and swiftly press the edges down into the sides of the pan between the edges of the fruit, taking care not to burn yourself.

Transfer the pan to the bottom rack and bake for 30 minutes without opening the oven. Reduce the oven temperature to 350°F / 180°C and rotate the pan 180 degrees. Continue cooking until the fruit's juices are thick and bubbly and the pastry is golden, 40 to 50 minutes. Check for doneness frequently near the end: the interior of the pastry's center vent should be a medium golden and crispy all the way through, with no visible grayish or wet-looking layers.

Remove the pan from the oven and use a rubber spatula to gently nudge the edges away from the pan. Invert a large serving plate over the pan. Quickly flip the pan, turning out the tart (taking care not to let the caramel seep out and burn you). Serve warm with ice cream, whipped cream, or crème fraîche.

APPLE, MAPLE, *and* BROWN BUTTER STREUSEL CAKE

Made with tender tart apple bits and sour cream, this cake is rich, moist, and completely different from some of the dry, crumbly coffee cakes you may have had in your lifetime. Maple sugar, the crystals that remain after maple sap has boiled into syrup, has just the right caramel notes to complement the nutty brown butter (it's also fantastic sprinkled on toast). You can usually find it at your local farmers' market or health food store, but regular brown sugar works fine.

Makes one 9-inch cake

CAKE	STREUSEL TOPPING
Nonstick cooking spray, as needed	½ cup / 70 g all-purpose flour
¼ cup / 55 g unsalted butter	½ cup / 60 g finely chopped toasted walnuts
1 cup / 140 g all-purpose flour	½ cup / 100 g maple sugar or packed light brown sugar
1 teaspoon baking powder	¼ teaspoon cinnamon
½ teaspoon ground cinnamon	⅛ teaspoon kosher salt
¼ teaspoon baking soda	5 tablespoons / 70 g unsalted butter, at room temperature
¼ teaspoon salt	
½ cup / 100 g maple sugar or granulated sugar	
1 large egg	
1 teaspoon pure vanilla extract	
½ cup / 120 ml sour cream	
2 cups peeled, cored, and finely chopped sweet-tart apples (see Apple Varieties chart, page 170–171)	

Preheat the oven to 350°F / 180°C. Press aluminum foil into the bottom and up the sides of a 9-inch / 23 cm round cake pan, allowing the edges to hang over the sides of the pan; coat the foil with cooking spray.

To make the cake, melt the butter in a small saucepan over medium heat. Cook until the foam subsides and the butter turns a deep nut brown (watch carefully to see that it does not burn: it may take as long as 5 minutes). Remove the pan from the heat and let the butter cool completely.

In a large bowl, whisk together the flour, baking powder, cinnamon, baking soda, and salt. In a separate bowl, beat together the cooled butter, sugar, egg, and vanilla. Using a wooden spoon, fold the flour mixture into the butter mixture in three additions, alternating with the sour cream. Fold in the apples.

Scrape the batter into the prepared pan. Bake for 20 minutes.

Meanwhile, prepare the streusel: Whisk together the flour, walnuts, sugar, cinnamon, and salt. Use your fingers to rub in the butter until coarse, pea-sized crumbs form. Sprinkle the streusel over the top of the cake. Return cake to oven and bake until it is golden brown and a toothpick inserted in the center emerges clean, 20 to 30 minutes more. Remove from the oven and let it cool for 15 minutes on a wire rack; grab the overhanging foil and lift the cake from the pan. Slice and serve.

Pears

HARVEST SEASON: LATE SUMMER to LATE AUTUMN;
AVAILABLE UNTIL EARLY SPRING

MY DAD LIKES TO SUM UP PEARS WITH A QUOTE BY Ralph Waldo Emerson: "There are only ten minutes in the life of a pear when it is perfect to eat." Wisely set down by Emerson over 150 years ago, it remains true today. A ripe pear, with its aromatic sweetness and melting texture, is a fleeting and elusive experience, one that requires plenty of patience. However, when you do capture a pear during its small window of perfection, it is pure pleasure.

one that seems ripe on the tree will have a disappointing flavor. For that reason, farmers almost always pick pears when they are still green and hard, then transfer them to cold storage for several weeks (and up to two months) to "cure" them. During this time, the starches gradually convert to sugar, yielding sweet flavor and smooth texture (The exception to this are Asian pears, which can be tree ripened).

Because the growing seasons are so entwined, pears

JOE'S GROWING TIPS:

• Pears' climate requirements are similar to those of apples and peaches: they prefer cool temperate zones, where cold winters allow a nice, long dormant period. Warm winters will inhibit spring budding. Pear trees root deeply, preferring heavier, well-drained soil in which to anchor.

• Unlike apple trees, pear trees' branches tend to grow upward rather than outward, which can lead to dense center foliage. Although excessive pruning of pear trees can lead to disease, make sure to annually clear the tree of branches that prevent light and air from reaching the fruit.

• To encourage strong fruit development and prevent overburdening of the tree, thin the fruit early in the summer. Pears grow in clusters; remove all but one or two pears per cluster, leaving 8 inches / 20.5 cm or so between the fruit. Take care not to break off the fruiting "spur," the small bud that holds the stem, as it will continue to bear fruit in future years.

• To avoid gritty texture, pick pears before they are fully ripened. They're ready once they have reached a full size and they separate easily from their fruit spur with a gentle twist. Store them in a cold place for several weeks and up to 60 days until they are tender and well-colored for their variety (see Pear Varieties chart, page 192).

The pear's fickleness is attributable, in large part, to its harvest conditions. Unlike any other orchard fruit, pears *must* be picked before they are fully ripened. If allowed to stay on the tree until tender, they develop a gritty texture and begin to rot from the inside out;

and apples often get lumped together like cousins, sometimes even in the same cooking pot. Though both are of the family Rosaceae, the pear offers more elegance than the reliable and eager-to-please apple, with an inherent muskiness open to sophisticated pairings and preparations. If you choose the juiciest varieties, like Bartlett or Comice, you have ample possibilities for serving the fruit raw. Nibble with cheeses such as a salty pecorino, creamy Brie, or pungent veiny blue; all provide a terrific counterpoint to the fruit's sweetness, as do briny cured meats like prosciutto. Pears also appreciate strong contrasting flavors, like the bitterness of radicchio and dandelion greens, the sharp bite of sweet onions and mustard, or the zing of lemon juice. The crisp, almost watery texture of raw Asian pears is especially excellent in salads. Pears also appreciate pecans, hazelnuts, and almonds.

For cooking, it is best to use firm varieties like Bosc, as they are less likely to fall apart under heat. Bake them into almond tarts, gingerbreads, and bittersweet chocolate cakes; roast them with honey; or braise them in fruity wines, like zinfandel, port, or sherry. Spike sweet or savory preparations with assertive peppercorn, bay leaf, star anise, or ginger; they're great in a chutney for slow-cooked pork, lamb, or beef. For herbal lift, try sage, rosemary, or thyme. When matching pears with another fruit, reach for those that share their spiced aroma, like black currants or quince.

Cooking pears are usually peeled with a paring knife or vegetable peeler. Remove the center seeds along with the stringy core. Their delicate flesh is prone to oxidization, so eat quickly or sprinkle with citrus or acidulated water if not using immediately.

SELECTION: Choose smooth, blemish-free fruit that is firm but not hard. Two signs tell you the fruit is ready: it will emit a sweet, musky perfume, and it will yield slightly to gentle pressure. Depending on the variety, the fruit may also change color as it ripens (see Pear Varieties chart, page 192). Pears, and especially Asian pears, have thin, delicate skin, so be sure to avoid bruised fruit.

STORAGE: Leave underripe pears in a paper bag at room temperature to aid in the maturation process. Ripe pears are highly perishable and must be refrigerated; at their peak, they will keep for several days. Don't stack them too closely together, as this might cause bruising and molding, and store them away from other foods, which easily absorb their fragrance. A perforated plastic bag in the crisper drawer is best. Raw pears don't stand up well to freezing, though you can freeze cooked purées (see Freezing Fruit, page 247).

PEAR VARIETIES

VARIETY	APPEARANCE	COLOR WHEN RIPE	FLAVOR	TEXTURE	BEST FOR
Anjou* (European)	Broad, slightly egg-shaped, lacking distinct shoulders	Pale green or maroon, depending on variety	Sweet, slightly acidic abundantly juicy	Fine to slightly granular	Baking, roasting, eating out of hand or with cheese
Bartlett (European)	Quintessential pear shape; bulbous bottom	Greenish-yellow or maroon, depending on variety	Musky, delicate, aromatic	Juicy, buttery smooth, fine-fleshed	Baking, eating out of hand, canning
Bosc (European)	Slender, tapered neck; curved stem	Earthy bronze	Sweetly perfumed, mildly spicy	Firm, sandy texture; papery skin	Excellent for poaching, baking, sautéing, and eating out of hand
Comice*	Blunt, large-bottomed shape with short neck	Yellow-green with some pink russeting	Buttery, floral, sweet	Soft, very juicy, and smooth; thin tender skin	Excellent out of hand or on a cheese platter
Harrow Crisp	Bulbous; similar to Bartlett	Golden with yellow cheeks	Rich, sweet	Juicy, buttery, and fine-fleshed	Excellent all-purpose
Seckel (European)	Tiny, palm-sized pear shape	Moss green with burgundy blush	Rich, sweet	Crisp, slightly granular, juicy	Raw in salads or as garnish; gently cooked or pickled
Ya Li (Asian)	Plump, short-necked pear shape	Pale green to golden yellow	Sweet with melon undertones	Crisp, watery, but softer than other Asian pears	Eating out of hand or salads; baking

*Indicate varieties that we do not grow

PEAR AND PUMPKIN SOUP *with* SAGE CROUTONS

This is the soup to make when you're trying to please a crowd. Its warm, saffron glow and sweetly spiced aroma is hard to resist on brisk fall days. Buttery Bartlett pears are a terrific variety to use here—their fine texture purées smoothly with the dense, rich pumpkin. Sage croutons add crunch and infuse the soup with subtle herbal notes.

Makes 4 to 6 servings

PEAR-PUMPKIN SOUP

6 tablespoons / 85 g unsalted butter

1 large onion, sliced

2 celery stalks, diced

2 pounds / 910 g pumpkin or kabocha squash, peeled, seeded and cut into 1-inch / 2.5 cm cubes

1 tablespoon chopped fresh thyme leaves

1 tablespoon chili powder

3 medium Bartlett pears, peeled, cored, and diced

1 bay leaf

2½ teaspoons sea salt, plus more as needed

¼ teaspoon freshly ground black pepper

SAGE CROUTONS

¼ cup / 60 ml extra-virgin olive oil

20 fresh sage leaves

Large pinch of kosher salt

Large pinch of freshly ground black pepper

3 slices country-style bread, cut into ¼-inch / 6 mm cubes (about 1 cup)

Crème fraîche, to serve

To make the soup, melt the butter in a large pot over medium heat. Add the onion and celery; cook until the vegetables are very soft, 15 to 20 minutes. Add the pumpkin and cook until it is lightly caramelized, about 10 minutes. Stir in the thyme and chili powder; cook for 1 minute.

Stir in the pear, bay leaf, salt, and pepper, and pour in 4 cups / 1 L of water. Bring the mixture to a simmer. Cover the pot and simmer until the vegetables are tender, 30 to 40 minutes. Remove and discard the bay leaf. Purée the soup using an immersion blender or transfer it in batches to a food processor or blender. Return the soup to the pot, cover, and keep it warm over low heat.

To make the croutons, heat the oil in a small pot over medium heat. Add the sage leaves. Cook until leaves turn a deep, almost translucent green, about 5 seconds. Use a slotted spoon to transfer the leaves to a paper towel–lined plate. Crumble the leaves into a bowl with a pinch of salt and pepper.

Add the bread to the pot of oil. Cook, stirring occasionally, until the bread is golden and crisp, about 3 minutes. Transfer the bread to a paper towel–lined plate (reserve the oil). Sprinkle the croutons with the sage seasoning.

To serve, ladle the soup into warm bowls. Top each serving with a dollop of crème fraîche and a drizzle of sage oil. Sprinkle with croutons.

ROASTED PEAR *and* BARLEY PILAF

Roasting, typically a cool-weather technique applied to herb-flecked meats and sturdy root vegetables, is ideal for firm, musky pears, which commingle with these foods just fine. Tossed with warm barley, roasted pears make for a filling autumn side dish, but they would also be satisfying with a platter of chicken or a wedge of stinky cheese.

Makes 4 servings

1 large Bartlett pear, cut into 8 wedges and cored	¾ cup / 150 g pearled barley
2 teaspoons extra-virgin olive oil	1 cup / 240 ml chicken stock
½ teaspoon salt, plus more as needed	1 bay leaf
Freshly ground black pepper	½ cup / 60 g chopped toasted walnuts
1 tablespoon unsalted butter	3 tablespoons chopped fresh parsley
1 small yellow onion, finely chopped	1 teaspoon lemon zest
1 celery stalk, thinly sliced	

Preheat the oven to 425°F / 220°C. In a medium bowl, toss the pear wedges with the oil and season them lightly with salt and pepper. Arrange the pears in a single layer on a large baking sheet. Roast the pears for 20 minutes, turning once halfway through, until they are golden and tender. Remove the baking sheet from the oven and let the pears stand at room temperature until they are cool enough to handle, then chop them into bite-sized pieces and set them aside.

Melt the butter in a medium saucepan over medium heat. Add the onion and celery and sprinkle with salt and pepper to taste. Cook until the vegetables are soft, about 10 minutes. Add the barley and cook, stirring frequently, for 3 minutes. Pour in the stock, 1 cup / 240 ml of water, the bay leaf, and the ½ teaspoon of salt. Bring the mixture to a boil; reduce the heat to medium-low and simmer, covered, until the barley is tender and most of the liquid has evaporated, about 25 minutes. Remove the pan from the heat and let it stand at room temperature, covered, for 10 minutes. Remove and discard the bay leaf. Fluff the barley with a fork and fold in the pears, nuts, parsley, and lemon zest. Season to taste with salt and pepper, and serve immediately.

SESAME NOODLES *with* ASIAN PEAR AND BOK CHOY

Jeff and Adina Bialas's farm stand has been a welcome sight at the Greenmarket for years. Everything they bring to market always seems like the best of its kind—the sweetest corn, the crispest carrots, the most fragrant basil. The trick to this Bialas family favorite is to purchase greens so fresh and tender that they need just the briefest sauté. The juicy Asian pear is a crisp surprise, providing the perfect foil for the spicy peanut sauce.

Makes 4 servings

1 (8-ounce / 230 g) package soba noodles	¾ teaspoon kosher salt, divided
2 tablespoons sesame seeds	Thai chili sauce, such as Sriracha
3 tablespoons smooth peanut butter	1 tablespoon grapeseed oil
1½ tablespoons soy sauce	1 pound / 455 g bok choy, thinly sliced
1 tablespoon rice wine vinegar	1 Asian pear, peeled, cored and cut into ⅛-inch / 3 mm matchsticks
2 teaspoons sesame oil	1 large carrot, peeled and cut into ⅛-inch / 3 mm matchsticks
2 teaspoons hoisin sauce	
2 teaspoons peeled and finely grated fresh ginger	3 tablespoons chopped fresh cilantro

Bring a large pot of salted water to a boil. Cook the noodles according to the package instructions until al dente. Drain the noodles in a colander, reserving 1 cup / 240 ml of the cooking water for thinning the sauce, and rinse them under cold running water to cool slightly and prevent sticking.

In a medium skillet over medium heat, toast the sesame seeds until light golden and fragrant; remove the pan from the heat and let the seeds cool at room temperature.

In a small saucepan over medium-high heat, stir together the peanut butter, soy sauce, vinegar, sesame oil, hoisin sauce, ginger, ¼ teaspoon of the salt, and the chili sauce. Simmer for 10 minutes, adding enough reserved water until the sauce has a consistency slightly thicker than heavy cream. Cover the pan and keep it warm over low heat.

Heat the grapeseed oil in a large skillet over medium-high heat. Add the bok choy and the remaining ½ teaspoon of salt; cook, stirring constantly, until the greens are tender and wilted, about 2 minutes.

In a large bowl, mix the noodles with the warm sauce until well coated. Toss in the bok choy, Asian pear, and carrots. Garnish with the cilantro and sesame seeds and serve immediately.

CHICORY SALAD *with* PEAR, PECORINO, AND HAZELNUTS

Bill Telepan cooked in some of the world's top kitchens before settling into his own down-to-earth Manhattan restaurant, Telepan, in 2005. His menus are ideal for our fruit—genuinely ingredient-driven and stripped of excessive seasoning, it's all about showcasing the best of what he finds at the market. In this light, fresh salad, he contrasts juicy, aromatic pears with salty cheese and delicate hazelnuts. Using hazelnut oil instead of the usual olive oil subtly unites all of the flavors.

Makes 4 servings

2 tablespoons red wine vinegar

6 tablespoons hazelnut oil

Kosher salt and freshly ground black pepper

1 medium head radicchio

1 medium head endive, cut into ½-inch / 1.3 cm-thick rounds

1 head frisée, outer leaves and core removed; tender greens torn into 1-inch / 2.5 cm pieces

½ cup / 80 g chopped toasted hazelnuts, divided

2 ripe Bartlett pears, halved, cored, and cut into 8 slices each

4 ounces / 110 g Pecorino Romano cheese, shaved (1 cup)

In a small bowl, whisk together the vinegar and oil; season to taste with salt and pepper.

Trim the bottom core from the radicchio; discard any damaged outside leaves. Remove 4 large outer leaves to use as cups and set aside. Tear the remaining radicchio into 1-inch / 2.5 cm pieces.

In a large bowl, toss together the torn radicchio, endive, frisée, and three-quarters of the hazelnuts with the vinaigrette. Place a radicchio cup on each plate. Divide the salad equally among the cups, mounding it nice and high. Arrange the pears around the sides of the cups and sprinkle with the remaining hazelnuts and shaved cheese.

BRAISED PORK SHOULDER *with* LEEKS AND PEARS

This is one of those instances where a ton of flavor is born out of a small shopping list. Slow-cooking the pork makes for juicy, tender meat, while the pears and leeks melt into a luscious, mellow gravy. Inserting garlic slivers into the meat infuses the entire roast with garlicky fragrance; you could also add fennel seed or fresh rosemary.

Makes 8 servings

1 (4½-pound / 2 kg) bone-in pork shoulder, such as Boston butt	2 pounds / 910 g leeks, halved lengthwise and rinsed of grit
2 garlic cloves, peeled and thinly sliced	1 cup / 240 ml dry white wine
4½ teaspoons kosher salt, divided, plus more as needed	1 cup / 240 ml chicken stock
2 teaspoons freshly ground black pepper, plus more as needed	2 bay leaves
2 tablespoons extra-virgin olive oil	3 firm Bosc pears, peeled, cored, and cut into 1-inch /2.5 cm chunks

Pat the meat dry and score the skin and fat, cutting as deeply as you can without slicing the meat. Insert the garlic slivers into the slits. Rub 4 teaspoons of salt and the 2 teaspoons of pepper all over the meat. Place the meat in a large bowl and cover it with plastic wrap. Transfer to the refrigerator for at least 3 hours or overnight. Let the meat stand at room temperature for 30 minutes before cooking.

Preheat the oven to 325°F / 165°C.

Heat the oil over high heat in a 4- to 5-quart / 4- to 5-L Dutch oven. Add the meat and cook, turning occasionally, until it is well-browned on all sides, about 10 minutes. Transfer the meat to a plate.

Remove and discard the dark green leek tops and root ends; thinly slice the white and light green bottoms. Add the leeks to the pot and cook over medium-high heat until they are soft and turning golden, about 5 minutes. Stir in the remaining ½ teaspoon of salt and continue cooking until the leeks are caramelized, 2 to 3 minutes more. Return the meat to the pot. Stir in the wine and broth, scraping up any browned bits stuck to the bottom of the pan. Drop in the bay leaves. Bring the liquid to a simmer. Cover the pot tightly and transfer it to the oven; cook for 2½ to 3 hours, turning the meat every hour, until it is very tender. Stir in the pears after 2 hours of cooking.

Remove the pot from the oven and transfer the meat to a cutting board. Skim off the fat from the pan juices and return the pot to medium-high heat. Simmer the juices until the sauce thickens to a gravy like consistency, about 10 minutes. Taste the gravy and add salt and pepper if necessary. Slice the meat and arrange it on a platter; spoon the gravy over the top and serve immediately.

PEAR-CHOCOLATE UPSIDE-DOWN CAKE

Pears are equal opportunists when it comes to chocolate and caramel. A poached pear dipped in molten chocolate sauce is as undeniably delicious as one drizzled with butterscotch. To do both at the same time is usually overkill, but this cake unites all three in an ideal blend of flavor and texture—the pears turn golden and toffee-edged while the airy cake topping bakes up gently bittersweet. Pears release a lot of moisture when cooking, so make this recipe in a cast-iron skillet. A great conductor of heat, cast iron will aid the caramelization process. Like anything chocolate (or caramel), this cake is delicious topped with whipped cream.

Makes one 10-inch cake

¾ cup plus 2 tablespoons / 200 g unsalted butter, at room temperature, divided, plus 1 tablespoon melted

½ cup / 50 g packed light brown sugar

2 firm but ripe pears, such as Bosc or Bartlett, peeled, cored, and thinly sliced

½ cup / 50 g unsweetened Dutch-processed cocoa powder, divided

⅔ cup / 160 ml boiling water

4 large egg yolks

2 teaspoons pure vanilla extract

1½ cups / 150 g sifted cake flour

1 cup /200 g granulated sugar

2 teaspoons baking powder

½ teaspoon kosher salt

½ teaspoon ground cinnamon

¼ teaspoon ground cloves

Preheat the oven to 350°F / 180°C.

Melt ¼ cup / 55 g of the butter in a 10-inch / 25.5 cm cast-iron skillet over medium heat. Stir in the brown sugar until well combined and remove the skillet from the heat. Arrange the pear slices in tight, overlapping circles on top of the sugar mixture, with the thin ends facing toward the center. Brush the sides of the pan with the melted butter.

In a small bowl, whisk together the cocoa powder and boiling water. Let the mixture cool to room temperature. In a separate bowl, whisk together the egg yolks, one quarter of the cocoa mixture, and the vanilla.

In the bowl of an electric mixer fitted with the paddle attachment, lightly mix together the flour, sugar, baking powder, salt, cinnamon, and cloves. Beat in the remaining 10 tablespoons / 145 g of the butter and the remaining cocoa mixture. Beat on medium speed for 2 minutes. Scrape down the sides. Beat in the egg mixture, a third at a time, beating the mixture for 15 to 20 seconds between each addition.

Spoon the batter over the pears, smoothing it evenly with an offset spatula. Bake until a cake tester emerges clean, 40 to 45 minutes. Remove the skillet from the oven and let the cake cool for 5 minutes in the pan on a wire rack. Run an offset spatula around the edges of the cake. Place a large plate on top of the skillet and carefully flip the cake over onto the plate. Let the cake stand for 2 minutes before lifting the skillet. Cool completely before serving.

MAPLE PEAR SQUARES

Sarah Kanneh, along with Erika Williams and Carolyn Bane, is one of the cooking wizards/owners behind the ever-popular Brooklyn eatery Pies n' Thighs. Inspired by the Slow Food movement and the farm-fresh emphasis of California cuisine, the focus at Pies n' Thighs is turning out good, old-fashioned American food made with high-quality ingredients (think fried catfish, cornbread, and, of course, pie!). Baked on a sheet pan, these bars fall somewhere between a slab pie and a turnover, contrasting the flakiest crust ever with the sweet softness of cooked, maple-infused pears. Look out—they go down easy.

Makes 12 servings

CRUST

1 cup / 225 g cold unsalted butter

2½ cups / 330 g all-purpose flour

2 tablespoons granulated sugar

1 teaspoon kosher salt

½ to ¾ cup / 120 to 180 ml ice water, as needed

FILLING

4 ripe Bosc pears, peeled, cored, and sliced ¼ inch / 6 mm thick

¼ cup / 50 g packed light brown sugar

2 tablespoons maple sugar or granulated sugar, plus more for sprinkling

2 tablespoons pure maple syrup

1 tablespoon cornstarch

1 tablespoon unsalted butter, at room temperature

1½ teaspoons finely grated lemon zest

1½ teaspoons freshly squeezed lemon juice

¼ teaspoon peeled and grated fresh ginger

Pinch kosher salt

1 large egg

1 tablespoon heavy whipping cream

To make the crust, cut the butter into ½-inch / 1.3 cm cubes and stick them in the freezer for 10 minutes; they won't freeze, but will be nice and chilly when you're ready for them.

In a large bowl, whisk together the flour, sugar, and salt. Add half the flour mixture and all of the butter to the bowl of a food processor. Pulse several times until the butter is incorporated in chunky nubs. Transfer the mixture to the bowl with the remaining flour mixture; toss lightly with your hands to incorporate. Add the ice water to the mixture, a little at a time, mixing quickly and lightly with your hands so as not to overwork the dough or melt the butter. Mix in just enough water until the dough is shaggy and moist (but not wet), and just barely holds together. Divide the dough into 2 equal-sized balls, wrap each tightly with plastic wrap, and flatten the balls into disks with the palm of your hand. Refrigerate for at least an hour.

Preheat the oven to 375°F / 190°C. Arrange a rack in the lower third of your oven.

To prepare the filling, in a large bowl, toss the pears with the sugars, syrup, cornstarch, butter, lemon zest and juice, ginger, and salt.

On a lightly floured surface, roll out one ball of dough until it fits a 13 x 9-inch / 33 x 23 cm sheet pan, with an inch of overhanging dough on each side; it will be about ⅛ inch / 3 mm thick. Transfer the pan to the refrigerator while you roll out the top layer to a size that fits just inside the perimeter of the pan.

Remove the pan from the fridge; scoop the pear mixture evenly over the crust, leaving behind ¼ cup / 60 ml of juices in the bottom of the bowl. Arrange the top crust over the fruit. Fold the overhanging dough up over the top crust, pinching and crimping the edges together to seal. With a sharp knife, make several slashes in the top of the crust to allow steam to exit. In a small bowl, whisk together the egg and cream; using a pastry brush, brush the egg wash over the crust's surface. Sprinkle with maple sugar (demerara sugar works too).

Transfer the pan to the prepared oven rack. Bake until the crust is firm and golden brown and the filling is bubbling, 30 to 40 minutes. Remove the pan from the oven and transfer it to a wire rack to cool for at least 30 minutes. Slice the pie into triangular, baklava-shaped slices and serve.

ASIAN PEAR MARTINI

A lot of fruity cocktails are overly sweet and completely devoid of any actual fruit. This one gets its fresh, floral flavor from a ripe Asian pear muddled and mixed with a potent combination of vodka and pear-infused brandy.

Makes 1 serving

¼ cup / 40 g peeled and finely diced Asian pear
½ teaspoon granulated sugar
2 ounces / 60 ml good-quality vodka
1 ounce / 30 ml pear brandy, such as Poire William
1 lime wedge
Thin Asian pear slice, for serving

Combine the chopped pear and sugar in the bottom of a cocktail shaker. Muddle the mixture until it forms a juicy mash. Fill the shaker three quarters of the way with ice and add the vodka, brandy, and a squeeze of lime juice. Shake thoroughly, and strain the mixture into a chilled martini glass. Garnish with the pear slice.

PEAR GINGERBREAD CAKE *with* WHISKEY CREAM FROSTING

The incredible, nostalgic scent of this gingerbread will waft its way into every room of your house as it bakes, reminding you of Christmases past. A richly dark, sticky cake filled with sweet, tender pears and spicy ginger, it makes a fine ending to a hearty winter meal or even a nice alternative to Thanksgiving pie.

Makes one 9-inch cake

Nonstick cooking spray, as needed

2 cups / 280 g all-purpose flour

1 teaspoon baking soda

¼ teaspoon fine sea salt

1 teaspoon ground cinnamon

1 teaspoon ground ginger

⅛ teaspoon ground allspice

½ cup / 115 g unsalted butter, at room temperature

½ cup / 110 g packed dark brown sugar

2 large eggs, at room temperature

⅔ cup / 160 ml unsulfured molasses

¾ cup / 180 ml whole milk

1¼ cups / 210 g peeled, cored, and diced pear. Such as Anjou, Bosc, or Bartlett

1½ cups / 350 ml heavy whipping cream

8 ounces / 230 g mascarpone

¼ cup / 30 g confectioners' sugar

3 tablespoons whiskey

Preheat the oven to 350°F / 180°C and lightly oil a 9-inch / 23 cm square baking pan with nonstick cooking spray.

In a large bowl, whisk together the flour, baking soda, salt, cinnamon, ginger, and allspice.

In the bowl of an electric mixer fitted with the paddle attachment, beat the butter and sugar together until fluffy. Beat in the eggs, one at a time, until fully incorporated, then beat in the molasses. Add the milk and the dry ingredients in three batches each, alternating between the two and beating well between each addition. Using a wooden spoon, gently fold in the pears.

Scrape the batter into the prepared pan and transfer the pan to the oven. Bake until a toothpick inserted in the center of the cake emerges clean, 40 to 45 minutes. Remove the pan from the oven and place it on a wire rack to cool completely.

While the cake cools, combine the cream, mascarpone, and confectioners' sugar in the bowl of an electric mixer fitted with the whisk attachment. Whip the mixture until it forms soft peaks. Beat in the whiskey, and spoon the topping over the cooled cake before serving.

Grapes

GRAPES ARE OFTEN ASSOCIATED WITH WINE-SWILLING Europe or California, where long rows of gnarled vines climb the sun-soaked hills and valleys of warmer climes. But the Eastern Atlantic seaboard has always been home to a trove of wild grape varieties discovered long ago by Native Americans. For centuries, New York was the epi-

wine and grapes diminished further, effectively stamping out our state's growing industry.

In recent years, New York has steadily regained its foothold in the wine world, but at Red Jacket we grow only *labrusca* grapes, the Eastern American species of table grapes. *Labrusca* grapes are different from *vinifera* grapes

JOE'S GROWING TIPS:

- Choose a grape variety that grows well in your region. *Lambrusca* grapes like cold winters followed by a fairly long warm period in which to mature. *Rotundifolia* grapes, a Southern slip-skin grape variety that includes Muscadines, prefer steady, warm periods.

- Ideally, you should plant in sandy or rocky ground, where the vine will produce the highest quality fruit. Getting full sun and excellent air circulation helps the vines root deeply, providing protection against periods of drought. They need less water than other fruits, requiring the most precipitation to nurture spring shoots. Little water is required during fall ripening and too much can actually do more harm than good. A well-maintained grapevine can produce for as long as five decades.

- Unlike many other fruits, grapes are pollinated by wind, not insects, so it is important to plant the pollinating varieties near each other (aim for 6 to 8 feet / 1.8 to 2.4 m apart) in order to set the fruit.

- Grapes are borne on each season's new growth. Prune in late fall or winter, just enough to control the amount of grapes that will produce in the following season; the key is to strive for a smaller amount of grapes on each vine. Less fruit per vine yields higher quality and flavor (because this comes at a cost of production and yield, it is also why great wines are often more expensive).

- Grapes do not continue to ripen once picked, so allow them to ripen fully on the vine until they are sweet, aromatic, and covered with a silvery bloom. Clip the berries with sharp shears and protect the fruit by handling them by the stems, not the berries.

center of our nation's viticulture. It only began to slow when the railroad expansion of the late nineteenth century enabled California to ship grapes to the East. With the arrival of Prohibition in the 1920s, the demand for

like Chardonnay or Cabernet Sauvignon, which are only suitable for making wine. *Labrusca* varieties, on the other hand, make a very grapey-tasting wine and are excellent for eating and food-processing; they are characterized by a thick skin that slides easily away from the pulp and a flavor frequently referred to as "foxy," a hard-to-pin-down description that implies a rich, brooding quality.

Perhaps the most common *labrusca* grape, and our most popular at the market, is the Concord. Concords boast a blue-black, chalky bloom and full-bodied, aromatic sweetness. The first thing a customer always remarks when tasting one is, "Grape jelly!" The purple, grapey flavor we associate with jams, juice, and soda is that of the Concord; in fact, much of the Concords grown in this country are put to commercial use. Our orchards also produce two other varieties: Fredonia, an early-ripening, subtly spicy grape similar to Concords, and Niagara, an amber-green grape with lush floral notes.

Many of our customers view these grapes as a delicacy, anticipating their arrival each year for the sheer pleasure of slipping them down their throats like oysters, spitting out the tiny pips as they go. Eating them this way is easiest, though they can also be clipped into single-serving clusters and placed next to slabs of chalky goat's milk cheese, sliced walnut bread, or cured sausage. The raw grapes are surprisingly good in salads; crisp, fresh celery and endive are refreshing partners, especially when dressed with sharp sherry vinaigrette and sprinkled with toasted hazelnuts. If cooking, a quick high-heat method like roasting or sautéing is almost essential to concentrate their juices; either of these methods works well alongside rich dark meat like rabbit, duck, or chicken legs. In savory dishes, it may be necessary to cut the grapes' sweetness with seasonings like shallots, garlic, rosemary, or black pepper. Round out the flavors with a finishing pinch of coarse sea salt such as fleur de sel.

The seedy flesh is often the greatest hurdle when it comes to working with any of these grapes. You can cut each grape in half and dig out the pips with a paring knife, a somewhat tedious job. Or, if you don't mind the crunchy texture and slightly tannic flavor the seeds impart, just leave them in. Many sweet preparations work around the seed problem altogether by simmering and straining the fruit, leaving only the jammy pulp behind.

Rinse grapes thoroughly under cool water just before serving. You can then trim the bunch into smaller ones.

SELECTION: Grapes don't continue to ripen off of the vine, so choose plump, succulent-looking fruit from the outset. The fruit should be firmly attached to flexible stems; avoid any fruit that is shriveled, discolored, or sticky.

STORAGE: Moisture and heat cause grapes to ferment, and they quickly go bad at room temperature. Store unwashed grapes in a paper towel-lined, perforated plastic bag in the refrigerator, where they should keep for one to two weeks. Remove and discard any wrinkled or soft-looking berries from the bunch first. Grapes absorb other foods' aromas, so keep them away from anything strongly flavored like onions or cabbage. Whole grapes don't freeze well, but you can freeze the cooked and strained pulp (see Freezing Fruit, page 247).

CONCORD MOSTARDA *with* SALUMI AND PEARS

An Italian condiment of candied fruit and pungent mustard seed, mostarda is traditionally paired with roasted or boiled meats, but it's great with cured meats and cheese boards, too. This shortcut version skips the candying step, for a preparation that's fast and fresh-tasting. Once you've made it a few times, adjust the seasonings to your liking—spoon in a little extra mustard if you prefer it strong and sinus-awakening, or splash some red wine into the simmering pot for deeper complexity.

Yield 1 cup

1 pound / 455 g Concord grapes, seeds removed (see tip, below)

½ cup / 60 g thinly sliced shallot

¼ cup / 50 g packed light brown sugar

¼ cup / 60 ml red wine vinegar

2 teaspoons minced fresh sage

Pinch chili flakes

1 tablespoon whole-grain mustard, plus more as needed

Mixed salumi, such as prosciutto, speck, coppa, or finocchiona, for serving

Sliced ripe seckel pears or roasted pears (see Pear and Barley Pilaf, page 194), for serving

Crusty bread, for serving

In a medium pot over medium heat, combine the grapes, shallot, sugar, vinegar, sage, and chili flakes. Simmer the mixture, stirring occasionally, until the juices are thick and syrupy, about 30 minutes. Stir in the mustard. Remove the pot from the heat and let it cool to room temperature. Serve the mostarda alongside a board of salumi, pears, and crusty bread.

Note: Seeding Concords can be a messy labor of love. You can leave in the seeds if you're okay with a little extra texture, or to make things easier, spread the grapes on a baking sheet and freeze them for 20 minutes or so. Slice the semisolid fruit in half and remove the seeds with the tip of a paring knife.

CONCORD GRAPE FOCACCIA

In Jody Williams's West Village bistro, Buvette, French country cooking meets Italian peasant food. It adds up to simple, hearty fare like pork rillettes and croques monsieurs, with menu rotations inspired by the changing seasons. This Italian *schiacciata* (known as *uva de fragola* in Italy) is a focaccia-type flatbread spiced with fennel seeds and dimpled with juicy Concord grapes. Jody serves it any time of day—with morning coffee, alongside an after-dinner cheese plate, or late into the evening with a glass of vin santo.

Makes one 17³/₄- x 12³/₈-inch pan

⅓ cup / 80 ml extra-virgin olive oil, divided, plus more as needed

2 sprigs fresh rosemary (leaves only)

3 cups / 420 g all-purpose flour

1½ teaspoons active dry yeast

1½ teaspoons granulated sugar, plus more for garnish

1 teaspoon coarse sea salt, plus more for garnish

½ teaspoon crushed fennel seeds, plus more for garnish

1 to 1½ cups / 240 to 350 ml room-temperature water, plus more as needed

1 pound / 455 g Concord grapes, stemmed and seeded

In a small bowl, combine the olive oil and rosemary leaves. Let the mixture stand for 30 minutes, then strain it through a fine-mesh sieve into a small bowl and reserve the oil and leaves separately.

In a large bowl, combine the flour, yeast, sugar, salt, and crushed fennel seeds. Add about 3 tablespoons of the olive oil and slowly add 1 cup / 240 ml of the water in three intervals; you want to mix the dough by hand until the ingredients are well combined, adding just enough additional water to create a moist yet well-defined dough. Knead the dough on a lightly floured board for 15 minutes until it is smooth and elastic.

Stretch out the dough to a large rectangle; spread two thirds of the grapes and half of the reserved rosemary leaves over the surface. Gently dimple the dough with your fingertips, and then fold it in half repeatedly until the grapes and rosemary are mixed throughout. Transfer the dough to a lightly oiled bowl and cover it with plastic wrap. Let the dough rise and rest in the refrigerator overnight.

The next day, preheat the oven to 425°F / 220°C. Lightly oil a 18 x 13-inch / 46 x 34 cm rimmed baking sheet. Remove the dough from the refrigerator and stretch it to fit the prepared pan. Let the dough rise at room temperature, loosely covered with a clean towel, for 45 minutes. Uncover the dough and drizzle it with the remaining 2 tablespoons plus 1 teaspoon of olive oil; sprinkle with the remaining grapes, rosemary, and a large pinch of fennel seeds. Sprinkle with sugar and salt. Use your fingertips to dimple the dough. Let the dough rest for another 15 minutes at room temperature, then transfer the pan to the oven and bake until the bread is golden brown and the grapes begin to burst, about 25 minutes. Serve warm.

PEPPERY CHICKEN THIGHS *with* BRANDY-ROASTED GRAPES

It's essential to crank up the heat for this one. A hot oven gets the chicken good and crispy and tempts the grapes' full-bodied juices from their skins. This is a toss-and-bake recipe: everything is thrown in the oven, even the grapes' stems and crunchy, edible pips. Serve the meat, grapes, and pan juices over a mound of steamed farro or other nutty, firm-textured grain.

Makes 4 servings

2 pounds / 910 g bone-in chicken thighs	1 tablespoon extra-virgin olive oil
1½ teaspoons kosher salt, plus more as needed	12 ounces / 340 g Concord grapes, cut into small bunches
1 teaspoon freshly ground black pepper	2 tablespoons brandy
1 tablespoon minced fresh rosemary	1 tablespoon melted unsalted butter
2 garlic cloves, smashed and peeled	

In a large bowl, toss the chicken with the salt, pepper, rosemary, garlic, and oil. Cover the bowl with plastic wrap and refrigerate for 1 hour, then remove the bowl from the refrigerator and let it stand at room temperature for 20 minutes before cooking.

Preheat the oven to 450°F / 230°C. Scatter the chicken in the bottom of a lightly oiled roasting pan and roast for 30 minutes. In a medium bowl, toss the grapes with the brandy, butter, and a large pinch of salt; add the mixture to the roasting pan, tucking bunches of grapes around the chicken. Continue cooking until the grapes have begun to burst through their skins and the chicken juices run clear when pierced with the tip of a sharp knife, about 15 minutes.

Remove the pan from the oven and serve the chicken and grapes immediately..

INDIAN SUMMER GRAPE CREAMSICLES

Concords' late summer arrival signals that autumn is just around the bend, but plenty of years the weather hasn't quite caught up. These easy, four-ingredient popsicles are for those last sweltering days when you long for cooler days but are still trying to beat the heat. Tangy buttermilk cuts the grapes' intense sweetness and creates a frozen yogurtlike creaminess.

Makes 8 creamsicles

1 pound / 455 g Concord grapes	1 scant cup / 230 ml buttermilk
⅓ cup / 70 g granulated sugar	

In a large, heavy saucepan over medium heat, combine the grapes and sugar. Cook until the grapes' pulp separates from the skin, about 30 minutes.

Place a double layer of cheesecloth in a strainer set over a large bowl. Pour in the grape mixture to strain; once it is cool enough to handle, wrap the cheesecloth in a bundle and squeeze as much juice through the strainer as possible (you should have about 2 cups / 470 ml). Stir the buttermilk into the juice.

Divide the mixture among the popsicle molds, allowing at least ¼ inch / 6 mm of space at the top of the mold for expansion. Freeze completely, at least 4 hours.

GRAPE BROWN BETTY *with* LEMON WHIPPED CREAM

This is a classic, humble recipe that will get dog-eared, juice-splattered, and flour-smudged in your file box. Basically a bread pudding without the heavy custard or time investment, it's so uncomplicated that you can almost always scrape one together, even if your wallet is looking slim or your pantry is in a sadly barren state. A few slices of bread and a bunch of grapes, and you're pretty much good to go.

Makes 4 to 6 servings

1 pound / 455 g Niagara and/or Concord grapes, halved and seeded (see note, page 211)

¼ cup plus 1½ tablespoons / 78 g granulated sugar, divided

2½ teaspoons freshly squeezed lemon juice, divided

1½ tablespoons all-purpose flour

Pinch of fine sea salt

4 ounces / 110 g soft white bread, torn into small pieces (2 to 2½ cups)

2 tablespoons unsalted butter, at room temperature

¾ cup / 180 ml heavy whipping cream

2 teaspoons finely grated lemon zest

Preheat the oven to 375°F / 190°C. Toss together the grapes, ¼ cup / 50 g of the sugar, 1 teaspoon of the lemon juice, the flour, and the salt. Transfer the mixture to an 8-inch / 20.5 cm square baking dish or a 2-quart / 1.9 L gratin dish. Sprinkle the torn bread pieces over the fruit and dot with butter. Cover the dish with aluminum foil and transfer it to the oven.

Bake until the fruit mixture is bubbling, about 30 minutes. Uncover the dish and continue baking until the bread is golden brown, 15 to 20 minutes. Remove the dish from the oven.

Combine the cream, remaining 1½ tablespoons of sugar, the remaining 1½ teaspoons of lemon juice, and the lemon zest in the bowl of an electric mixer fitted with the whisk attachment; whip the mixture until soft peaks form.

To serve, cut the warm Brown Betty into slabs and top each slab with a dollop of whipped cream.

NIAGARA GRAPE *and* JASMINE RICE PUDDING

Rice pudding has many incarnations—sticky and custardy, steaming hot and porridge-y, or, like this easy stovetop version, creamy and cold. Standing in for traditional golden raisins are plump, sweetly floral Niagara grapes, which pair beautifully with aromatic jasmine rice. Folding the whipped cream into the cold pudding just before serving adds airiness, but warm rice pudding eaters can do it sooner, so long as the rice has cooled slightly—10 minutes or so off the burner should do it.

Makes 8 servings

2½ cups / 590 ml whole milk	2 teaspoons unsalted butter
2 cups / 470 ml heavy whipping cream, divided	1 cup / 160 g Niagara grapes, halved and seeded
1 cinnamon stick	1 teaspoon lemon zest
½ teaspoon kosher salt	1½ teaspoons pure vanilla extract
1¼ cups / 240 g jasmine rice, rinsed and drained	Ground cinnamon, as needed
⅔ cup plus 1 tablespoon / 172 g granulated sugar, divided	

In a medium pot over high heat, combine the milk, 1 cup / 240 ml of the cream, the cinnamon stick, and the salt. Bring the mixture to a boil, stir in the rice, and reduce the heat to medium. Simmer, uncovered, until the rice is tender, 25 to 30 minutes. Remove the pot from the heat and immediately stir in ⅔ cup / 133 g of the sugar.

While the rice cooks, melt the butter in a small skillet. Add the grapes and sprinkle with 1 tablespoon of the sugar. Cook over medium-low heat, stirring only once or twice, until the grapes are caramelized, 15 to 20 minutes. Stir in the lemon zest. Fold the grapes into the rice mixture and set the pot aside to cool to room temperature. Cover and refrigerate until cold, at least one hour and up to overnight.

Before serving, place the remaining 1 cup / 240 ml of cream in the bowl of an electric mixer fitted with the whisk attachment. Whip the cream to soft peaks, and beat in the vanilla. Using a wooden spoon, fold the whipped cream into the rice.

Spoon the rice pudding into bowls and sprinkle each serving with cinnamon.

MOM'S CONCORD GRAPE PIE

Oftentimes it starts like this: "Mom, can you make us some of that grape pie?" We have to be extra nice, because we know it's not the easiest job, cooking and straining all those grapes. My mom is known for her amazing pies, but the grape is special. Not just because fresh Concords are only available for a short time, but because nothing really compares to that rich, deep grape sensation. Be aware, you'll know who's been eating it—just ask to see their tongue.

Makes one 9-inch

---

1 recipe Double Pie Crust (page 111), disks wrapped in plastic and chilled

2 pounds / 910 g Concord grapes, stemmed and washed

¾ cup / 150 g granulated sugar

1½ tablespoons freshly squeezed lemon juice

1½ tablespoons quick-cooking tapioca

¼ teaspoon fine sea salt

1 large egg, whisked with 1 tablespoon water

To make the pie filling, slip the skins from the grapes; place the skins and pulp in separate bowls. Transfer the pulp to a medium pot over medium heat; cook until the seeds loosen from the pulp, 5 to 10 minutes. Working over a large bowl, press the pulp through a medium-mesh sieve or colander to separate out the seeds. Discard the seeds and stir the skins into the strained pulp.

Preheat the oven to 450°F / 230°C.

To the grape mixture, add the sugar, lemon juice, tapioca, and salt. Stir to combine, and let the filling stand for 15 minutes at room temperature while you roll out the crust.

On a clean, lightly floured surface, roll each disc of dough into a 12-inch / 30.5 cm circle. Transfer one round to the bottom of a 9-inch metal pie pan. Pour in the filling. Cut the remaining crust into ½-inch / 1.3 cm-thick strips and create a lattice crust (see Triple-Cherry Lattice Pie, page 111). Brush the top of the pie with the egg wash.

Place the pie on a rimmed baking sheet to catch any dripping juices during baking. Bake the pie for 15 minutes, then reduce the oven temperature to 350°F / 180°C and bake until the crust is golden and the juices are bubbling thickly, about 40 minutes longer. Remove the pie from the oven and let it cool completely on a wire rack before serving.

Quinces

IF YOU AREN'T PAYING CLOSE ATTENTION, YOUR EYES might wander right over the quinces at market. They usually take up less real estate than the sea of apples and pears hogging the tables, and their downy, yellow complexion blends right in with the crimson, copper, and gold of the season. Even the shape, a lumpy, awkward approximation of a pear, could easily be mistaken for the real deal. Really, they don't stand out at be enjoyed raw. When uncooked, the texture is dense, dry, and astringent. It takes a trusting cook to simmer, roast, or bake the fruit until its bitter tannins soften and mellow, turning the cream-colored flesh a flaming, semi-translucent pink.

This cooking limitation is hardly limiting, however. You can do plenty with a quince in the kitchen. After the enticing aroma, quince's next-best quality is its

JOE'S GROWING TIPS:

- Quince grows best in temperate climates where winters are cool, and it prefers full sun and moist, well-drained soil. It can tolerate some wetness and drought, but it dislikes drastic weather fluctuations, so plant it in a slightly sheltered area away from wind.

- Typically a small to medium-sized fruit tree (usually about 15 feet high / 4.6 m at most), quince can be pruned to a tree shape or allowed to sucker freely into a bush. Fruit is borne each year on new growth, so take time each year to remove any weak or dead branches from the ground level of the plant; this helps stimulate new, fruit-bearing shoots.

- Patience is required when planting a quince tree. They grow slowly and won't bear fruit for at least four years, with heavy crops taking another four or five years to appear. However, once the tree is fruiting well, you can expect at least two decades of fertility.

- Pick quince as you would an apple, twisting it gently from the tree (you can also use strong pruning shears). Harvest the fruit just before it is fully ripe, when the coloring changes from green to yellow. It can continue to mature in a cool root cellar or on a countertop at home.

all until you get a whiff of their perfume, an alluring blend of pineapple, rose, and honey, reminiscent of exotic places. The fruit is most prized in far flung Middle Eastern and Mediterranean cuisines, where the distinctive flavor, like that of a musky, tropical apple, is much esteemed. Here in America it remains something of a mystery fruit, possibly because it's not one to high level of pectin, which yields superior jams, jellies, and fruit butters. A classic example of this is *membrillo*, a Spanish condiment in which quince is thickened to a sliceable paste to serve with sheep's milk cheese or charcuterie. Because its flavor is so singular and it maintains its shape so well when cooked, quince is also very comfortable with the simplest preparations—gently poached in a brandy-based syrup, honey-glazed and roasted until its edges candy, or buttered, sugared, and baked. From there it can be sliced over ice cream, spooned atop almond cake, or served warm with a drizzle of rich, fresh cream. Related to pears and apples, quince is also sometimes slipped into these fruits' pies, crumbles, and sauces for added aroma and rosy color (though dice it smaller than the other fruits, since quince takes longer to cook). It imbues lamb or beef stew with a heady floral fragrance, marrying nicely with cinnamon, ginger, cardamom, and cumin.

You may find quince covered in pale gray fuzz. Give the fruit a rinse under cool water and gently wipe away this coating with a clean towel. The thick, tart, skin must also be removed. Cut the fruit into quarters and then peel the skin with a paring knife or vegetable peeler. Alternatively, you can bake the rinsed fruit in its jacket first; it should then pull smoothly away from the tender cooked flesh. The seeds and core can be discarded unless you plan to use the fruit for jam, in which case you should leave them in; both are especially high in pectin. Strain them out at the end, after they've helped set the preserve. Quince oxidizes very rapidly, so be sure to sprinkle the fruit with lemon juice or drop slices into acidulated water until you are ready to use them.

SELECTION: Choose plump, firm (not hard) fruit that is free of discoloration, bruises, and spots. Look for fruit that is fully ripe or almost ripe, with a mostly yellow or completely golden color. More mature fruit is usually covered in less fuzz, but if the fruit has good coloring, the downy coat can be brushed away.

STORAGE: Ripen slightly green fruit on the counter for up to one week in a bowl, where it can perfume the entire kitchen. Once ripe, transfer it to the refrigerator for up to three weeks. Quince contains the naturally occurring gas ethylene, which hastens the ripening of other fruits and vegetables, so store them individually wrapped in newspaper in a plastic bag away from other foods (the crisper drawer is a good choice). This also prevents food from absorbing the fruit's strong fragrance.

BUCKWHEAT-QUINCE PANCAKES *with* SPICED QUINCE SYRUP

In my house, every weekend morning is "fry-up" time, and my kids have become essentially the "sous chefs." Their favorite and mine is locally milled buckwheat pancakes. These fluffy, whole-grain pancakes, filled with sweet, tender chunks of poached quince, provide a hearty start to crisp fall mornings. The fruit's poaching liquid does double duty, creating its own aromatic syrup for spooning over the pancakes; a less heavy alternative to maple syrup, it won't overwhelm quince's delicate flavors. You can poach the quince up to three days ahead; refrigerate the fruit in its syrup in an airtight container until ready to use.

Makes about 12 pancakes

SPICED QUINCE SYRUP	BUCKWHEAT-QUINCE PANCAKES
1¾ pounds / 795 g quince, peeled, quartered, and cored	¾ cup / 90 g buckwheat flour
3 cinnamon sticks	¾ cup / 110 g all-purpose flour
3 whole star anise	1½ teaspoons baking powder
1 strip lemon peel, white pith removed	½ teaspoon baking soda
½ cup / 100 g packed light brown sugar	½ teaspoon grated nutmeg
½ teaspoon pure vanilla extract	¼ teaspoon fine sea salt
	2 large eggs
	1 cup / 240 ml buttermilk
	¾ cup / 180 ml whole milk
	4 tablespoons canola oil, divided
	Melted butter, for serving

In a small saucepan over medium heat, combine 4 cups / 1 L of water with the quince, cinnamon sticks, star anise, and lemon peel. Simmer until the fruit is just tender, about 30 to 40 minutes. Using a slotted spoon, remove 6 of the quince quarters and transfer them to a bowl; once they are cool enough to handle, dice the quince and refrigerate, covered, until ready to use. Using a potato masher, mash the fruit remaining in the poaching liquid.

Pour the mashed quince into a colander lined with a double layer of cheesecloth and set over a bowl. Cover the colander and bowl with a large sheet of plastic wrap. Transfer to the refrigerator and allow the mixture to drain completely, about 3 hours or up to overnight. Do not press on the solids or the syrup will be cloudy. The yield should be about 1 cup / 240 ml of juice.

Return the juice to the saucepan and stir in the sugar. Simmer until the syrup is slightly thickened, 10 to 15 minutes (it will continue to thicken as it cools). Remove the pot from the heat and stir in the vanilla; allow the syrup to cool completely at room temperature.

To make the pancakes, in a small bowl, toss the diced quince with 1 tablespoon of the quince syrup. In a large bowl, whisk together the flours, baking powder, baking soda, nutmeg, and salt. In a separate bowl, whisk together the eggs, buttermilk, milk, and 2 tablespoons of the oil. Using a wooden spoon, fold the wet ingredients into the flour mixture. Fold in the quince-syrup mixture.

Heat 1 tablespoon of the oil in a large skillet over medium-high heat. Working in batches, drop the batter into the skillet (about ¼ cup / 60 ml per pancake). Cook without moving, until the edges appear firm and the bubbles on the surface of the pancake have subsided, about 2 minutes. Flip and cook until golden, 1 to 2 minutes longer. Repeat with the remaining oil and batter. Top the pancakes with melted butter and drizzle them with quince syrup.

MANCHEGO CRACKERS *with* CANDIED QUINCE

Manchego and quince are a classic pairing in Spain, where slices of the salty sheep's' milk cheese are often served with a sliver of *membrillo*, a sweet, slow-cooked quince paste. In this quick cheaters' version, the fragrant fruit is poached in honey until sticky and tender, rendering it a perfect topping for the addictive, savory crackers. Both are excellent companions to an appetizer tray and can be made ahead; the crackers will keep in an airtight container for up to one week, and you can store any leftover quince in its cooking syrup in the fridge for up to one month.

Makes 3½ dozen crisps

CANDIED QUINCE

1 cup / 240 ml honey

2 medium quince (12 ounces / 340 g),
peeled, cored and cut into ¼-inch / 6 mm cubes

MANCHEGO CRACKER CRISPS

¼ cup / 20 g roasted, salted, coarsely chopped almonds

⅔ cup / 90 g all-purpose flour

½ teaspoon fine sea salt

½ teaspoon freshly ground black pepper

4 ounces / 110 g aged Manchego cheese,
finely grated (1 cup)

¼ cup / 55 g unsalted butter, cold and cubed

2 to 3 tablespoons heavy whipping cream, as needed

To make the candied quince, combine 1 cup / 240 ml of water with the honey in a medium, heavy-bottomed saucepan. Bring the mixture to a simmer over medium-low heat and cook until the honey dissolves, about 5 minutes. Stir in the quince. Reduce the heat to low and simmer very gently until the fruit is tender and translucent, 45 to 50 minutes. Remove the pan from the heat and use a slotted spoon to transfer the fruit to a bowl. Cool the fruit and the syrup separately; recombine to store.

To make the crackers, pulse the almonds in a food processor until they are finely ground, then pulse in the flour, salt, and pepper until combined. Add the cheese and butter and pulse until the mixture forms coarse crumbs, then pulse in the cream, one tablespoon at a time, until the dough comes together into a ball. Turn out the dough onto a clean work surface and roll it into a 1½-inch / 4 cm-diameter log. Wrap the log tightly with plastic and refrigerate it for at least 3 hours or overnight.

Preheat the oven to 350°F / 180°C. Line 2 baking sheets with a Silpat liners or parchment paper.

Slice the dough into ¼-inch / 6 mm-thick rounds. Arrange the rounds on the prepared baking sheets, allowing 1 inch / 2.5 cm between each cracker (you will need to bake the crackers in two batches, or four trays). Transfer the baking sheets to the oven and bake the crackers until they are golden, 10 to 12 minutes. Immediately remove the baking pan from the oven and transfer the crackers to a wire rack to cool.

To serve, top each cracker with a small spoonful of candied quince.

PAIRING FRUIT *with* CHEESE

The contrast of savory cheese and sweet succulent fruit often makes them a natural pairing. While that ubiquitous cluster of grapes is a classic complement to any cheeseboard, most fruit—in the right context—can be enjoyed in the company of cheese. The trick to successfully uniting the two is in thinking in terms of complementary characteristics: consider Gruyère's nuttiness against the sweet, winey crispness of apple, or fresh ricotta's creaminess offset by a strawberry's delicate floral notes.

When serving fresh, seasonal fruit, select only the sweetest, most aromatic, recently harvested fruit available—you are relying on the fruit's balance of sugars, acids, and juices to enhance the inherent qualities of the cheese. However, prepared fruit can also complement cheese quite nicely, as with honey-roasted plums over mascarpone, piquant chutney with sturdy farmhouse Cheddar, or dried apricots stuffed with goat cheese. In fact, fruits that lack natural sweetness, like gooseberries, rhubarb, or currants, pretty much demand a cooked preparation when it comes to cheese pairing. You can also experiment with mixing the two in salads, sandwiches, and desserts.

Below is a list of tried-and-true combinations, but let your palate be your guide. Cheese and fruit are both highly nuanced foods; you might be surprised by what works well together.

CHEESE	SOFT, FRESH (Mascarpone, Ricotta, Farmer Cheese)	SOFT-RIPENED (Brie, Camembert)	SEMISOFT (Fontia, Fresh Mozzarella, Port Salut)	GOAT'S MILK (Chévre, Feta)	SEMIHARD (Mild Cheddar, Gruyère, Comte, Manchego)	HARD (Aged Cheddar, Gouda, Parmesan, Pecorino)	BLUE-VEINED (Gorgonzola, Roquefort, Stilton)
FRUIT							
Apples	X	X		X	X	X	X
Apricots	X	X	X	X			
Blackberries	X	X					
Blueberries	X	X		X			
Cherries	X	X			X		X
Grapes	X	X		X	X	X	X
Nectarines	X	X	X	X			X
Peaches	X	X	X	X			X
Pears	X	X	X	X	X	X	X
Plums	X			X	X	X	X
Quince					X	X	X
Raspberries	X	X		X			
Strawberries	X	X	X	X			
Chutneys and sharp Jams (Gooseberry, Currant, Rhubarb)	X	X		X	X	X	X

LAMB *and* QUINCE TAGINE

Left for a day or two in the fridge, the flavors of this tagine become rounder and deeper, so don't worry if you can't finish it in one go. You'll be glad you didn't. Traditionally, North African tagines don't call for browning the meat, but doing so adds an extra layer of flavor. Make sure to do it in batches—if you overcrowd the pot, the meat won't be able to form its delicious caramelized crust.

Makes 6 servings

LAMB	QUINCE
2 teaspoons whole coriander seeds	1¼ pounds / 570 g fresh quince (about 2 medium), peeled, quartered, and cored
2 teaspoons whole cumin seeds	
1 cinnamon stick, broken into pieces	¼ cup / 60 ml honey
2½ pounds / 1.2 kg lamb shoulder, trimmed and cut into 2-inch / 5 cm chunks	2 strips lemon zest
	Juice of 1 lemon
2 teaspoons kosher salt	1 tablespoon unsalted butter
2 teaspoons ground ginger	
½ teaspoon cayenne pepper	Cooked couscous, for serving
2 tablespoons extra-virgin olive oil	Sliced almonds, for serving
1 yellow onion, finely chopped	Fresh cilantro, for serving
3 garlic cloves, finely chopped	
½ teaspoon crumbled saffron threads	

Preheat the oven to 325°F / 165°C.

In a small, dry skillet over medium heat, toast the coriander, cumin, and cinnamon until fragrant, 1 to 2 minutes; transfer the mixture to a spice grinder and finely grind. (If you don't have a grinder you can skip the toasting step and substitute 2 teaspoons of ground coriander, 2 teaspoons of ground cumin, and 1 teaspoon of ground cinnamon.) In a large bowl or platter, toss the lamb with the ground toasted spices, salt, ginger, and cayenne. Cover the bowl with plastic wrap and refrigerate for 2 hours. Let the meat come to room temperature for 30 minutes before cooking.

Preheat a large Dutch oven over medium-high heat. Add the oil. Working in batches, brown the meat, turning only occasionally, until it is golden all over, 3 to 4 minutes per batch. Transfer the browned meat to a large clean bowl.

Add the onion to the Dutch oven and cook, scraping up any browned bits in the bottom of the pot, until it has softened, about 5 minutes. Stir in the garlic and cook for 1 minute. Return the lamb to the pot and pour in enough water to cover the meat by two thirds. Bring the liquid to a simmer over high heat; crumble in the saffron. Cover the pot and transfer it to the oven. Cook the meat until it is very tender and falling apart, 1½ to 2 hours.

Meanwhile, to prepare the quince, place the quince in a small pot and add enough water to just cover it. Stir in the honey, lemon zest, and lemon juice. Simmer, uncovered, until the quince is tender but still slightly firm, 15 to 20 minutes. Remove the pot from the heat and use a slotted spoon to transfer the poached quince to a cutting board; reserve ½ cup / 120 ml of the poaching liquid.

Remove the tagine from the oven and skim the fat from the surface of the liquid; transfer the lamb to a plate with a slotted spoon. Stir ¼ cup / 60 ml of the reserved quince poaching liquid into the tagine juices, and return the Dutch oven to the stove over medium-high heat. Simmer vigorously, stirring occasionally, until the mixture reduces to a saucy consistency. Return the lamb to the pot; cover the pot and keep warm over low heat.

Slice the quince into ½-inch / 1.3 cm pieces. In a large skillet over medium-high heat, melt the butter until the foam subsides. Add the quince pieces in a single layer. Cook, without moving, until the undersides are caramelized, about 2 minutes; flip and brown the other sides. Add the remaining ¼ cup / 60 ml of reserved poaching liquid and cook, stirring the fruit, until it is well glazed.

To serve the tagine, portion the couscous among 6 bowls or plates and spoon the lamb and sauce over top. Arrange the glazed quince pieces on top of the lamb, and garnish with almonds and cilantro.

Putting Up
for Winter

CANNING AND PRESERVING

VENTUALLY, THE LAST APPLE IS PLUCKED FROM AUTUMN'S TREES. FOR MONTHS IT FEELS AS IF THE FULL-TILT PACE OF HARVEST SEASON WILL NEVER END AND THEN—ABRUPTLY—IT DOES, USUALLY RIGHT AROUND THANKSGIVING. IT'S NO WONDER THAT THE HOLIDAY COUNTS AS A FAVORITE FOR ALL OF MY FAMILY—TRUE TO ITS ORIGINS, WE GATHER AND GIVE THANKS, CELEBRATE THE CLOSE OF ANOTHER HARVEST, AND REFLECT ON THE ACCOMPLISHMENTS OF THE SEASONS AS WE LOOK TO THE LONG WINTER AHEAD.

Meanwhile, Geneva and the Finger Lakes settle slowly into winter, resuming a sleepy, small-town feel. Summer tourists have long since fled and the autumn wine season draws to a close. Winter sports enthusiasts gleefully anticipate the first snow, when at last they can take advantage of the many ski slopes gracing the region's lakes and the hundreds of miles of snowmobile trails. But for us at the orchard, we look forward to a slower pace as everyone catches up on a little sleep and breathes a small sigh of relief. Most of our crew is not needed again until springtime and head out in search of other work. The handful of us who remain prepare the tractors for a winters' rest, stack the emptied apple totes, and tend to minor orchard work. An ideal winter is one that arrives softly and then stays consistently cold. Like us, the fruit trees need rest, requiring a certain amount of cold temperatures each year to lie dormant and gather energy for the next growing season; the longer it remains cold without abnormal warm spells, the better.

Although the orchard's slumbering trees are now bare, we still find ourselves surrounded by fruit. Our packhouse hums like a buzz saw, with cold-stored apples to pack; like potatoes and onions, apples are a natural for long-term storage and the only crop we can offer all winter long. We also have fresh juices to be pressed each day from the "culls" (apples that don't make fresh sales), something my family has been doing for almost half a century. At home, there is the comfort of a sunny jar of apricot jam at breakfast, or a snack of bread slathered thickly with apple butter.

For many years, my grandmother Emily was the canner of the family. She would start each year with June's berry crops, then move on to canning cherries (sour varieties were always canned without pits so she could mix them more easily into pies), apricot jams, syrupy prune plums (usually elongated European varieties or the Green Gage plums), and of course, slow-simmered apple butter in the fall. She would always use the tangiest apples in the orchard—our Staymans, Northern Spys, or Cortlands—and sweeten them with just a bit of cider and spices like nutmeg and cinnamon. My dad recalls a particularly excellent pepper relish, piquant with onion and vinegar, that she would make at the end of each summer before the first frost, always serving it with cold cuts and one of her legendary fresh salads. Today, my mom and dad carry on the tradition, taking time each summer to put up jams, jellies, and pickles that, along with our juices, will satisfy some of our fruit cravings until the spring harvest arrives. Just like the generations before us, we continue to live off our "cellared stock."

If the harvest season is about living in the moment, winter's theme is preparation and looking ahead, whether we are stocking our larder or reflecting on the farm's future. Lists are drawn, detailing what worked and what needs fixing for the next year. Orchards essentially take a full decade to become productive and profitable. As tastes change, weather patterns and climates shift, and generations of owners adapt, foresight becomes crucial. We spend the winter cultivating ideas, scouring tree cat- alogs, and plotting out land; my dad takes time to visit different growing regions and markets in search of inno- vation and inspiration. Winter can pass by so quickly and before we know it, the March thaw arrives, and well—it's back to chapter one.

When all is said and done, one of the purest pleasures of the orchard is exactly this timeless cycle. No two years are alike, we enjoy constant anticipation of the next seasonal focus and the rich knowledge that our craft provides for those around us. My family and I often remark to each other that we are in the nurturing business: working hand in hand with Mother Nature, we nurture our trees, which in turn gives us sustenance to nurture our staff, our family, and our larger commu- nity. It is a symbiotic and sustainable process.

Preserving Fruit: Getting Started

THE GOLDEN RULE: BEGIN WITH EXCELLENT FRUIT

When it comes to putting up foods for long-term storage, "preserving" is exactly as it sounds—you are capturing the true essence of a food (here, fruit) at its peak ripeness. On a scientific level, you also extend the life of a living organism, slowing or destroying the enzyme activity that causes fresh fruit to deteriorate and eliminating any lurking microorganisms that might cause contamination. This can be done through freezing (whole fruit or purées), heating (jams, jellies, and butters), alcohol (cordials and liqueurs), or vinegar (pickles, infusions, and chutneys). But no matter what method you choose, the first hard and fast rule is always the same: It begins with excellent fruit.

Fresh, tree-ripened fruit contains just the right balance of sugar, acid—and when necessary, pectin, nature's setting agent—to produce superior flavor and texture. It is also less likely to harbor bacteria or fungi than fruit past its prime. Because locally grown fruit can be picked when it is so much closer to ideal ripeness, purchasing the best-quality produce at your farmers' market, the kind that you would happily eat out of hand, will yield the best results. Of course, if you have an excess of fruit lingering in the fridge at home or are able to negotiate a good price for slightly bruised cast-offs at the close of market day, you should absolutely preserve them. Just make sure to prepare the fruit as soon as possible, slicing away and discarding any particularly soft or discolored parts.

EQUIPMENT

Your kitchen is probably already stocked with almost everything you need to kick off a canning project. As you become increasingly experienced, you may want to upgrade some of your basic equipment to specialty gear designed to make certain tasks easier. The items essential to getting started include the following:

A LARGE, HEAVY-BOTTOMED POT WITH LID. Traditional preserving pans for jamming have a wide shape that allows moisture to evaporate quickly (providing a quicker set) and are made of an excellent heat-conducting material, such as copper. A good-quality pot made of stainless steel or other nonreactive metal is a good stand-in for your first projects; avoid aluminum pans, which interact with the fruit's acids and create unpleasant flavor **SPOONS.** Three spoons will come in handy: a wooden spoon, for stirring simmering mixtures; a slotted stainless steel spoon for skimming foam and pulling whole pieces of fruit from a pan; and a shallow ladle, for transferring hot preserves from the pot to the waiting jars.

CANDY THERMOMETER. A clip-on candy thermometer or deep-fat thermometer allows you to gauge when your preserve has reached necessary temperatures.

FINE-MESH SIEVE LINED WITH CHEESECLOTH. This is particularly important for jelly-making when you need to carefully strain a fruit's clear juices, leaving all solids behind. You can also purchase a jelly bag that is specifically designed for this purpose.

CANNING JARS AND BOTTLES. Made from sturdy, heat-tempered glass that won't break at high temperatures, canning jars are essential. Look for unchipped jars with a noncorrosive two-part lid that includes a screw-on band (an excellent supplier is Ball Canning). Choose dark-colored bottles for light-susceptible alcohols and vinegars. All jars must be sterilized before use.

JAM FUNNEL. This wide-mouthed funnel fits over the opening of a jar, making it easier to ladle in preserves without making a mess.

Other things you might wish to purchase along the way include:

KITCHEN SCALE. For greater accuracy, some canning recipes rely on the weight of ingredients, not volume. A digital kitchen scale can tell you exactly how much an item weighs down to the gram or fraction of an ounce.

BOILING WATER CANNER AND/OR CANNING RACK. A canner is a large, deep saucepan that can fit your canning jars and enough water to immerse them by 1 inch / 2.4 cm during sterilization and processing. They are often fitted with a rack that elevates your jars away from the direct heat of the stove. Any deep, heavy pot and round cake cooling rack will work for beginners.

CANNING TONGS. These wide, angled tongs fit perfectly over the curved shape of canning jars, making it easier to remove hot jars from boiling water. Rubber bands wrapped around each clamp end of a regular set of tongs can also provide the nonslip grip you need.

BUBBLE REMOVER. Usually made of plastic or another non-metallic material, this long, thin tool is slid along the side of a jar to eliminate air bubbles, which can interfere with canning effectiveness. A wooden chopstick also works well for this.

STERILIZING AND PROCESSING: THE BOILING WATER METHOD

Once you've successfully simmered and sauced your way to lasting fruit flavor, you're still only halfway there. Creating a hygienic environment for your preserves is essential for long-term storage. To achieve this, preserved fruit must be heat processed in a boiling water bath. Not only does this sterilize your storage vessel, eliminating spoilage-causing microbes, it also expands and releases the air in the filled jars, creating a vacuum-sealed, inhospitable environment for future microbial growth. While vinegar and alcohol preserved fruits should always be stored in sterilized containers, it is not always necessary to process them a second time in the water bath; recipes will usually specify when this is the case. Hot water bath canning is pretty much as easy as boiling water:

STEP 1: Start with a clean kitchen. Make sure that all countertops, equipment, and tools are thoroughly clean and organized; have ready a stack of freshly laundered dish towels for wiping up spills.

STEP 2: Sterilize your jars or bottles. Wash your jars, lids, and screw tops in hot soapy water. Transfer jars to a boiling water canner fitted with a canning rack, or place them in a deep pot fitted with a round cooling rack. Do not overload the pot; you should have space between the vessels. Cover the jars with water and bring to a boil for 10 minutes to sterilize. Place lids and screw tops in a large, heatproof bowl and cover with boiling water; if you are using a jelly bag or cheesecloth, place them in a separate heatproof bowl and cover with boiling water as well.

STEP 3: Fill your jars. Prepare your recipe as instructed. Remove jars from boiling water to a clean work surface. Carefully ladle the hot mixture into the jars, allowing the recipe's recommended headspace at the top of the jar to allow for food expansion. Slide a bubble remover or long wooden skewer around the inside of the jar to eliminate any trapped air; top off jar with more of the preserve if necessary.

STEP 4: Screw on your lids. Using a clean towel, carefully wipe any food from the rim of your jar. Place the lid over the jar's mouth and gently screw on the ring until it just stops securely. If it's too loose, water will sneak in during processing; too tight and the jar will not seal properly.

STEP 5: Process jars. Return filled jars to the water canner; make sure jars are covered by at least 1 inch / 2.5 cm of water. Boil according to a recipe's suggested processing time (you may need to make adjustments if you live at an exceedingly high altitude). Remove the pot from the heat and let the jars stand in hot water for 5 minutes. Transfer the jars to a towel-lined countertop and let them stand upright, without disturbing, for at least 12 hours and up to 24.

STEP 6: Check the seal. Press down on the center of your lids to see that the vacuum as sealed properly. If the center springs back on any of the jars, store them in the refrigerator and consume first. Label jars with contents and date, and store them in a cool, dark place.

Jams, Jellies, Sauces, and Butters

Probably the most popular and familiar types of preserves are those that fall loosely into the jam category. Usually made with fresh fruit, sugar, lemon juice, and occasionally commercial pectin, they are almost universally pleasing and easy to use—spread them onto toast or sandwich between cake layers, whisk into vinaigrettes and sauces, or glaze over meats. While all share similarities in preparation (and are sometimes referred to interchangeably), there is a difference between them; grape jam is not the same as grape jelly and applesauce is prepared differently than apple butter.

JAM: Consisting of fruit that is cooked and mashed or cooked until it falls apart in small pieces, jams are simmered with sugar, lemon juice, and occasionally pectin until they gel to a thick, spoonable consistency.

JELLY: A clear spread made only from extracted fruit juice, jelly does not have any pieces of fruit in it. Like jam, it is combined with sugar, lemon, and occasionally pectin and boiled until it gels to a firm, somewhat wobbly consistency. They are typically made from very juicy or high-pectin fruits, like quince, Concord grapes, or currants.

CONSERVE: Conserves are a delicate preserve in which large pieces of fruit are suspended in thick sugar syrup. The fruit is often macerated in sugar before cooking to strengthen its cell walls and prevent breaking down during cooking. This method is ideal for highly succulent or flavorful fruits, like perfectly ripe apricots, whole, just-picked strawberries, or Green Gage plums.

MARMALADE: Made from the highest-pectin fruits—often citrus like orange or grapefruit—marmalade requires no added thickeners: just sugar and sometimes lemon juice, for flavor. It is more textured than other preserves, often containing thinly sliced peel.

FRUIT SAUCE: Almost any fruit can be cooked into a sauce, but soft fruits that fall apart easily when cooked, like apples, pears, and plums, are frequently used. Fruit is simmered with sugar until a loose, spoonable consistency is reached; for the smoothest texture, cooks sometimes run the final product through a food mill.

BUTTER: Most fruit sauces can be transformed into fruit butter with a little patience. Fruit butter is a sweetened fruit purée simmered slowly and gently until it concentrates into a thick, full-flavored spread. The key to making fruit butter is abundance, since it requires starting with more fresh fruit than other preserves.

FRUIT PASTE OR "CHEESE": One step beyond fruit butter is fruit paste. The fruit must be cooked until it concentrates enough to reach a solid, sliceable texture. A famous example of a fruit paste is the Spanish quince paste, *membrillo.* High-pectin fruits with good gelling power make the best pastes.

The Relationship Between Sugar, Acid, and Pectin

Sweet preserves rely on a balance between sugars, acid, and pectin to thicken and achieve their characteristic gelled consistency. All fruit naturally contains all three, but the proportion between them varies depending on the type of fruit and its degree of ripeness; achieving a properly set preserve is dependent on understanding how these elements interact with each other.

SUGAR

Sugar plays multiple roles in preserving fruit. It provides additional sweetness to balance out fruits' natural acidity; adds vibrant color and gloss; and, most importantly, contributes body and thickening power. Fruits with higher levels of pectin naturally absorb more sugar as they cook and set (high-pectin gooseberry jam, for example, will require more sugar than low-pectin blueberry). Because sugar also fortifies the cell walls of fruit, it can inhibit a fruit's ability to break down. This is desirable in coarsely textured preserves such as conserves, but for most jams and jellies, where the goal is to soften fruit, sugar is typically added after the fruit has fallen apart in cooking. Sugar also works as a natural preservative—highly sugared jams (such as those with equal proportions of fruit to sugar) have a longer storage life than those with less sugar; of course, this also makes them sweeter.

ACID

Like sugar, acid also aids in the release of pectin. All fruits, even those that taste very sweet, contain acid; however, those with the highest levels of acid also tend to contain the highest levels of pectin. This is why using a portion of slightly underripe fruit is sometimes suggested for preserving. You've probably tasted an unripe grape or apple and observed that they taste sour; their natural sugars have not yet fully developed, making them more acidic. At this point they also contain high levels of pectin. Of course, if you used all underripe fruit, you would miss out on the balance of sugars present in perfectly ripe fruit. A good rule of thumb is to use about one quarter slightly underripe fruit to three-quarters ripe fruit, or if that's not possible, use exclusively ripe fruit. Never use overripe fruit, which has the least amount of acid and pectin.

Most recipes call for the addition of acid, such as lemon juice. In part, this helps brighten the flavor of a preserve, balancing its sweetness. It can also protect a fruit's color. But when a fruit's natural acid level is moderate or low, adding lemon juice enables the preserves to achieve a set. Usually the juice of 1 lemon (2 to 3 tablespoons) for every 2¼ pounds / 1 kg of fruit is sufficient to achieve proper gelling.

PECTIN

Pectin is a natural carbohydrate found in fruit. When combined with sugar and acid, it forms a bond that gives structure and gel to a preserve. Its presence is especially high in a fruit's peels, cores, and seeds. All fruits have different pectin levels. Some, like currants, are naturally high in pectin; others, such as pears, are very low in pectin. Pectin levels are always at their peak in slightly underripe to perfectly ripe fruit. In cases where a fruit's pectin levels are low, various methods can be employed to achieve a set preserve, including combining the fruit with one that contains higher levels of pectin, cooking the fruit for a longer period of time, adding higher quantities of acid, or mixing in commercial pectin (available at most supermarkets). If using commercial pectin, it is very important to follow the recipe's instructions carefully, as different types of pectin require different quantities and techniques to work properly.

Setting

A fruit's ability to set, or "gel" is a function of its natural pectin level as well as its ratio of acid to sugar. For example, high-pectin, high-acid fruit like grapes gel beautifully, making them a good choice for jellies or pastes, where sweetness and a firm set are desirable. Fruits with a more moderate setting ability may gel more softly, which can be pleasant in jams and sauces; they may also require a slightly longer cooking time. Fruit with the lowest level of pectin and acid are more difficult to set without the addition of extra acid and/or pectin. Except where stated, this chart refers to perfectly ripe fruit.

FRUIT	PECTIN LEVEL	ACID LEVEL	SET ABILITY	BEST FOR
Concord grapes	High	High	High	Jams, jellies, conserves, sauces, butters
Currants (black, white, and red),	High	High	High	Jam, jellies, conserves, sauces, butters, pastes
Gooseberries	High	High	High	Jams, jellies, conserves, sauces, butters, pastes
Niagara grapes	High	High	High	Jams, jellies, conserves, sauces, butters, pastes
Tart/underripe plums, such as Damson or Green Gage	High	High	High	Jams, jellies, conserves, sauces, butters, pastes
Quince	High	High	High	Jams, jellies, conserves, sauces, butters, pastes, marmalade
Tart/underripe apples, such as Granny Smith	High	High	High to moderate	Jams, jellies, conserves, sauces, butters, pastes
Sweet to sweet-tart apples	High to Moderate	High to Moderate	Moderate	Jams, jellies, sauces, butters, pastes

FRUIT	PECTIN LEVEL	ACID LEVEL	SET ABILITY	BEST FOR
Apricots	Moderate	Moderate	Moderate to Low	Jams, conserves, sauces, butters, pastes
Sour cherries	Moderate	Moderate	Moderate	Jams, conserves, jellies (with added pectin)
Sweet ripe plums	Moderate	Moderate	High to Moderate	Jams, conserves, sauces, butters, pastes
Raspberries	Moderate	Moderate	Moderate to Low	Jams, jellies (with added pectin), conserves, sauces
Blackberries	Moderate to low	Moderate to low	Moderate to low	Jams, jellies (with added pectin), conserves, sauces
Blueberries	Low	Moderate to Low	Moderate to low	Jams, jellies (with added pectin), conserves, sauces
Sweet cherries	Low	Low	Moderate to low	Jams, jellies (with added pectin), conserves, sauces
Nectarines	Low	Low	Moderate to low	Jams, conserves, sauces, butters
Peaches	Low	Low	Moderate to low	Jams, conserves, sauces, butters
Pears	Low	Low	Low	Jams, conserves, sauces, butters
Rhubarb	Low	High	Moderate to low	Jam, sauces
Strawberries	Low	Moderate to Low	Moderate to low	Jams, jellies (with added pectin), conserves, sauces

CHECKING THE SET

You can do everything right—secure fresh-picked fruit, sterilize every inch of your kitchen, and use the perfect amount of sugar and acid—but if you don't know when your jam is ready, you can end up with frustrating results: either watery, undercooked spreads or rubbery, overcooked blobs. You can tell when your jam or jelly is almost ready by using a few different methods:

TEMPERATURE. Jams and jellies reach the gel stage at 220°F / 105°C; you can clip a candy thermometer to your pot and wait for it to hit the sweet spot. But be careful: if your thermometer is not well calibrated, it might give you a misreading. Use the thermometer as a guide and test jam using a second method as it approaches temperature.

READ THE POT. Preserves often give telltale visual signs that they have almost reached the set point; the color will deepen, the preserves will begin to take on a glossy sheen, and any foam on the surface will gradually subside.

FREEZER TEST. This is a simple, reliable way to see if your preserves have set. While you are prepping the preserves, stick a small, clean plate in the freezer. Pull the plate out as you approach the set point. Spoon a few drops of hot jam onto the plate and allow it to cool briefly. Prod the jam with your finger. If it wrinkles slightly and doesn't run down the plate, it is ready.

Note: When checking the progress of sauces, butters, and pastes, visual clues are best. A sauce is often up to personal preference, but in general, once it has reached a smooth mass with no pooling, watery liquid on the surface it is ready. Butters will darken in color and reach a consistency thick enough for the back of a spoon to leave an impression. Pastes should be cooked until the mixture bubbles slowly and thickly, and a spoon dragged across the bottom of the pan leaves a clear, firm trail.

PROBLEMS WITH JAMS AND JELLIES

Making fruit preserves is part artistry and part science. Sometimes a jam comes together in a magical marriage of flavor and texture; other times, something goes awry. The good news is that preventative measures exist for almost any necessary fix.

PROBLEM: A jam refuses to set or sets too softly.

SOLUTION: Lots of factors can contribute to a soft-setting jam, but in general it's usually because it lacked sufficient pectin, sugar, or acid. It can also happen when the preserve isn't cooked long enough to reach the proper setting temperature. To fix it, you will need to open up your jars and cook it again. This time, while it heats, stir in 1½ teaspoons of liquid pectin, 3 tablespoons of sugar, and 1½ teaspoons of lemon juice for every cup / 240 ml of jam you're trying to fix. Bring the mixture to a rolling boil for 1 minute, stirring constantly. Remove from the heat; skim off the foam. Re-sterilize the jars before filling, sealing, and processing.

PROBLEM: Your jam is thick and gummy.

SOLUTION: This is almost always the result of overcooking. While it is important to reach 220°F / 105°C for a set point, it is equally important not to surpass this temperature as it will quickly harden your preserve. It's best to begin checking early; if you aren't sure about temperature, err on the side of a lower, not a higher temperature. Many soft-set jams and conserves still have wonderful texture and flavor. If you know you've surpassed the temperature, you can usually thin it out with a small amount of water; just return the jam to a boil for a moment to heat through before ladling it into jars.

PROBLEM: Your jelly takes on a clouded appearance.

SOLUTION: Jellies require more patience than other preserves. In order to achieve a clear jelly, it's important not to press down on the draining juices during extraction. This can cause tiny pieces of fruit solids to leach into the mixture. Though this won't affect the flavor, it may create an opaque preserve.

PROBLEM: A jar develops "fruit float," with a mass of fruit collecting at the top of the jar rather than evenly suspending throughout the preserve.

SOLUTION: Overripe fruit can interfere with the pectin's ability to create a proper suspension. Overprocessing (boiling the jars longer than the recommended time) can also interfere with a uniform suspension. Use fresh, ripe fruit and follow the recipe's processing instructions carefully.

PROBLEM: Liquid leaks from the preserve, leaving a wet "weeping" consistency.

SOLUTION: Also called syneresis, this problem might be a result of too much acid, which can create an unstable environment for pectin. This can also happen as a result of too-warm storage conditions. Make sure to use the recommended amount of lemon juice and store the preserve in a cool, dry place until opened.

PROBLEM: You notice a layer of mold or fermentation inside the stored jar.

SOLUTION: Mold can happen if a preserve does not contain enough sugar, but it's more likely that your jars were not properly sterilized or sealed: the contents of these jars should be discarded. Always make sure to work in a clean environment and follow processing instructions carefully. Double-check the seal before storing the jams in a cool, dry place. Air bubbles are harmless unless they are fizzing or rise to the surface of the jar when opened. This can indicate contamination; these preserves should be discarded.

Freezing Fruit

Freezing is a fast and convenient way to preserve fruit. When food is stored at a temperature below 32°F / 0°C, the rate at which microorganisms can flourish is considerably slowed; fruit is kept fresh-flavored and nutritious for up to a year. Some fruits freeze better than others, and you may notice that the thawed fruit has a softer texture than the fresh.

THE CONTAINER

As with any preserving method, the container in which you store the food is an important part of successful long-term storage. Choose only containers that are sturdy, moisture-vapor resistant, and easy to seal. Heavy-duty plastic containers, freezer-safe resealable plastic bags, and wide-mouthed freezer jars all work; avoid fragile canning jars and flimsy plastic containers that shatter easily at cold temperatures.

FREEZING METHODS

Different freezing methods suit different needs. There are multiple ways to package fruits for freezing, including open freeze, syrup pack, sugar pack, or purée pack. Packing in sugar or syrup helps preserve a fruit's flavor, but it is not necessary. If you do choose to sweeten your fruit before freezing, make a note of it on the package so that you can adjust the recipe's quantity of sugar accordingly.

OPEN FREEZE: Ideal for loose berries and small stone fruits like plums and apricots, open freezing involves spreading fruit in a single layer on a parchment-lined baking sheet (halve and pit larger fruit), then transferring it to the freezer for several hours until solid. For final storage, it is repackaged in an airtight, freezer-safe container. To prevent freezer burn, fruit should be repackaged as soon as it is fully frozen. Fruits that are preserved this way can often go straight into a recipe without thawing.

SUGAR PACK: In this method, fruit is sprinkled lightly with sugar before freezing. Sometimes this method is combined with an open freeze (sugar is scattered over fruit on the baking sheet before freezing); other times, as with juicy fruits like sliced peaches or pitted cherries, fruits are tossed with the sugar until it dissolves into a syrup. The benefit to this method is that it strengthens the cell walls of the fruit, helping to preserve the fruit's texture as well as flavor. This method is better for general baking and cooking purposes than syrup packing, since the product contains less liquid.

SYRUP PACK: Application of the syrup pack, in which fruit is preserved in a simple sugar syrup, is dependent on what kind of fruit is being frozen. For most fruits, a concentration of 2¾ cup / 350 g sugar to 4 cups / 1 L water is ideal; prepare a heavier syrup (a higher proportion of sugar to water) for tart fruits, such as sour cherries. Usually best for sauces or uncooked desserts.

PURÉE PACK: Raw and cooked purées freeze beautifully. Those preserved with sweetener and lemon juice last longest, but it's not strictly necessary. For easy storage, freeze purées first in a resealable plastic bag set inside the bottom of a wide, shallow, freezer-safe container; once frozen, remove the bag from the container.

FREEZING TIPS:

- To prevent ice crystals from forming on the fruit, thoroughly drain rinsed fruit before freezing. Discard any fruit that seems bruised or damaged.
- Dip sliced fruit like apples and peaches in lemon juice before freezing to prevent discoloration.
- Leave at least ¾ inch / 2 cm of headspace at the top of any freezer container to allow for the expansion of the food when frozen. Wipe the container of any spills or excess moisture. If using a plastic bag, press out excess air before sealing.
- Fruit will usually maintain excellent quality for six months to one year, with unsweetened fruit having a shorter freezer life than sugar- or syrup-packed fruit. Label and date your containers so you will know when a fruit is nearing its expiration period. Frozen food past its expiration date won't make you sick, but its texture and flavor will suffer.
- As with any frozen food, defrost frozen fruit in the refrigerator to protect against food-borne illness. Once defrosted, enzyme activity in fruit resumes and fruit should be used quickly.

MIXED BERRY FREEZER JAM

Freezer jam is great for so many reasons: it requires no stovetop time, it is easily adapted to small batches, and it preserves the flavor of fresh-fruit jam for up to an entire year. Though ideal for low-acid, usually hard-to-set berries, it is also excellent with juicy, succulent fruit like peaches and cherries (for more ideas, see the next oage). You can also play with the flavors, adding chopped mint, grated ginger, or a pinch of spice.

Makes 3 (8-ounce / 240 ml) jars

1¼ pounds / 570 g mixed fresh berries, such as strawberries, raspberries, and blueberries

1 cup / 200 g granulated sugar

3 tablespoons instant pectin powder

Have ready 3 clean, dry freezer-safe containers; glass freezer jars or small, sturdy plastic containers are best.

In a large bowl, mash the berries with a potato masher or pastry blender until they are juicy and crushed. In a separate, smaller bowl, whisk together the sugar and pectin (this is an important step; if you add them to the fruit separately, you will get lumps). Sprinkle the mixture over the fruit; stir constantly for 3 minutes.

Ladle the jam into the prepared jars, leaving ½ inch / 1.3 cm of headspace; cover the jars and refrigerate them for 1 hour until set. Label the jams and freeze them for up to 1 year.

FRUIT AND APPROPRIATE
FREEZER METHODS

FRUIT	OPEN FREEZE	SUGAR PACK	SYRUP PACK (raw or blanched)	PURÉE (raw or cooked)	FREEZER JAM
Apples	X	X	X	X (cooked only)	
Apricots	X	X	X	X	X
Blackberries	X	X	X	X	X
Blueberries	X	X	X	X	X
Cherries	X	X	X	X	X
Currants	X	X	X	X	X
Gooseberries	X	X	X	X	
Grapes (Concord, Niagara, Fredonia)				X (strain seeds pre-freezing)	
Nectarines	X	X	X	X	X
Peaches	X	X	X	X	X
Pears			X (cooked only)	X (cooked only)	X
Plums	X	X	X	X	X
Quince	X	X	X	X (cooked only)	
Raspberries	X	X	X	X	X
Rhubarb	X	X	X	X (cooked only)	X
Strawberries	X	X	X	X	X

QUICK STRAWBERRY JAM

Karen Demasco, the pastry chef at Locanda Verde, swirls this simple but tasty jam into her Strawberry Olive Oil Cake (page 39), but it's also an excellent spread in its own right. Because it's not processed like other jams, store it in the refrigerator, where it will keep for two to three weeks. Apricots have a modest amount of pectin and may take a few days or even a week or so to set fully; don't worry if yours seems slightly loose at first.

Makes about 1 ¼ cups / 300 ml

1 pound / 455 g ripe strawberries, hulled and quartered (about 2 ⅔ cups quartered)

1⅓ cups / 270 g granulated sugar

2½ tablespoons freshly squeezed lemon juice

In a small saucepan over medium-high heat, combine the strawberries, sugar, and lemon juice. Stir frequently and cook until the berries become dark and the juices thicken, 15 to 25 minutes.

Remove from the heat and ladle the hot jam into a sterilized jar. Wipe the rim and cool, uncovered, to room temperature. Cover tightly and refrigerate the jam for up to 3 weeks.

GOOSEBERRY-ELDERFLOWER JAM

Gooseberries and elderflower blossoms come to season at the same time, making them a natural and classic pairing, with the elderflower's floral notes bringing out the tart gooseberries' more delicate flavors. A high-pectin, high-acid fruit, gooseberries are ideal for jams.

Makes 4 to 5 (8-ounce / 240 ml) jars

2 pounds / 910 g green gooseberries, tops and tails removed

4 cups / 800 g granulated sugar

½ teaspoon finely grated lemon zest

2 tablespoons elderflower cordial

In a large, heavy-bottomed pot or preserving pan, combine the gooseberries and ½ cup / 120 ml of water. Bring the mixture to a boil over medium-high heat; reduce the heat to medium-low and simmer the berries, stirring often and crushing them lightly, until they are pulpy and broken down, 10 to 15 minutes.

Stir in the sugar, lemon zest, and cordial. Bring the mixture to a boil and cook, skimming off any foam that rises to the surface, until the jam reaches the setting point (see page 245), 15 to 20 minutes more.

Ladle the hot jam into sterilized jars, leaving ¼ inch / 6 mm of headspace. Wipe the rims of the jars and apply the lids and bands; process the jars in a boiling water canner for 5 minutes. Allow the jars to seal, and store them in a cool, dark place. Refrigerate after opening.

CLASSIC BLUEBERRY JAM

Heading out to a blueberry patch and filling up baskets of ripe, jam-worthy berries is a rite of passage for most canners—nothing says summer quite like the glossy purple spread. Because blueberries don't have as much pectin as other fruits, they tend to yield a softer setting jam. The lemon juice in this recipe helps with gelling; you can also add liquid or powdered pectin (follow the package instructions).

Makes 4 to 5 (8-ounce / 240 ml) jars

2 pounds / 910 g fresh blueberries	3 tablespoons freshly squeezed lemon juice
3½ cups / 690 g granulated sugar	

In a large, heavy-bottomed pot or preserving pan, combine the blueberries, and ½ cup / 120 ml of water. Bring the mixture to a boil over medium-high heat; reduce the heat to medium-low and simmer the berries, stirring often and crushing the fruit lightly with a spoon, until the fruit is softened, about 10 minutes.

Stir in the sugar and lemon juice; return to a boil and cook, skimming off any foam that rises to the surface, until the jam reaches the setting point (see page 245), 10 to 15 minutes more.

Ladle the hot jam into sterilized jars, leaving ¼ inch / 6 mm of headspace. Wipe the rims of the jars and apply the lids and bands; process the jars in a boiling water canner for 5 minutes. Allow the jars to seal, and store them in a cool, dark place. Refrigerate after opening.

EMILY'S APRICOT JAM

Sometime over the years, my grandmother Emily's actual jam recipe was misplaced, but luckily my dad long ago committed the basics to memory. It's a perfect traditional jam, with sweetness tempered by the subtle tartness of the unpeeled fruit. Made with just about equal parts fruit to sugar, this jam easily keeps all winter long. It uses liquid pectin; if you plan to use powdered instead, adapt the recipe based on the package directions. Apricots have a modest amount of pectin and may take a few days or even a week or so to set fully; don't worry if yours seems slightly loose at first.

Makes about 4 (8-ounce / 240 ml) jars

1¼ pounds / 560 g apricots, pitted and cut into eighths (3 cups)	3 tablespoons freshly squeezed lemon juice
3 cups / 600 g granulated sugar	3 tablespoons liquid pectin

In a large, heavy-bottomed pot or preserving pan, combine the apricots with the sugar and lemon juice. Bring the mixture to a full boil over medium-high heat. Add the pectin immediately; continue to boil hard for 1 minute, stirring constantly. Remove the pot from the heat and skim off any foam from the surface.

Ladle the hot jam into sterilized jars, leaving ¼ inch / 6 mm of headspace. Wipe the rims of the jars and apply the lids and bands; process the jars in a boiling water canner for 5 minutes. Allow the jars to seal, and store them in a cool, dark place for at least 1 week. Refrigerate after opening.

BOOZY BOURBON PEACH JAM

Jessica Quon and Sabrina Valle, "the Jam Ladies," are two of the friendliest, most positive people in the food business, full of genuine entrepreneurial spirit and creative flair. They've successfully transformed our fruit into one of the hippest and most delicious products to come out of the New York food scene. This tasty peach jam gets an extra jolt from a pinch of hot spice and a dram of bourbon.

Makes about 2 (8-ounce / 240 ml) jars

1¾ pounds / 795 g ripe peaches (about 4 medium), peeled, pitted, and quartered

1 teaspoon freshly squeezed lemon juice

1 cup / 200 g granulated sugar

¼ teaspoon cayenne pepper

¼ teaspoon chili powder

2 teaspoons bourbon

In a large, heavy-bottomed pot or preserving pan, combine the peach slices, lemon juice, sugar, cayenne, and chili powder, and bring the mixture to a simmer over medium heat. Cook, stirring occasionally to make sure the bottom doesn't scorch, until the mixture reaches the setting point (see page 245), 25 to 30 minutes. Remove the pot from the heat and stir in the bourbon. Skim off any foam from the top.

Ladle the hot jam into sterilized jars, leaving ¼ inch / 6 mm of headspace. Wipe the rims of the jars and apply the lids and bands; process the jars in a boiling water canner for 5 minutes. Allow the jars to seal, and store them in a cool, dark place. Refrigerate after opening.

APPLE, BLACKBERRY, *and* WALNUT CONSERVE

This orange-scented, walnut-studded, nutmeg-spiced conserve has all the makings of crustless apple pie. Stir it into plain yogurt at breakfast or use as the base for a quick, oat-topped crumble.

Makes 3 to 4 (8-ounce / 240 ml) jars

1¼ pounds / 570 g baking apples, such as Fuji (see Apple Varieties chart, page 170–171), peeled, cored, and cut into ½-inch / 1.3 cm chunks

1¼ pounds / 570 g blackberries

2½ cups / 500 g granulated sugar

3 tablespoons freshly squeezed lemon juice

Finely grated zest of 1 orange

¼ cup / 30 g toasted, finely chopped walnuts

¼ teaspoon freshly grated nutmeg

In a large bowl, combine the apples, blackberries, sugar, and lemon juice. Cover the bowl and let it stand at room temperature for 2 hours.

Place the fruit and its accumulated juices in a large, heavy-bottomed pot or preserving pan. Stir in the orange zest. Cook over medium-low heat until the apples are just tender, about 5 minutes. Increase the heat until the mixture reaches a steady boil (not too fast or too slow) and cook, stirring as little as possible to prevent breaking up the fruit, until it just reaches the setting point (see page 245), about 15 minutes.

Ladle the hot jam into sterilized jars, leaving ¼ inch / 6 mm of headspace. Wipe the rims of the jars and apply the lids and bands; process the jars in a boiling water canner for 5 minutes. Allow the jars to seal, and store them in a cool, dark place. Refrigerate after opening.

GREEN GAGE PLUM CONSERVE

Considered by many to be the prize plum in an orchardist's garden, Green Gage plums appear briefly in summer, provided that the weather cooperates with this delicate fruit. The fine, tart-yet-honeyed flavor shines brightest without the interference of added ingredients. It's especially well-suited for fruit conserve, a preparation in which the fruit is left in larger pieces and cooked more gently than for a jam or jelly. Green Gage plums are also excellent for pickling, fruit butters, and curds.

Makes about 3 (8-ounce / 240 ml) jars

2 pounds / 910 g ripe but firm Green Gage plums, halved and pitted	3 cups / 600 g granulated sugar
	3 tablespoons freshly squeezed lemon juice

In a large bowl, combine the plums, sugar, and lemon juice. Cover and let the mixture stand at room temperature for 2 hours.

Place the fruit and its accumulated juices in a large, heavy-bottomed pot or preserving pan over medium heat. Bring the mixture to a steady boil (not too fast or too slow) and cook, stirring as little as possible to prevent breaking up the fruit completely, until it reaches the setting point (see page 245), about 10 minutes.

Ladle the hot jam into sterilized jars, leaving ¼ inch / 6 mm of headspace. Wipe the rims of the jars and apply the lids and bands; process the jars in a boiling water canner for 5 minutes. Allow the jars to seal, and store them in a cool, dark place. Refrigerate after opening.

RED CURRANT JELLY

Luminous and ruby-hued, red currant jelly is considered a delicacy in the preserving world, especially in France, where the famed Bar-le-Duc jelly uses berries individually de-seeded with goose quills. Because of its sweet-tart bite, currant jelly is often served with savory foods like lamb or pate, but it's delicious slathered on muffins and scones, too.

Makes about 3 (8-ounce / 240 ml) jars

2 pounds / 910 g red currants, rinsed with stems intact	Granulated sugar, as needed

Place the currants and stems in a medium saucepan and cover them with 1 cup / 240 ml of water. Bring the mixture to a boil over medium heat, then reduce the heat to a simmer and allow the berries to soften, 5 to 10 minutes. Mash the currants lightly with a potato masher or fork.

Transfer the mixture to a clean, damp jelly bag or a cheesecloth-lined fine sieve set over a large bowl; leave to drip for several hours or overnight. Do not squeeze the bag, or you will risk clouding the jelly.

When the juice has fully drained, measure the liquid into a clean preserving pot (you should have about 3½ cups / 830 ml of juice). Add an equal amount of sugar to the juice in the pot. Stir the mixture over medium heat until the sugar is completely dissolved. Bring the mixture to a boil and cook until the setting point is reached (see page 245), about 10 minutes. Skim off any foam that rises to the surface.

Ladle the jelly into hot, sterilized jars, leaving ¼ inch / 6 mm of headspace. Wipe the rims and apply the lids and bands; process in a hot water bath for 5 minutes. Allow the jars to seal, and store them in a cool, dark place. Refrigerate after opening.

HABAÑERO JELLY

Serving belly-filling eats like fried pickles with buttermilk dip, shrimp and grits, and grasshopper pie, Tipsy Parson, in Manhattan's Chelsea neighborhood, has nailed Southern comfort food. Owner Julie Taras Wallach first added this five-alarm pepper jelly to the menu a few years ago in an effort to use up a bumper crop of chile peppers. Her husband is so crazy about the sweet-hot flavor combo that he still makes her bring home a jar every week to spread over grilled chicken. They joke that it's the easiest way to add spice to a marriage. If habaneros are too fiery for you, substitute a milder pepper, like jalapeno.

Makes 3 (8-ounce / 240 ml) jars

⅔ cup / 160 ml cider vinegar

3 cups / 550 g granulated sugar

¾ cup / 30 g coarsely grated carrot

½ cup / 40 g minced red bell pepper
(remove the seeds and membrane first)

½ cup / 60 g minced habañero peppers
(remove the seeds and membrane first)

1 (3-ounce / 90 ml) package liquid fruit pectin

In a large, heavy-bottomed pot or preserving pan, combine the vinegar and sugar over medium-high heat. Stir until the sugar dissolves. Stir in the carrots and red pepper. Bring the mixture to a boil and then reduce the heat to medium and simmer for 5 minutes. Stir in the habaneros and simmer for 5 minutes longer. Increase the heat to high and bring the mixture to a boil. Add the pectin and continue to boil hard for 1 minute, stirring constantly. Remove the pot from the heat and skim off any foam from the surface.

Ladle the jelly into hot, sterilized jars, leaving ¼ inch / 6 mm of headspace. Wipe the rims and apply the lids and bands; process in a hot water bath for 5 minutes. Allow the jars to seal, and store them in a cool, dark place. Refrigerate after opening.

NIAGARA GRAPE-APPLE JELLY

Beautifully amber-hued, this jelly is more delicately flavored than one made with Concord grapes. Grape jellies are sometimes susceptible to crystallization, formed by tartrate crystals in grape juice. To remove them, allow the extracted grape juice to settle in the refrigerator overnight, and strain it once more through a cheesecloth-lined sieve before cooking the jelly.

Makes about 4 (8-ounce / 240 ml) jars

---

1 tart or underripe apple, such as Granny Smith

4 ½ pounds / 2 kg Niagara grapes, stems removed

2¼ to 3 cups / 450 g to 600 g granulated sugar, or as needed

Coarsely chop the apple (do not peel it or remove the seeds) and place it in a large, heavy-bottomed pot or preserving pan. Add the grapes and ¾ cup / 180 ml of water. Bring the mixture to a boil over medium-high heat, then reduce the heat to a simmer and cook, covered, until the fruit is juicy and tender, about 10 minutes. Mash the mixture occasionally with a spoon.

Transfer the mixture to a clean, damp jelly bag or a cheesecloth-lined fine sieve set over a large bowl; leave to drip, covered, overnight in the refrigerator. Do not squeeze the bag, or you will risk clouding the jelly.

Strain the liquid a second time through a cheesecloth-lined sieve set over a liquid measuring cup (you should have 3½ to 4 cups / 830 ml to 1 L of juice).

Pour the strained juice into a large, heavy-bottomed pot or preserving pan over medium-high heat. Stir in ¾ cup / 150 g of sugar for each cup / 240 ml of juice. Simmer the mixture over medium heat until the sugar is completely dissolved. Bring the mixture to a boil and cook until the setting point is reached (see page 245), 10 to 20 minutes. Skim off any foam that rises to the surface.

Ladle the jelly into hot, sterilized jars, leaving ¼ inch / 6 mm of headspace. Wipe the rims and apply the lids and bands; process in a hot water bath for 5 minutes. Allow the jars to seal, and store them in a cool, dark place. Refrigerate after opening.

QUINCE JELLY

Much of the rich pectin in quince lies in its skin and seeds, so there's no need to peel or core the fruit for jellies. They'll help create a good set and are ultimately strained out. The pale flesh of raw quince is a bit of a chameleon; once cooked it turns a deep, glowing pink, and this jelly takes on that rosy hue. Quince matches well with added seasonings like ginger, citrus, vanilla, and rosehip. If you decide to embellish the flavor of your jam, add a small amount to the simmering fruit in the first step.

Makes about 3 (8-ounce / 240 ml) jars

1½ pounds / 680 g quince, rinsed and wiped dry of fuzz

3 to 4 cups / 550 g to 800 g granulated sugar, or as needed

1 tablespoon freshly squeezed lemon juice

Cut the quince into large chunks. Place them in a large, heavy-bottomed pot or preserving pan. Add enough water to cover the fruit by barely 1 inch / 2.5 cm. Bring the water to a boil over medium-high heat; reduce the heat to a simmer and cook, occasionally mashing the fruit with a spoon or potato masher, until the quince is very tender, about 45 minutes. (It may take more or less time depending on the ripeness of your fruit.) The mixture should be the consistency of a very loose applesauce; if it is thicker, add a little more water to reach the proper texture.

Transfer the mixture to a clean, damp jelly bag or a cheesecloth-lined fine sieve set over a large bowl; leave the mixture to drip, covered, in the refrigerator, for several hours or overnight. Do not squeeze the bag, or you will risk clouding the jelly.

When most of the juice has drained, measure the liquid into a clean preserving pot (you should have about 3 to 4 cups / 710 ml to 1 L of juice). Stir in one cup of sugar for each cup of juice and add the lemon juice to the pot. Simmer the mixture over medium heat until the sugar is completely dissolved. Bring the mixture to a boil and cook until the setting point is reached (see page 245), 10 to 20 minutes. Skim off any foam that rises to the surface.

Ladle the jelly into hot, sterilized jars, leaving ¼ inch / 6 mm of headspace. Wipe the rims and apply the lids and bands; process in a hot water bath for 5 minutes. Allow the jars to seal, and store them in a cool, dark place. Refrigerate after opening.

PEACH-VANILLA BUTTER

This cheerful, coppery-colored butter provides a hit of summer on cold winter days. Its bright, sweet flavor is especially suited to buttery, crumbly baked goods like biscuits, scones, and white layer cakes.

Makes about 3 (8-ounce / 240 ml) jars

4 pounds / 1.8 kg ripe peaches, peeled, pitted and cut into chunks	3 tablespoons freshly squeezed lemon juice
1¾ cups / 350 g granulated sugar	1 vanilla bean, split and scraped
	⅛ teaspoon kosher salt

Place the peaches in a large, heavy-bottomed pot or preserving pan. Cover with ¾ cup / 180 ml of water. Bring the mixture to a boil; reduce the heat and simmer until the peaches are very tender, about 15 minutes. Mash the fruit occasionally with a spoon as it cooks.

Run the mixture through the fine mesh attachment of a food mill or blend in a food processor until very smooth. Return the purée to the pot and stir in the sugar, lemon juice, vanilla bean seeds, and salt. Simmer the mixture over low heat, stirring often to prevent scorching, until it is very thick, jammy, and deeply colored, 1½ to 2 hours more. You'll know it's ready when a spoon pressed into the sauce leaves an indentation.

Ladle the hot sauce or butter into sterilized jars, leaving ¼ inch / 6 mm of headspace. Wipe the rims and apply the lids and bands; process the jars in a boiling water canner for 10 minutes. Allow the jars to seal, and store them in a cool, dark place. Refrigerate after opening.

PLUM-PEAR SAUCE *with* CARDAMOM

When this sauce is bubbling on the stovetop it smells like the farmers' market in autumn, all crisp sweetness and musky spice. Eat it as is or spread the cooked-down butter on warm slices of pumpkin bread.

Makes 2 to 3 (8-ounce / 240 ml) jars

2 pounds / 910 g soft, ripe pears such as Bartlett or Anjou,

2 pounds / 910 g Italian plums, pitted and chopped

⅓ cup / 80 ml pear brandy, such as Poire William, or regular brandy

⅔ cup / 130 g packed light brown sugar

2 tablespoons freshly squeezed lemon juice

½ teaspoon ground cardamom

⅛ teaspoon salt

Coarsely chop the pears, leaving the skin and seeds intact. Put the pears and plums in a large, heavy-bottomed pot or pre-serving pan. Cover them with 1½ cups / 350 ml of water and the brandy and place the pot over medium-high heat. Bring the mixture to a boil; reduce the heat and simmer until the fruit is very soft and pulpy, 30 to 45 minutes. Mash the fruit occasionally with a spoon as it cooks.

Run the mixture through the fine-mesh attachment of a food mill to remove the seeds and skin. Return the purée to the pot and stir in the sugar, lemon juice, cardamom, and salt. Bring the mixture to a simmer over low heat, stirring often to prevent scorching, and cook until the mixture is thick and a dollop of sauce spooned onto a plate doesn't weep liquid, about 30 minutes.

Ladle the hot sauce into sterilized jars, leaving ¼ inch / 6 mm of headspace. Wipe the rims and apply the lids and bands; process the jars in a boiling water canner for 10 minutes. Allow the jars to seal, and store them in a cool, dark place. Refrigerate after opening.

Variation

To make pear butter instead, run the finished sauce through the fine-mesh attachment of a food mill. Return the purée to the pot and continue to cook the sauce until it is thick, jammy, and chestnut-colored, about 1½ hours more. You'll know it's ready when a spoon pressed into the sauce leaves an indentation. Process the jars in a water bath as directed. Makes 1 to 2 (8-ounce / 240 ml) jars.

CIDER-SWEETENED APPLESAUCE

While I was growing up, this was the kind of sauce my grandmother made, simple and straight from the orchard. Make sure to use a tangy apple like Stayman, Northern Spy, or Cortland. If you have a spice grinder, it's worth grinding a fresh cinnamon stick for this sauce rather than using pre-ground cinnamon; it will lend vibrant warmth to this chunky sauce.

Makes about 3 (8-ounce / 240 ml) jars

3½ pounds / 1.6 kg tangy apples, peeled and cored

1¾ cup / 410 ml favorite apple cider, such as Red Jacket, plus more as needed

2 tablespoons freshly squeezed lemon juice

½ teaspoon freshly ground cinnamon (from 1 cinnamon stick)

¼ teaspoon freshly grated nutmeg.

Coarsely chop the apples and place them in a large, heavy-bottomed pot or preserving pan. Pour in the cider and lemon juice, and place the pot over medium-high heat. Bring the mixture to a boil; reduce the heat and simmer, mashing the fruit occasionally with a spoon as it cooks, until the apples are very tender and a dollop of the sauce spooned onto a plate doesn't weep liquid, about 30 minutes. Add additional cider, as needed if the liquid evaporates before the apples are tender. Stir in the cinnamon and nutmeg.

Ladle the hot sauce into sterilized jars, leaving ¼ inch / 6 mm of headspace. Wipe the rims and apply the lids and bands; process in a boiling water canner for 10 minutes. Allow the jars to seal, and store them in a cool, dark place. Refrigerate after opening.

Variation

To make apple butter instead, run the finished sauce through the fine-mesh attachment of a food mill. Return the purée to the pot and continue to cook the sauce until it is thick, jammy, and chestnut-colored, about 1½ hours longer. You'll know it is ready when a spoon pressed into the sauce leaves an indentation. Process the butter in a water bath as directed. Makes 2 (8-ounce / 240 ml) jars.

Pickled Fruits and Chutneys

WHEN PRESERVING FRUIT, MOST MINDS AUTOMATICALLY run to the sweet end of the spectrum, where jams, jellies, and marmalades reside. This makes sense, since these methods exalt a fruit's natural sweetness, concentrating it for long-term storage. Pickles and chutneys, on the other hand, approach fruit from the opposite, savory side. Instead of enhancing a fruit's sweetness, they contrast and balance it with the tartness of vinegar and unexpected aromatics like garlic, peppercorn, and bay leaf.

If you aren't sure how you feel about blending sweet and sour flavors, start with the chutneys, which have a jamlike consistency. Although they rely on vinegar for their preserving power, they are still sweetened and simmered like jams, but with any number of complementary ingredients, including ginger, spices, onion, herbs, dried fruit, and chopped nuts. Since they simmer slowly until a tender, uniform texture emerges, chutneys are best prepared with fruit that has some meatiness to it; apples, quince, pears, rhubarb, and plums are all good choices. You will know chutney is ready when you can drag a spatula across the bottom of the pot and the mixture doesn't flood back into the empty space. Chutneys have intense flavor, and are usually treated as a condiment for savory foods like roasted or cured meats and salty cheeses, such as a good aged Cheddar or dry goat cheese.

If you like a little mouth-puckering flavor every now and then, you will enjoy pickled fruit, which is "cooked" by submerging it for an extended period in a lightly sweetened and spiced vinegar solution. Pickled fruit can have an addictive effect once you've grown accustomed to its piquancy. That sharp flavor comes from acetic acid, an organic compound present in varying levels in different types of vinegar. To ensure safe long-term storage, it is recommended that you stick to high-grade vinegars containing at least 5 percent acetic acid, like cider vinegar, white distilled vinegar, or wine vinegar. Rice vinegar has a level of about 4.3 percent acetic acid; though its mellow flavor goes nicely with fruit, only use it if you plan to refrigerate your pickles and eat them within a week or two. Enjoy pickles on their own or serve them as a condiment for savory foods; heavily sweetened pickled fruit are even nice as a sauce for ice cream or cake.

Although chutneys and fruit pickles contain two natural preservatives, vinegar and sugar, it is still recommended that you process filled jars in a canner for long-term storage. As always, begin with a clean workspace and sterilized, nonreactive equipment, such as stainless steel.

NECTARINE-FENNEL CHUTNEY

Made with aromatic nectarines, herbaceous fennel, and a kick of spice, this light, fresh chutney is ideal for stuffing into lean pork tenderloin. You can also mix it with mayonnaise and roast turkey for a quick, Thanksgiving leftover feast.

Makes 2 to 3 (8-ounce / 240 ml) jars

1¾ pounds / 795 g firm, ripe nectarine, peeled (see page 125) and pitted

½ teaspoon fennel seeds

¾ cup / 150 g packed light brown sugar

½ cup / 120 ml white wine vinegar

½ cup / 70 g finely chopped red onion

½ cup / 60 g finely diced fennel

1 small jalapeño pepper, seeded and chopped

⅓ cup / 60 g golden raisins

½ teaspoon freshly ground black pepper

½ teaspoon salt

Cut the nectarines into ½-inch / 1.3 cm-thick wedges.

In a heavy, dry pot over medium heat, toast the fennel seeds until fragrant, about 1 minute. Stir in the sugar and vinegar, and bring the mixture to a boil. Stir in the onion, fennel, jalapeño, raisins, black pepper, and salt. Reduce the heat and simmer very gently for 10 minutes. Stir in the nectarine and simmer, stirring occasionally, until the fruit is tender and the juices are thick enough that they don't pool when dragged with a spoon, about 10 minutes (if the juices need more time, remove the nectarines with a slotted spoon and continue to cook the juices until syrupy; return the nectarines to the pan to heat through before processing).

Ladle the hot chutney into jars, leaving ¼ inch / 6 mm of headspace. Wipe the rims and apply the lids and bands; process in a boiling water canner for 10 minutes. Allow the jars to seal, and store them in a cool, dark place. Refrigerate after opening.

APPLE, QUINCE, *and* DATE CHUTNEY

This warm and wintry chutney goes nicely with cold-weather comfort food—serve it alongside broiled sausages or spread some onto a grilled cheese sandwich. Quince has a denser texture than apple and usually takes longer to become tender, so make sure to chop it more finely to ensure even cooking.

Makes about 2 (8-ounce / 240 ml) jars

1 cup / 200 g packed light brown sugar

¾ cup / 180 ml cider vinegar, plus more to taste

⅓ cup / 100 g dried pitted dates, coarsely chopped

1 shallot, finely chopped

1 tablespoon peeled and grated fresh ginger

1 garlic clove, finely chopped

¼ teaspoon kosher salt

12 ounces / 340 g firm, tart-sweet cooking apples (see Apple Varieties chart, pages 170–171), peeled, cored, and diced

12 ounces / 340 g ripe quince, peeled, cored, and finely diced

In a heavy-bottomed pot over medium heat, combine the sugar and vinegar; bring the mixture to a boil. Stir in the dates, shallot, ginger, garlic, and salt, and simmer over low heat for 10 minutes. Add the apple and quince to the pot and simmer, stirring occasionally, until the fruit is tender and juices are thick enough that they don¹t pool when dragged with a spoon, 25 to 30 minutes. Add water, as needed, if the juices thicken before the fruit is completely tender. Taste and adjust seasonings, if desired.

Ladle the hot chutney into jars, leaving ¼ inch / 6 mm of headspace. Wipe the rims and apply the lids and bands; process in a boiling water canner for 10 minutes. Allow the jars to seal, and store them in a cool, dark place. Refrigerate after opening.

RHUBARB PICKLES

A little sour, a little sweet, and a little spicy, these pickles make a wonderful springtime treat. Snack on them straight from the jar, chop and toss them into vinaigrettes, or serve them alongside the cheeseboard at your next party.

Makes about 1 quart / 1 liter

1 pound / 455 g rhubarb stalks, rinsed and trimmed

4 (½-inch / 1.3 cm-thick) strips orange peel, pith removed

1 teaspoon coriander seeds

1 small dried chile, such as chile de arbol

1½ cups / 350 ml cider vinegar

1⅓ cups / 270 g granulated sugar

2 teaspoons kosher salt

Cut the rhubarb into equal-sized batons, about ½ inch / 1.3 cm thick and 3 inches / 7.5 cm long. Place the rhubarb in a sterilized 1-quart / 9.5 ml canning jar, along with the orange peel and coriander seeds; crumble in the chile.

In a medium, nonreactive pot, combine ½ cup / 120 ml of water with the vinegar, sugar, and salt. Bring the mixture to a boil over high heat, then reduce the heat to medium-low and simmer for 5 minutes until the sugar and salt are completely dissolved.

Pour the hot liquid over the rhubarb, leaving ½ inch / 1.3 cm of headspace. Give the rhubarb a quick stir and top it off with more pickling liquid, if necessary. Wipe the rim and apply the lid and band; process in a boiling water canner for 10 minutes. Allow the jar to seal, and store it in a cool, dark place. Refrigerate after opening.

PICKLED SECKEL PEARS

Palm-sized Seckel pears are the perfect size for pickling. They require little prep work, and they also look great in the jar, making them excellent holiday gifts. Be sure to start with nice crisp pears, since their tender flesh readily absorbs the pickling liquid.

Makes 3 (8-ounce / 240 ml) jars

1½ pounds / 680 g firm Seckel pears, peeled and halved

½ teaspoon allspice berries

3 bay leaves

¾ cup / 180 ml white wine vinegar

½ cup / 100 g granulated sugar

1 teaspoons kosher salt

1 inch / 2.5 cm fresh ginger, peeled and thinly sliced

Using a small spoon, scoop out the seeds from the center of each pear half. Divide the pear halves, allspice berries, and bay leaves between 2 sterilized 8-ounce canning jars.

In a medium, nonreactive pot, combine ¾ cup / 180 ml of water with the vinegar, sugar, salt, and ginger. Bring the mixture to a boil over high heat; reduce the heat to medium-low and simmer for 5 minutes, until the sugar and salt are completely dissolved.

Strain the hot pickling liquid over the pears (it should completely submerge them), leaving ½ inch / 1.3 cm of headspace. Give the pears a quick stir and top off the jars with more pickling liquid, if necessary. Wipe the rims and apply the lids and bands; process the jars in a boiling water canner for 10 minutes. Allow the jars to seal, and store them in a cool, dark place. Refrigerate after opening.

SPICED PICKLED PLUMS

The longer you store these pickled plums, the better—the rich, deep flavor of the plum will just continue to enrich the spiced pickling brine. Crack this one open at Christmastime to serve with the holiday ham or roast.

Makes about 2 quarts / 2 liters

2 pounds / 910 g firm Italian plums	2 cardamom pods
2 cups / 450 g packed dark brown sugar	1 cinnamon stick
1½ cups / 350 ml red wine vinegar	1 whole star anise
4 whole cloves	1 teaspoon black peppercorns

Using a sharp paring knife, cut a slit from top to bottom along the side of each plum in three places. Loosely pack the plums into 2 large sterilized jars.

In a dry, nonreactive pot over medium-high heat, toast the spices until fragrant, about 30 seconds. Stir in the sugar, vinegar, and 1½ cups / 350 ml of water. Bring the mixture to a boil, then reduce the heat to medium-low and simmer for 15 minutes.

Using a fine-mesh strainer, strain the hot pickling liquid over the plums (it should completely submerge the plums), leaving ½ inch / 1.3 cm of headspace. Give the plums a quick stir and top off with more pickling liquid, if necessary. Wipe the rims and apply the lids and bands; process the jars in a boiling water canner for 10 minutes. Allow the jars to seal, and store it in a cool, dark place. Refrigerate after opening.

PICKLED APRICOTS

The firm, dense flesh of apricots makes them a good choice for pickling; their shape holds up nicely in storage. Sweeter than some pickled fruits, this preserve provides just enough tang to cut through the richness of roast pork, but can also be spooned on top of vanilla ice cream for an easy dessert.

Makes about 1 quart / 1 liter

1 pound / 455 g apricots	¾ cup / 150 g granulated sugar
½ cup / 120 ml cider vinegar	1 cinnamon stick

Prick each apricot in several places with the tip of a paring knife. In a medium, nonreactive pot over medium-high heat, combine the vinegar, ½ cup / 120 ml of water, and the sugar; bring the mixture to a simmer and cook for 5 minutes. Stir in the apricots and cinnamon stick. Return the syrup to a simmer and cook the apricots gently until just tender, 3 to 5 minutes (do not overcook).

Using a slotted spoon, transfer the apricots to a sterilized, 1-quart / 1 L canning jar. Pour the hot syrup over the fruit, leaving ½ inch / 1.3 cm of headspace. Give the mixture a quick stir and top off with more pickling liquid if necessary. Wipe the rim and apply the lid and band; process in a boiling water canner for 10 minutes. Allow the jar to seal, and store it in a cool, dark place. Refrigerate after opening.

Infused and Spirited Preserves

IT'S ALMOST IMPOSSIBLE TO GO AWRY WITH FRUIT-
infused alcohol. For starters, alcohol is such a willing
partner, readily absorbing the flavor of whatever you
plunk into it; with the right mix of ingredients, any
fruit can be transformed into a tasty liqueur or cordial.
The process is simple: layer fruit with sugar and seasonings in a sterilized, wide-necked bottle, top it off with
alcohol, and set it aside to mature. It's really that easy.
Enhance the flavors with anything that sounds good to
you—citrus, chile peppers, herbs, ginger, and spices are
all possible companions.

Some infusions, like cordials, are strained after a
period of time; others, like maraschino cherries, continue to mature and develop their flavors until the last
drop has been spooned. Although extended steeping
develops more nuanced flavor, you can control the intensity—if you're after a mild kick, strain the mixture after
a few weeks; if you're looking for a serious punch, let it
go for several months. You can even adjust the sweetness
or dryness as it ages, giving it an occasional sip and stirring in more sugar or booze to suit your taste. Most are

good for sipping on their own (though potent), or they
can be mixed into cocktails, drizzled over desserts, or
splashed into sauces.

Infused spirits are among the most economical
preserves; you'll find that the cost of your ingredients
is usually about what you'd pay for a single cocktail at
a high-end bar—except you'll yield truer, fruitier flavor
and a lot more alcohol than you could fit in a martini
glass. High-proof spirits like vodka, gin, brandy, or
bourbon are usually best, although some cordials are
made with wine. While you don't need to use top-shelf
liquor, you do intend to drink the stuff; aim for alcohol
of moderate quality.

Alcohol offers a naturally sterile environment,
alleviating food safety fears associated with preserves
like jams; it does not need to be processed (though you
should always begin with sterilized equipment as a matter of good habit). Alcohol is sensitive to light and heat,
so store it in a dark-colored glass container if possible,
and always stash in a cool, dark place, like a pantry or
liquor cabinet.

ANY BERRY VINEGAR

The juiciest berries you can get your hands on are best here; look for fruit that is almost (although not quite) on the other side of ripe. Add the strained infusion to vinaigrettes or drizzle into sweetened seltzer.

Makes 2 cups / 470 ml

2½ cups / 350 g ripe blueberries, raspberries, blackberries, or strawberries

2 cups / 470 ml white wine vinegar or distilled white vinegar

⅓ cup / 70 g granulated sugar

Place the berries in a nonreactive pot and crush them lightly with a potato masher. Place the pot over medium-high heat and stir in the vinegar and sugar; bring the mixture to a boil and simmer just until the sugar dissolves, about 2 minutes.

Pour the hot mixture into a sterilized quart / 1 L jar. Cover tightly with a nonreactive lid (to prevent corrosion); or wrap the opening with plastic wrap and screw the lid tightly on top. Shake well, and then place the jar in a cool, dark pantry to rest for at least 3 days and up to 1 week. Strain the vinegar through a fine-mesh sieve into a freshly sterilized pint / 500 ml jar. Store the vinegar in a cool, dark place. Refrigerate after opening.

BLUEBERRY SHRUB

Sometimes you wonder why a good idea ever fell out of favor. First popularized in Colonial America, berry shrub drinks are an old-fashioned cross between lemonade and a soda. Made with sweetened berry vinegars and seltzer, they have a refreshingly fruity, kombucha-like zing.

Makes 1 serving

3 fresh mint leaves

2 to 3 tablespoons blueberry or raspberry vinegar

1 tablespoon honey, plus more as needed

Seltzer, as needed

Fill a large iced tea glass with ice and mint. Stir in the vinegar and honey, and top off with seltzer. Taste the drink and add more vinegar and honey, if necessary. Serve immediately.

MARASCHINO CHERRIES

These boozy cherries, a far cry from the saccharine, candy-red orbs you sometimes find floating in Shirley Temples or perched atop ice-cream sundaes, are definitely for grownups. Steeped in genuine maraschino, a distinctive liqueur made from crushed cherries and their stones, these cherries are delicious dropped into cocktails or spooned over any dark chocolate dessert, from puddings to cakes.

Makes about 3 (8-ounce / 240 ml) jars

1½ pounds / 680 g sour cherries, stemmed and pitted (3 to 4 cups)	3 cups / 710 ml maraschino liqueur, such as Luxardo

Divide the cherries among 3 sterilized (8-ounce / 240 ml) jars. In a large, nonreactive pot over medium-high heat, bring the liqueur to a boil. Pour the hot alcohol over cherries. Wipe the rims of the jars and apply the lids and bands. Store the cherries in a cool, dark, dry place for at least 1 month before opening. Refrigerate after opening.

SOUR CHERRY OLD-FASHIONED

Bourbon drinkers usually take this classic cocktail on the rocks with a garnish of cherries. This version adds a splash of maraschino liqueur for an extra hit of sweet-tart cherry flavor.

Makes 1 serving

1 sugar cube or 1 teaspoon granulated sugar

2 to 3 dashes Angostura bitters

2 ounces / 60 ml rye or bourbon whiskey

2 Maraschino Cherries (above), plus ½ ounce of their infusing liqueur

1 strip orange peel, white pith removed

Place the sugar in the bottom of an old-fashioned glass, add the bitters and a tiny splash of water (no more than 1 teaspoon), and muddle the mixture until the sugar dissolves. Fill the glass with ice and pour in the whiskey and cherry liqueur. Serve, garnished with the cherries and the orange peel.

PEACH-CARDAMOM CORDIAL

Peach-based cocktails should always be made with real peaches, no exceptions. Nothing at the liquor store labeled "peach-flavored" will ever capture the sweet, juicy, slightly tangy essence of the ripe fruit. Make several bottles of this fragrant cordial in the summertime when the peach getting is good; you'll enjoy the fruits of your labor for many months.

Makes about 1 quart

3 pounds / 1.4 kg peaches, pitted and diced

2 cups / 400 g superfine sugar

4 strips lemon peel, white pith removed

3 cardamom pods, lightly crushed

4 cups / 1 L vodka

Layer the peaches, sugar, lemon, and cardamom in a large, sterilized jar. Pour the vodka over the fruit and screw on the lid. Turn and shake the jar a few times to help dissolve the sugar. Label the jar and store it in a cool, dark, dry place for at least 3 months. Taste the cordial every few weeks to see if it is sweetened to your taste; add another spoonful or so of sugar if you would like it sweeter.

Strain the cordial through a fine-mesh sieve into a clean, sterilized jar. Store it in a cool, dark place for up to 6 months.

HOMEMADE CRÈME DE CASSIS

Cassis, a deep violet liqueur made from rich, intensely flavored black currants, has an elegant, French café feel to it. Though it is often mixed with white wine or champagne (see Kir, page 52), it can also be served alone as an after-dinner drink. A few currant leaves are traditionally stuffed into the jars during steeping, but if you don't have access to any, don't worry—you'll still love the results.

Makes 1 to 1½ quarts

2 pounds / 910 g black currants, stems removed (about 3 cups)	15 small black currant leaves (optional)
6 cups / 1.5 L vodka, gin, or brandy	2¾ cups / 550 g granulated sugar

In a large, sterilized jar with a tight fitting lid, combine the currants, alcohol, and leaves, if using. Cover tightly and refrigerate for at least 2 (and up to 5) months; the longer the mixture steeps, the more fully flavored it will be.

Strain the alcohol through a cheesecloth-lined sieve into a bowl; mash the currants gently to extract as much liquid as possible. Tie the cheesecloth into a bundle and squeeze out any excess juice (you should have a generous 2 cups / 470 ml of liquid).

In a small pot over medium heat, simmer the sugar and 1 cup / 240 ml of water until the sugar mixture completely dissolves, about 5 minutes. Cool completely. Pour the syrup into the alcohol, a little at a time. Taste often and stop when it reaches your desired sweetness. Decant the infused alcohol into freshly sterilized, airtight bottles and store them in a cool, dry place.

DAMSON GIN

This sweet-tart damson cordial is made with whole ripe plums steeped in sugar and gin for several months, and it is a terrific way to use up an excess of September's plums. In England, where the beverage is more common, plums are often swapped out for sloes, a relative of the plum. The sloes are usually picked after the first frost to ensure soft texture and sweet flavor; use well-ripened plums here to achieve the same effect. To maintain its beautiful amethyst hue, store it in a dark-colored bottle, away from light.

Makes 1 quart / 1 liter

1½ pounds / 680 g ripe Damson plums	6 juniper berries, lightly crushed
1⅔ cups / 330 g superfine sugar	3 cups / 710 ml gin

Rinse the plums and prick each fruit all over with a fine needle.

Layer the plums, sugar, and juniper berries in a large, sterilized jar. Pour the gin over fruit and screw on the lid. Turn and shake the jar a few times to help dissolve the sugar. Label the jar and store it in a cool, dark, dry place for at least 3 months. Taste the cordial every few weeks to see if it is sweetened to your taste; add another spoonful or so of sugar if you would like it sweeter.

Strain the cordial through a fine-mesh sieve into a clean, sterilized jar. Store it in a cool, dark place for up to 6 months.

DAMSON GIN FIZZ

First popularized at the turn of the last century, fizzes are simple gin- or vodka-based drinks mixed with lemon, seltzer, and sugar. This recipe doesn't add any extra sugar; the homemade Damson gin is sweet enough. You can also substitute store-bought sloe gin, but you'll want to add a teaspoon or so of sugar to the cocktail shaker. With a rich, striking berry color and moderate potency, this cocktail makes a great addition to a brunch table.

Makes 1 serving

2½ ounces / 75 ml Damson Gin (above), or sloe gin
½ ounce / 15 ml freshly squeezed lemon juice
Seltzer water, as needed

Fill a cocktail shaker three quarters of the way full of ice. Pour in the gin and lemon juice; shake well. Strain into a chilled Collins glass and top with seltzer.

QUINCE-RUM RATAFIA

Italian in origin, ratafia is a general term for a liqueur that has been seasoned with any number of fruits, herbs, or spices. This rum-based version, spiced with quince, ginger, mace, and vanilla bean, has a Caribbean feel just right for sipping on frigid winter evenings when you could use a little island inspiration. It also makes a terrific addition to the holiday punch bowl.

Makes 1 scant quart

2 large quince	½ teaspoon ground mace
1 cup / 200 g superfine sugar	1 vanilla bean pod, split
1 (2-inch / 5 cm) piece fresh ginger, peeled and thinly sliced	Dark rum, as needed

Rinse the quince and wipe off any of the downy coating with a towel. Without peeling, cut the quince into quarters and remove the core. Finely chop or grate the fruit and peel.

Transfer fruit to a clean, sterilized quart-sized / 1 L jar. Stir in the sugar, ginger, and mace. Scrape in the vanilla seeds and drop in the pod. Top off the jar with dark rum; the fruit should be completely submerged in alcohol. Stir the mixture well.

Screw on the lid and store the jar in a cool, dry pantry for 1 month. Strain the ratafia through a fine-mesh sieve into a clean sterilized jar, and store it in a cool, dark dry place for up to 6 months.

BASIC BRANDIED FRUIT

Brandied fruit is best for juicy or soft fruits like peaches, pears, cherries, and berries, rather than firm apples or quince. You can also experiment with adding different seasonings to the steeping mixture, such as citrus rind, peppercorns, or star anise. Spoon the results over cake or ice cream.

Makes 1 generous quart / 1 liter

1½ pounds / 680 g fresh, ripe fruit	3½ cups / 830 ml brandy
1¼ to 1½ cups / 250 to 300 g superfine sugar	1 vanilla bean pod, split (optional)

Remove any stems or leaves from the fruit. Thickly slice and pit larger fruits like peaches and pears; leave berries whole; pit and halve cherries or leave them as is (the pits will lend a subtle almond aroma to the brandy).

Layer the fruit and sugar in the bottom of a large, sterilized jar. Drop in the vanilla bean (no need to scrape the seeds, they'll find their way into the liquor). Top with brandy, making sure the fruit is fully submerged in alcohol but leaving ½ inch / 1.3 cm of headspace. Seal the jar tightly and turn it a few times to help dissolve the sugar. Store it in a cool, dark, dry place for 2 to 3 months to mature before opening. Once opened, continue to store the brandy in a dark place for up to 9 months or keep it in the refrigerator for up to 1 year.

BRANDY AND FRUIT

Brandy and fruit have a long history of mingling; the French *eau de vie* ("water of life") and the German spirit-based *wasser* came about shortly after the discovery of distillation in the seventeenth century. These clear fruit brandies are made by fermenting and distilling fruit other than grapes; lightly flavored, they capture the fruit's fresh, lively character (an exception to this is barrel-aged apple Calvados, which is richer and more fruit-forward). Eau de vie can be produced from many fruits, including cherries (kirsch), pears (Poire William), plums (Mirabelle) and raspberries (framboise). When paired with their fresh counterparts, the flavors of both the fruit and the liqueur are heightened; splash a little kirsch into cherry pie, or drizzle framboise over raspberry sorbet to see the effect. Any of them are also excellent for sipping after a meal. Because of the processing involved, achieving the same delicate quality in the home kitchen is impossible, so, unfortunately, you must purchase eau de vie to enjoy it.

You can still successfully combine fruit with brandy at home, however. Both sweetened and strained fruit cordials and boozy, compote-like brandied fruit, like the recipe above, are terrific alternatives.

Pressing Juices

I love the scent of ripe, freshly smashed fruit. I never tire of it, even though it surrounds me in our juicing facility every day. To me, it's the orchard smell, a fragrance redolent of family tradition and decades spent living and working on this farm. For as long as I can remember, my grandfather made cider in the barn from the "culls" (apples sorted out that would not make fresh sales). We grow huge quantities of fruit and some of it never finds its way to market, often for minor reasons like a too-small size or negligible blemishes. Pressing the juice began as a sensible thing to do, a way for us to limit waste on the farm. Grandpa used a really old rack and cloth press, a simple, traditional process for pressing juice: you wash the fruit, crush it in a hammer mill, and pump the fruit "mash" into a large cider cloth (similar to a sturdy cheesecloth) that sits in a square frame. You fold the cider cloth, place another rack on top, and repeat the process until you've built up eight or so layers, depending on the size of your press. The old machine used a hand-crank to lower a hydraulic press onto the fruit, applying 1,500 to 2,000 pounds / 680 to 910 kg of pressure to extract the filtered juice, which was captured into a pan. My grandfather would sell the resultant cider at the farm stand and other markets in the area.

Even though times have changed and we now employ modern technology and food safety, we still rely on the same tried-and-true methods used by my grandfather fifty years ago. Our press is a larger, more efficient, but otherwise identical rack and cloth. We have found it remains the best way to ensure quality and flavor. From our perspective, fruit juice is easy: the tree, the grower, and the fruit have done all the hard work. We just need the juicer to help get that goodness into the bottle. Abiding by this philosophy has yielded a product that we couldn't be more proud of, with pure, fruit-forward flavor and lots of nutrients. If you ever see a bottle of our juice, you might notice that it's a little bit cloudy—that's all the good stuff from the fruit: the fiber, flavonoids, micronutrients, and antioxidants that fight disease and keep us healthy.

In larger production plants, it's easier to filter or cook out all these nutrients using heat, enzymes, centrifugal force, or concentration, but we wouldn't even consider it. In our mind, none of these methods respects the fruit's inherent integrity. We simply press the fruit and bottle it, always keeping it at a chilly 34°F / 1°C to maintain its freshness. In fact, our process is completely devoid of heat, save for the critical step in our flash pasteurization process that ensures food safety for all who drink it. For a total of 20 seconds the juice is flash-heated to about 170°F / 76°C, killing any possible bacteria, and then it is immediately rechilled to 34°F / 1°C. Cold-pressed, unfiltered, and all-natural processing

ensures a juice representative of fruit's natural character.

Juicing at home is not so different from what we do at the orchard. It's about taking the simple pleasure of biting into a fresh peach, apple, or cherry and distilling the experience. Treat it as you would any culinary project and let your taste buds steer you. The recipes provided here are meant only as a guide. Fruit varies tremendously in sweetness, juiciness, and degree of ripeness; an apple that yields ½ cup / 120 ml of juice one day might extract a little less the next. By the same token, the flavor you find just right might seem too tart to someone else. Once you get the hang of the basics, you will quickly discover how much flexibility juicing permits. You can even have fun playing with added seasonings like spices, herbs, citrus juice, or ginger. If it seems expensive or even a little bit shocking to watch a mountain of fresh fruit diminished to a slim glass of juice, remind yourself of all you're getting in return: a powerhouse of vitamins and minerals, a sense of vitality and well-being, and the pure, sublime flavor of tree-ripened fruit.

Juicing at Home

Choosing a Juicer

Juicers can be a hefty investment, so before you buy, it's important that you consider your needs and weigh your options. Most juicers fall into one of two categories, "centrifugal" and "masticating." A third option, not technically a juicer, but sometimes used as one, is the high-powered blender.

CENTRIFUGAL JUICERS

Equipped with a sharp blade that spins at high speed, a centrifugal juicer sucks in the item to be juiced through a feed tube, grinds it, and spins the juice away from the pulp, separating the two. Fans of this kind of juicer enjoy how quickly it operates; you can easily squeeze out a pitcher of juice in a few minutes. It's also a good choice if you dislike pulpy texture in your juice since any fiber is completely strained out. From a health standpoint, however, a lack of fiber means you are also missing out on one of fruit's great nutritional benefits. And because more of the juice comes into contact with the air, centrifugally produced juices oxidize very quickly. It's best to consume or freeze the juice as soon as possible.

MASTICATING JUICERS

Also referred to as "slow juicers," masticating juicers work in a way similar to how we chew our food—the ingredients are crushed and mashed until the juices are squeezed out. Though they take a few minutes longer than centrifugal juicers to extract juices, masticating juicers leaves behind less waste, making them ultimately more efficient. Masticating juicers also operate more quietly than other juicers, are easier to clean, and handle difficult-to-juice items like leafy greens, whole nuts, and soft-textured fruits better than centrifugal juicers. If you like pulp, this is the juicer for you; while masticating juicers also separate the fiber from fruit, they tend to retain more fiber than the centrifugal juicers do, resulting in a juice with thicker texture (and more nutrients, too).

HIGH-POWERED BLENDERS

In general, your home blender is not powerful enough to extract the full essence of fruits or vegetables as a juicing machine. Some exceptions exist, however, in commercial grade blenders equipped with high-powered motors (such as Vitamix or Blendtec brand blenders). Easy to use and clean, these blenders can process ingredients so finely that the texture is almost perfectly smooth, even though they don't separate out the fiber. High-powered blenders make up for their hefty price tags with superior utility; they are often able to grind flour, prepare nut milks, and operate as food processors, too.

MAINTAINING YOUR JUICER

Clean and dry the juicer as soon as you are finished using it. This helps ensure that no bits of fruit or vegetable matter cling to the machine, which can create an environment for bacterial growth.

Getting the Most from your Juice

CHOOSING YOUR FRUIT

Superior fruit is all about a balanced ratio of sugar to acid, and the same is true of the fruit juice. Too much of either throws off the flavor and can lead to a very flat drinking experience. Strike the proper equilibrium and you'll taste the heightened flavor. As with any fruit preparation, this means beginning with vibrant, ripe produce, preferably grown locally and in season.

Very few fruits can't be juiced. Dry, astringent quince is the lone outlier that comes to mind. Beyond that, some fruits juice exceptionally well, others take a little more fussing, but all will yield sweet, satisfying flavor if prepared properly. Berries, stone fruits, grapes, pears, melon, citrus, and tropical fruits are all good fodder for the juicer—but the best fruit of all is the apple, for several reasons: it has a high water content, an excellent sugar-acid balance, and it pairs almost universally with other fruits. Excellent-quality apples are also readily available all year long. At Red Jacket, we love apple juice so much that it serves as the base for all of our juices. Over the years we've paired it with a long list of fruits, including rhubarb, strawberries, currants, raspberries, blueberries, apricots, grapes, and cherries. It's excellent with so many more, too. If you enjoy vegetable-based juices like kale or cucumber, apples are also a good way to ground those earthier flavors and make them more palatable. A juicer's pantry should always be stocked with apples.

Of course, there are many different kinds of apples out there in the world, each rich with distinctive character, from lemony brightness to honeyed sweetness. This rich, broad palate is as desirable for juicing as it is for winemaking. The best apple juice depends on a mix of varieties, building as complex a flavor profile as possible. At the orchard, we strive for a certain proportion of sweet to tart apples in each batch, depending on what other fruits we will pair with the apples. Available apple varieties are different all over the world, but some common sweet ones to work with are Jonagold, Red Delicious, Fuji, Empire, Crispin, Golden Delicious, and Gala. Common tart apples include Ida Red, McIntosh, Granny Smith, and Cortland.

PREPPING THE FRUIT

Begin with cold, freshly rinsed fruit that has been grown as responsibly as possible. Most fruit does not require peeling unless the skin is tough or unpalatable, as with kiwi, pineapple, mango, melon, and citrus. Think of it in practical terms: if you would peel it to eat it out of hand, you should peel it for the juicer. Cut the fruit into pieces that will fit into the juicer and discard any pits, cores, or seeds.

Helpful Juicing Hints

As you will quickly discover, not all fruits juice equally. Firm fruit like apples and rhubarb produce thin, copious amounts of juice; softer fruits like strawberries, apricots, peaches, and pears tend to produce syrupy nectar that can be more difficult to fully extract. Taking your time with these kinds of fruit will produce significantly more juice. Many juicers even offer alternate speeds; rely on the high speed for firm fruit and lower speed for softer fruit. Because centrifugal juicers operate more quickly, they can be especially more finicky about extraction. A good way to check your juicing progress is to feel the discarded pulp; it should feel dry and stringy; if it is wet, you are losing juice.

Frozen fruit can be added straight to the juicer without thawing, but you may run into the same extraction problem. If you do, collect the pulp and run the fruit through the feed tube a second or even third time if necessary, until most of the juice has been pressed out.

You may also wonder what to do with all the leftover pulp you've collected. At the orchard we use it for compost, enriching the soil for our next round of fresh fruit. You could do the same thing in your own backyard, or try adding it to soups and baked goods like muffin or pancake batter for added fiber and flavor.

STORING JUICE

Once you've pressed that ice cold glass of frothy, jewel-toned juice, the best thing to do is drink it on the spot, preferably in a chilled glass. As soon as fruit is juiced, the flavor and nutrient content immediately begins to deteriorate (unless it undergoes a commercial preserving process, like flash-pasteurization). The next-best thing is to refrigerate it in an airtight container such as a mason jar for no more than one day. Be sure to give the juice a quick shake before drinking, as fine residual fibers can settle at the bottom of the jar. You will also likely notice that the color will begin to change pretty quickly as it sits. Although this doesn't adversely affect the flavor, it does appear less appetizing; you can help slow this oxidization process by adding a squeeze of lemon to the juice immediately after pressing it.

As with fresh fruit, juice freezes very well. Decant it into an airtight, freezer-safe container as soon as possible after juicing and store it for up to six months.

RHUBARB-APPLE JUICE

This is one of my favorites, and not only because of its attractive sunset hue. Too often we only eat rhubarb once it's been cooked, which is a shame. Raw rhubarb, in the right context, has a plucked-from-the-garden zing that is really refreshing. It also makes an excellent mate for sweet apples. The stringy skin can get stuck in the juicer, so give the stalks a light peel with a vegetable peeler before juicing.

Makes 2 cups / 470 ml

1½ pounds / 680 g sweet apples

4 ounces / 110 g fresh rhubarb,
cut into 2-inch / 5 cm lengths

½ teaspoon freshly squeezed lemon juice

Thoroughly rinse the apples and rhubarb. Core the apples and cut them into chunks that will just fit through the juicer's feed tube. Lightly peel away the fibrous rhubarb skin. Sprinkle the lemon juice into the bottom of a liquid measuring cup or whatever vessel you will be juicing into.

Following the manufacturer's directions, pass the apples and rhubarb through the juicer into the measuring cup, alternating between the two fruits. Run any wet pulp back through the juicer. Whisk the juice quickly to incorporate the lemon juice. Scrape off the foam, if desired. Pour the juice into chilled glasses and serve immediately.

STRAWBERRY-APPLE JUICE

When you're snacking on them by the bowlful, strawberries can seem candy-sweet, but in reality they are relatively tart and benefit from the addition of sugar, something you will discover once juicing. Here, we rely on the natural sweetness of apples, which helps coax out the strawberries' full flavor and body.

Makes about 2 cups / 470 ml

1½ pounds / 680 g mixed sweet apples	1 teaspoon freshly squeezed lemon juice
10 ounces / 285 g fresh strawberries, hulled	

Thoroughly rinse the apples and strawberries; core the apples and cut them into chunks that will just fit through the juicer's feed tube. Remove the strawberry hulls. Sprinkle the lemon juice into the bottom of a liquid measuring cup or whatever vessel you will be juicing into.

Following the manufacturer's directions, pass the apples and berries through the juicer into the measuring cup, alternating between the two fruits. Run any wet pulp back through the juicer. Whisk the juice quickly to incorporate the lemon juice. Scrape off the foam, if desired. Pour the juice into chilled glasses and serve immediately.

BRIAN'S STRAWBERRY-CHAI SUN TEA

I began making this when my wife Kirstin was pregnant with our twins, during a long, hot summer. She found the combination of strawberries and chai soothing and refreshing on sweltering days and loved that it wasn't overly sweet. Our twins are now eight and we're still brewing it. If you don't have all day to make it, you can combine the tea with 4 cups / 1 L of boiling water and steep it for 5 minutes. Chill thoroughly before stirring in the juice.

Makes 4 to 6 servings

4 cups / 1 L cold water

4 chai tea bags (you can use decaf for the kids)

1⅓ cups / 320 ml Strawberry-Apple Juice (Fuji, Cherry, and Raspberry are other favorites)

In the morning, place the tea bags in a large glass pitcher with a lid. Pour the water over the tea bags, and place the pitcher in a warm spot outside where it will get full sun. Let it steep for most of the day. When the tea is steeped to your liking, squeeze out and discard the tea bags.

For each serving, fill a tall glass with ice. Fill the glass two-thirds full with tea and top it off with the juice.

BLACK CURRANT-APPLE JUICE

The ripe, brooding flavor of black currant really stands out in this sweet-tart juice. We find the more apple types we plunk into the juicer, the merrier. If your currants are on the tart side, skew the mix of apple proportions towards sweeter varieties.

Makes about 2 cups / 470 ml

1 pound / 455 g sweet apples	4 ounces / 110 g black currants
8 ounces / 230 g tart apples	1 teaspoon freshly squeezed lemon juice

Thoroughly rinse the apples and currants; core the apples and cut them into chunks that will just fit through the juicer's feed tube. Remove the currants from their stems. Sprinkle the lemon juice into the bottom of a liquid measuring cup or whatever vessel you will be juicing into.

Following the manufacturer's directions, pass the apples and currants through the juicer into the measuring cup, alternating between the three fruits. Run any wet pulp back through the juicer. Whisk the juice quickly to incorporate the lemon juice. Scrape off the foam, if desired. Pour the juice into chilled glasses and serve immediately.

SPICED BLACK CURRANT GLÖGG

This hot mulled wine is a Yuletide tradition in Scandinavia, where it is sometimes made with black currant juice instead of alcohol. You can also use Grape-Apple Juice (page 309) in place of the black currant.

Makes about 6 cups / 1.5 liters

1 (750-ml) bottle fruity red wine, such as Beaujolais

2 cups / 470 ml Black Currant-Apple Juice (above)

1 cup / 240 ml brandy

¾ cup / 150 g granulated sugar

5 cardamom pods

3 whole cloves

1 cinnamon stick

4 strips orange peel, white pith removed

½ cup / 80 g raisins

½ cup / 40 g sliced blanched almonds

In a large, heavy-bottomed pot over medium heat, combine the wine, juice, brandy, sugar, cardamom, cloves, cinnamon stick, and orange peel. Simmer gently for 45 minutes, stirring occasionally. Ladle the glog into warm mugs (strain if desired), and garnish each serving with raisins and almonds.

RASPBERRY-APPLE JUICE

Like strawberries, raspberries are more tart than you might think, so we like to use all sweet apple varieties in this blend. To extract as much juice as possible from the berries, be sure to alternate them with the apples in the feed tube; the juicy apples will help pull out the concentrated raspberry flavor.

Makes about 2 cups / 470 ml

1½ pounds / 680 g mixed sweet apples, cored and sliced (see page 170–171)

5 to 8 ounces / 150 to 230 g fresh raspberries, or to taste
1 teaspoon freshly squeezed lemon juice

Thoroughly rinse the apples and raspberries; core the apples and cut them into chunks that will just fit through the juicer's feed tube. Sprinkle the lemon juice into the bottom of a liquid measuring cup or whatever vessel you will be juicing into.

Following the manufacturer's directions, pass the apples and berries through the juicer into the measuring cup, alternating between the two fruits. Run any wet pulp back through the juicer. Whisk the juice quickly to incorporate the lemon juice. Scrape off the foam, if desired. Pour the juice into chilled glasses and serve immediately.

APRICOT STOMP

With its rich, nectar-like quality and a beautiful sherbet color, this juice is the true essence of apricot. Because apricots can have an almost custardy texture, you might sometimes read that they aren't a great choice for juicing. Ignore that advice. As long as you mix the apricots with something juicy and sweet, such as apples, you'll have great results, though I usually run the apricot pulp through the juicer a second time to squeeze out every last drop of flavor.

Makes 2 cups / 470 ml

1½ pounds / 680 g sweet apples	1 teaspoon freshly squeezed lemon juice
8 ounces / 230 g apricots	

Thoroughly rinse the fruit. Core the apples and cut them into chunks to fit through the juicer's feed tube; quarter the apricots and discard the pits. Sprinkle the lemon juice into a liquid measuring cup or whatever vessel you will be juicing into.

Following the manufacturer's directions, pass the apples and apricots through the juicer into the measuring cup, alternating between the two fruits. Run any wet pulp back through the juicer. Whisk the juice quickly to incorporate the lemon juice. Scrape off the foam, if desired. Pour the juice into chilled glasses and serve immediately.

APRICOT MARGARITA

After sipping our juices straight all day, it's nice to head to Geneva's Red Dove Tavern some evenings to sample them spiked. Owners Giulietta and Rune Hilt are master mixologists—this version of their margarita makes great use of our Apricot Stomp, but try it with Concord Grape Juice and Tart Cherry Stomp, too.

Makes 1 serving

Salt for rimming the glass (optional)
2 ounces / 60 ml tequila
1 ounce / 30 ml triple sec
½ ounce / 15 ml Rose's lime juice
Apricot Stomp (above), or apricot nectar, as needed

If using salt, place it in a shallow dish. Moisten the rim of a chilled margarita glass with a dampened paper towel, and then dip it in the salt.

Fill a cocktail shaker three quarters of the way with ice. Add the tequila, triple sec, and lime juice. Shake well. Pour the mixture into the prepared glass and top it off with Apricot Stomp.

TART CHERRY STOMP

Every summer during cherry season, we sell this vibrant, ruby-red juice at the market, where it attracts a cult-like following among sour cherry lovers. It's an intense, full-bodied drink, and a good one to make with a mix of apples or even a splash of apple cider instead, since it can really take on a complex flavor profile. Cherry juice has also recently been dubbed "Advil in a juice bottle"—due to its high levels of antioxidants and anthocyanin, a natural anti-inflammatory—so this one is extra good for you, too.

Makes about 2 cups / 470 ml

1½ pounds / 680 g sour cherries	1 teaspoon freshly squeezed lemon juice
8 to 12 ounces / 230 to 340 g sweet or sweet-tart apples	

Thoroughly rinse the cherries and apples. Stem and pit the cherries; core the apples and cut them into chunks that will just fit through the juicer's feed tube. Sprinkle the lemon juice into the bottom of a liquid measuring cup or whatever vessel you will be juicing into.

Following the manufacturer's directions, pass the cherries and apples through the juicer into the measuring cup, alternating between the two fruits. Run any wet pulp back through the juicer. Whisk the juice quickly to incorporate the lemon juice. Scrape off the foam, if desired. Pour the juice into chilled glasses and serve immediately.

JOE'S SUMMER BLEND

The two Joes in the family will debate about who invented this favorite (my money is on my brother Joe III, who, while on a Fuji juice diet, discovered that a squeeze of lemon added a refreshing twist), but they both get the headline name so I think they're happy. While you can put lemons and other citrus through a juicer (just slice away the skin and white pith first), it's easiest to squeeze a couple of halves into a bowl and stir it in at the end. At the orchard, we go heavy on the lemon so that the juice has a pure, summery lemonade flavor, but stir in a little at a time until it hits your personal sweet spot.

Makes 2 cups / 470 ml

2 pounds / 910 g sweet apples	2 to 4 tablespoons freshly squeezed lemon juice, as needed

Thoroughly rinse the apples, then core them and cut them into chunks that will just fit through the juicer's feed tube. Sprinkle 1 tablespoon of the lemon juice into the bottom of a liquid measuring cup or whatever vessel you will be juicing into.

Following the manufacturer's directions, pass the apples through the juicer into the measuring cup. Run any wet pulp back through the juicer. Whisk the juice quickly to incorporate the lemon juice. Whisk in additional lemon juice, a little at a time, until the juice reaches your desired flavor. Scrape off the foam, if desired. Pour the juice into chilled glasses and serve immediately.

PLUM STOMP

When plums are in high season and you find a market table covered with a colorful array of varieties, that's the best time to experiment with this juice. Choose your apples according to the flavor of your plums—sweet ones to temper slightly sour plums, or tarter apples if your plums are mature and syrupy.

Makes 2 cups / 470 ml

1 pound / 455 g sweet or sweet-tart apples	1 teaspoon freshly squeezed lemon juice
1 pound / 455 g mixed plums	

Thoroughly rinse the apples and plums. Core the apples and cut them into chunks that will just fit through the juicer's feed tube; quarter the plums and discard the pits. Sprinkle the lemon juice into the bottom of a liquid measuring cup or whatever vessel you will be juicing into.

Following the manufacturer's directions, pass the apples and plums through the juicer into the measuring cup, alternating between the two fruits. Run any wet pulp back through the juicer. Whisk the juice quickly to incorporate the lemon juice. Scrape off the foam, if desired. Pour the juice into chilled glasses and serve immediately.

FUJI APPLE JUICE

Apple juice sounds so basic, but superb apple juice is anything but. Customers constantly ask us why our varietal Fuji juice tastes so pure and apple-y. First, it starts with the incredibly mellow, sweet and almost pearlike flavor of the Fuji apple. In the same way that the best apple pies combine fruit with a mix of flavor profiles, we like to create a blend of mid-range sweet apples (like Empire, McIntosh, and Golden Delicious) to complement but not overpower Fuji's subtle essence. You can experiment with your own varietal juices. The more varieties you use the better, but you can make a terrifically complex juice with just three. Cut 1 line

Makes about 2 cups / 470 ml

2 pounds / 910 g mostly Fuji apples mixed with other sweet varieties	1 teaspoon freshly squeezed lemon juice, if desired

Thoroughly rinse the apples; core the apples and cut them into chunks that will just fit through the juicer's feed tube. Sprinkle the lemon juice into the bottom of a liquid measuring cup or whatever vessel you will be juicing into.

Following the manufacturer's directions, pass the apples through the juicer into the measuring cup. Run any wet pulp back through the juicer. Whisk the juice quickly to incorporate the lemon juice. Scrape off the foam, if desired. Pour the juice into chilled glasses and serve immediately.

HOT BUTTERED RUM CIDER

This rich, warming cocktail is the sort of drink to be enjoyed around a roaring fire on a snowy night. Take a sip of your cider before using it; if it's on the sweet side, leave out the brown sugar in this recipe.

Makes 1 serving

¾ cup / 180 ml apple cider, Fuji Apple Juice, or other favorite apple cider

1 teaspoon unsalted butter, at room temperature

1 teaspoon packed light brown sugar (optional)

¼ teaspoon ground cinnamon

½ teaspoon pure vanilla extract

3 tablespoons / 45 ml ml dark rum

Freshly grated nutmeg, for garnish

In a small pot, heat the cider until bubbling.

In the bottom of an Irish whiskey glass, muddle the butter, sugar, cinnamon, and vanilla. Pour in the rum, and top it off with cider; stir briskly. Dust with nutmeg and serve immediately.

FUJI APPLE SODA

How can you not love a restaurant named after one of New York State's classic heirloom apples? Northern Spy credits a long list of local bakers, cheesemongers, coffee roasters, and butchers on their menu, and it's an honor for our orchard to be included among them. Owner Chris Ronis usually serves this fizzy apple soda as an alcohol-free, kid-friendly refreshment, but you can swap out the seltzer for sparkling wine if you're in the mood for something stronger.

Makes 2 to 3 servings

½ cup / 100 g granulated sugar
¼ cup / 60 ml freshly squeezed lemon juice
2 cups / 470 ml Fuji Apple Juice (page 305), or other favorite apple juice
1½ to 2 cups / 350 to 470 ml plain seltzer, as needed

In a small saucepan over medium-high heat, bring the sugar and ½ cup / 120 ml of water to a boil, stirring occasionally until all of sugar has dissolved and the mixture is clear. Boil the mixture for 2 more minutes, and then reduce the heat to low and simmer for 5 minutes. Immediately pour the syrup into a bowl to cool completely.

In a small pitcher or a large liquid measuring cup with a spout, stir together the cooled simple syrup, the lemon juice, and the Fuji Apple Juice. For each serving, fill a tall glass with ice. Fill the glass two-thirds full with the juice mixture and top it off with seltzer to taste.

CRANBERRY-APPLE JUICE

This is a nice, tart option for fruit lovers who don't like their juice too sweet. Though we rely on a mix of tart and sweet apples, we tend to lean toward slightly more tart varieties. If you find this one too mouth-puckering for your taste, use all sweet apples instead.

Makes 2 cups / 470 ml

1½ pounds / 680 g mixed sweet and tart apples

4 ounces / 110 g fresh cranberries

½ teaspoon freshly squeezed lemon juice

Thoroughly rinse the apples and berries; core the apples and cut them into chunks that will just fit through the juicer's feed tube. Sprinkle the lemon juice into the bottom of a liquid measuring cup or whatever vessel you will be juicing into.

Following the manufacturer's directions, pass the apples and berries through the juicer into the measuring cup, alternating between the two fruits. Run any wet pulp back through the juicer. Whisk the juice quickly to incorporate the lemon juice. Scrape off the foam, if desired. Pour the juice into chilled glasses and serve immediately.

GRAPE-APPLE JUICE

This juice tastes almost impossibly, truly grapey, thanks to the use of fresh, ripe Concord grapes, which is what jam and jelly producers rely on for that grape flavor you're accustomed to. Although the apples need to be cored, you can skip the arduous task of seeding the grapes here; your juicer will strain them out.

Makes about 2 cups / 470 ml

1½ pounds / 680 g mixed sweet and tart apples	1 teaspoon freshly squeezed lemon juice
8 ounces / 230 g Concord grapes	

Thoroughly rinse the apples and grapes; core the apples and cut them into chunks that will just fit through the juicer's feed tube. Remove the grapes from their stems. Sprinkle the lemon juice into the bottom of a liquid measuring cup or whatever vessel you will be juicing into.

Following the manufacturer's directions, pass the apples and grapes through the juicer into the measuring cup, alternating between the two fruits. Run any wet pulp back through the juicer. Whisk the juice quickly to incorporate the lemon juice. Scrape off the foam, if desired. Pour the juice into chilled glasses and serve immediately.

CONCORD GRAPE AND GALA APPLE SANGRIA

Just about everyone appreciates a pitcher of sangria. This one is not too sweet and not too strong. Fresh Concord grapes and crisp chunks of apple make this version a good one for your farewell-to-summer bash.

Makes about 8 cups / 2 liters

2 (750-ml) bottles hearty red wine, such as Rioja

1 cup / 240 ml Grape-Apple Juice (above) or other favorite grape juice

½ cup / 120 ml Cointreau

¼ cup / 50 g superfine sugar

1 pound / 455 g Concord grapes, halved and seeded

1 large Gala apple, cored and coarsely chopped

1 orange, thinly sliced

In a large pitcher, combine the wine, juice, and Cointreau. Stir in the sugar and fruit until the sugar dissolves. Chill thoroughly and serve over ice.

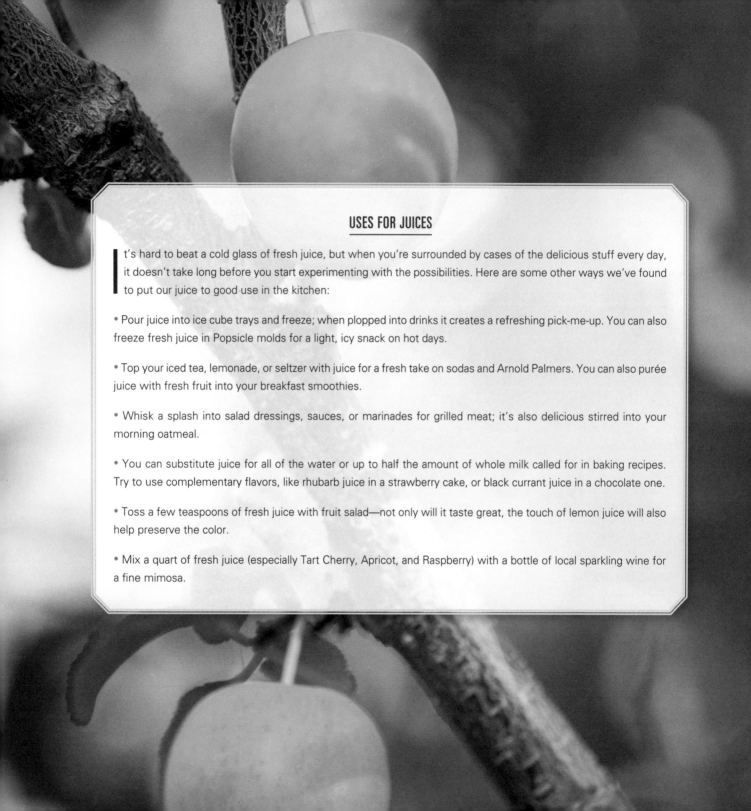

USES FOR JUICES

I t's hard to beat a cold glass of fresh juice, but when you're surrounded by cases of the delicious stuff every day, it doesn't take long before you start experimenting with the possibilities. Here are some other ways we've found to put our juice to good use in the kitchen:

• Pour juice into ice cube trays and freeze; when plopped into drinks it creates a refreshing pick-me-up. You can also freeze fresh juice in Popsicle molds for a light, icy snack on hot days.

• Top your iced tea, lemonade, or seltzer with juice for a fresh take on sodas and Arnold Palmers. You can also purée juice with fresh fruit into your breakfast smoothies.

• Whisk a splash into salad dressings, sauces, or marinades for grilled meat; it's also delicious stirred into your morning oatmeal.

• You can substitute juice for all of the water or up to half the amount of whole milk called for in baking recipes. Try to use complementary flavors, like rhubarb juice in a strawberry cake, or black currant juice in a chocolate one.

• Toss a few teaspoons of fresh juice with fruit salad—not only will it taste great, the touch of lemon juice will also help preserve the color.

• Mix a quart of fresh juice (especially Tart Cherry, Apricot, and Raspberry) with a bottle of local sparkling wine for a fine mimosa.

INDEX

Note: Page references in *italics* indicate photographs.

PHOTO CREDITS

Red Jacket Orchards Archive:
pages 1, 4, 6, 8, 60, 69, 178, 223

Thinkstockphotos:

page 53 © TRISTANBM; page 61 © FIOTA; page 164 © SYBANTO; page 189 © OKSANA SHUFRICH;
page 192 © DESIGN Page ICS; page 197 © SATORI13; page 207 © ARINA HABRICH;
page 219 © SLAVICA STAJIC; page 224 © ANGUS BEARE